WRITING FICTION

STEP BY STEP

WRITING FICTION
STEP BY STEP

JOSIP NOVAKOVICH

STORY PRESS
CINCINNATI, OHIO

Story Press Books are available from your local bookstore or direct from the publisher.

02 01 00 99 98   5 4 3 2 1

Library of Congress Cataloging-in-Publication Data

Novakovich, Josip.
    Writing fiction step by step / Josip Novakovich.
        p.   cm.
    Includes index.
    ISBN 1-884910-35-1 (alk. paper)
    1. Fiction—Technique. I. Title.
PN3355.N685   1998
808.3—dc21   98-7333
                                                                         CIP

Designed by Clare Finney

*To my children Eva and Joseph
in the hope that they will always love story telling.*

ACKNOWLEDGMENTS

I am especially grateful to Jack Heffron, who helped me immensely in conceiving and developing this book.

I am also thankful to my friends and colleagues, who have, in their conversations with me about fiction, helped me clarify many notions about writing it: Robert Shapard, Richard Duggin, Jim Heynen, Lois Rosenthal, Robin Hemley, Steve Yarbrough, Mikhail Iossel, Francine Prose, Margot Livesey, Ivor Irwin, Lon Otto, Thomas Palakeel, Al Davis, Jim Fogt, Erin McGraw, Louis Friedman, James Magnuson, Eric Nelson, John Drury, Eric Goodman, Mark Weingardner, and Manette Ansay.

CONTENTS

INTRODUCTION

Writing is a strenuous sport and a demanding art. You must be mentally fit to do it well. You must exercise your mind as well as your fingers. Many people imagine that to write well you need no preparation, other than research, and once you have something to say, you can move ahead. This is not true. If you can plunge into a novel and finish it without hesitation, great, you are a natural. But there's little that's natural about writing— it's an acquired skill.

You may say, "I can't imagine the great writers of the past bothered with something as artificial as exercises, so why should I?" Well, if you read the works of Fyodor Dostoyevsky, Thomas Mann or Henry James, you might notice that their published correspondence and journals are as voluminous as their literary works. They exercised by writing letters and by keeping journals and jotting down sketches. So even when they were not working on novels, they wrote frequently. Since we now have the telephone, few of us write long letters, and fewer keep journals. We do not stay in writing shape; most of us are quite sluggish with the written word, and when we are on the page, we feel awkward and brittle, like an unskilled skater on ice. I certainly recommend composing long letters and keeping journals, but to get in top shape, I invite you to follow my exercise plan. I promise you will enjoy it.

BUILDING FICTION BY CONNECTING THE EXERCISES

Sometimes writers feel that exercises are a waste of precious time because they don't lead to complete, publishable work. But in this book, I invite you to study your exercises, find the moments you like, and make stories out of them. Connect the exercises. The great thing about writing is that it needn't happen all at once, in one sitting. I'm sure you've often felt, while warming up in sports, *Wow, that was a nice shot, I wish I could save it for the game.* Here, you can. You can collect your best shots and connect them in a collage or use them as seeds for fiction.

Some exercises are narrowly focused; others are deliberately broad. For example, in one I ask you to remember the most intense experience you've had. Your recalling and dramatizing it may spark a story. If so, just keep writing. But other exercises may not trigger a flow beyond the assignment itself. In these cases, I offer, usually in the "tip" sections, possibilities for connecting with other exercises so you can enlarge a scene, pull in a setting you have already created and augment it with images, descriptions, and voices you have developed in other exercises.

The exercises thus build upon each other, and once you have finished the book, you might have drafts of a dozen stories and outlines with a couple of chapters for a novel or two.

The reason for connecting the exercises is simple: Putting different images together is the basic element of imagination. Some images obviously are related; for example, a romantic scene might benefit from descriptions of skin, sensations, and sounds.

Sometimes what works in imagination are the unexpected connections. So feel free to link the exercises that at first don't seem to have much to do with each other. Make the connections I haven't foreseen. The oddness of a connection may be the source of a story. For example, a bear belongs in a forest. Take the bear into an odd environment, a monastery or a restaurant, and you have a unique situation that could be full of tension and drama. You have created a reason for your reader to worry. Put together characters, settings, plot outlines that don't seem to belong together, and perhaps the odd juxtapositions will give you something to adjust, explain, and imagine. If sometimes you end up with a surreal story in this manner, all the better. Who says all your stories need to be realistic?

I have tried to structure the book so that the chapters build naturally upon each other—story ideas lead to characters, which lead to plots, and so on. However, you don't need to follow the chapters in order. You can skip around, flip back and forth, and still make connections and build sequences that will lead to completed stories.

GETTING THE MOST FROM THIS BOOK

I give some introductory remarks in the beginning of each chapter to alert you to some important aspects of the element (such as "voice" and "point of view") under discussion. These introductions give you some pointers and examples as well as the benefits of the experiences of many writers. I hope they are useful to you.

Now let's get started. The sooner you get to the keyboard to write your fiction, the better. Play with the assignments and watch your stories come to life.

CHAPTER ONE

IDEAS FOR FICTION

T he best source of fiction is the zone in which knowledge and the lack of knowledge meet, where you wonder. Aristotle said that wonder was the beginning of philosophy, and it is no less the beginning of good fiction. If you are intrigued by something and don't know enough about it, you can imagine what it is like, which may be more productive than merely relying on the information you already have.

But there's no reason to be dogmatic here. In some cases, a story comes mostly from experience; in others, it springs mostly from imagination.

EXPERIENCE

You experience a situation or event and write about it. You transform a real-life occurrence into fiction. If your life is full of strange events, what better source of fiction can you hope to find?

The advantage in writing autobiographically is that you can write vividly, directly, with the authority of your knowledge. There's a personal advantage to writing from your experience: You follow the Socratic dictum—Know thyself—and thereby reap benefits of introspection, philosophically and even psychologically.

Norman Mailer drew heavily from his war experiences to write *The Naked and the Dead*. Frederick Exley mined his years of alcoholism in *A Fan's Notes*. Mario Vargas Llosa used his experiences at the Radio Panamericana in Peru to write his novel *Aunt Julia and the Scriptwriter*. Perhaps everybody has enough material in his personal experience for at least one novel.

But you may run out of things to say if you are not an adventurer and if your memory is not amazingly detailed; and if you are an adventurer, you may not have the time to write. But writing from experience doesn't mean you need to be limited to your own; the experience could be somebody else's. If you've observed a strong conflict between two or more characters, you can disguise the characters and the places enough to protect the protagonists' privacy and take off from there. Since you don't thoroughly know the people you observe, you will naturally resort to imagination.

Look around, and when you are intrigued by a particular person's experience, imagine it and transform it into fiction. In Russia I once saw a woman send her son to beg. When he came back with a ruble, she would slap him so he'd be teary and then send him off to beg from another tourist. I think this would make a good setup for a story. You could transport the mother and her son to a country you know pretty well. And you could write it from either the child's perspective or the mother's. I'd say whoever has more of a choice about what's to be done is the better focal point for the story. Here, the woman's story intrigues me more than the child's. Suppose the woman faces the prospect of eviction from her apartment and she can't get a job. She has to resort either to prostitution or to forcing her child to beg. Later she could find some other options; that would be up to you to imagine if you write the story. This would, of course, be a departure from writing directly from experience, but all the better. Your observations are the starting point. Allow your imagination to take you from there. Don't limit yourself to the experienced facts, but be free to start from them.

IMAGINATION

When you work primarily from your imagination, you need not and cannot imagine everything. An imaginative painter does not have to invent colors, lines, geometric shapes—she works with these as the basic materials. Creativity may occur in the way a painter combines and recombines the familiar elements to come up with new images. Imagination means an ability to make images. As a writer, you need not invent airplanes, hairstyles, human behavior; you work with the elements of the world you know to construct images of something you have not experienced directly.

The crucial element in working from the imagination is to have a nearly empty canvas. You have all the paints and the shapes you want to work with, but you need the room to maneuver, which you get from not knowing the whole story and from wanting to know it.

Working from the imagination could be described as "Don't kiss and do tell as if you did kiss." For example, David Michael Kaplan, author of *Skating in the Dark*, says he wrote his story "Comfort" after visiting his girlfriend's daughter, a young woman who lived with another young woman. The visit was uneventful, but as he drove away, he wondered what complications would have happened if he had slept with one of the women. From those imaginings, he wrote the story from a woman's point of view and involving a man different from himself to ensure he was writing fiction.

Many people who work from the imagination do not need to know where the story is going. The uncertainty may work as a stimulant. The process can be as simple as one sentence leading to another, one image to another, and all you need is a good start. Maybe you are fortunate enough to be able to work that way. Peggy Shinner, a short story writer, says she works by association. Once she gets a sentence going, that sentence asks for another. But for this string of sentences to work, she needs a rhythm, usually clipped, fast-paced, with many commas or many periods.

To imagine a story, many writers need an intriguing life situation, and they must not know the rest. For example, Steve Yarbrough, author of *Mississippi History*, says he got the idea for his story "Stay-Gone Days" from a newspaper account of a woman confessing that she and a man robbed a store. After the first sentence of the newspaper story, Yarbrough quit reading. He did not want to know how the robbery actually happened; he imagined it, using as the protagonist one of his childhood friends in disguise.

PASSION

Imagination and knowledge by themselves may carry you far, but you need a specific enzyme for the right chemistry to happen: emotion. Ignite your imagination with emotion. Move your stories with desire, fear, love, grief, and other strong motives, and don't be afraid to make those emotions be yours. Live them through your characters.

It's possible to construct a story largely out of an emotion. For example, Dostoyevsky wrote his novel *The Double* by personifying his self-consciousness in a character. Leo Tolstoy was intrigued and terrified by death. He wrote many excruciatingly detailed scenes of dying in *War and Peace*. Tolstoy managed to express his own emotion and to let the fictional character live it for him. This is the basic Aristotelian notion of the use of drama: catharsis. You purge yourself of your own fears and vices by watching them enacted on the stage.

SUPPORTING THE IDEA FOR A STORY

You've probably experienced this: You have what seems like a great idea for a story, yet when you start to write, the story has no energy. It doesn't take hold. The problem is, you may have relied on the idea too much, without having the supporting materials. I have certainly experienced this. I thought once that I could write a story about a man who loses his soul in trying to gain it, and about another man who gains his soul in trying to lose it, according to the biblical verse, "He who wants to save his life will lose it, and he who loses it for my sake will gain it." But until I came up with convincing characters and a concrete setting, I could not go ahead with the story.

It's not enough to simply have an idea, a seed, for a story. Metaphorically speaking, you need the water, the right amount of light, and fertilizers. You might need to resort to research to develop your story ideas. In order to write *Sentimental Education*, Gustave Flaubert read more than thirty books dealing with the Revolution of 1830, even though politics were a secondary theme in the novel. Flaubert wanted to make sure his period details were authentic—and that his mob scenes and jail scenes rang true. Playing his ideas for the novel against this historical background stimulated his imagination to invent many new scenes, to develop the novel.

Most writers need to build scaffolding around their central ideas for pieces of fiction. This process involves moving beyond the major research. You must rely on your imagination and on your memory. A well-struck note here and there, an intriguing image, a line of dialogue overheard, a bizarre sensation you recall—they all come into play to support the growth of your story.

Of course, unless you have a photographic memory, you need not rely completely on recalling potentially useful details. Many writers keep journals and record whatever strikes them: a character portrait, a description of a group of people, a smell, a thought, a conversation, a joke, the atmosphere of a bus terminal. Thus, when you need a bus terminal in your story, you pull it out of your journal, or out of your memory, and with your accurately perceived details lend credibility to your fantastic plots.

This is where a whole series of sketches, whether noted beforehand or on the spot (whether simply in your mind or on the page), works for you. It's possible to write a novel straight out, without notes and journals to rely on, but having a storehouse of various moments you can use within your novel's framework will accelerate and sustain your work. A great many people who start their novels don't finish them, perhaps because they don't have the support of sketches, notes, journals, and other seemingly unimportant materials.

The exercises in this chapter and the chapters to follow should be useful for developing a whole arsenal of various elements you can use to make sure your story idea grows into a story. You can complete the exercises before having a story in progress; and you can also support your work in progress, sharpening images and scenes, running them through the exercise mill here.

Once you have identified your source of fiction, a story idea, especially when writing a novel, you'll need to grab whatever you can to keep the story going and growing.

VARIATION ON A THEME

Occasionally you may feel you have run out of fresh experience and out of ideas for fiction. Robin Hemley, author of *The Last Studebaker*, says: "Stories generate stories. You write one story and get the idea for another." From your writing, you may get ideas for new stories. And once you find a theme that works for you, use it to write not just one story but two or three. Cormac McCarthy wrote *All the Pretty Horses* about young Texans wandering and running into trouble in Mexico. The novel worked for him. So he then wrote *The Crossing*, about young Texans getting into trouble in Mexico. It worked. So he's writing another novel on that theme. Edgar Allan Poe wrote several short stories about guilt driving the murderer to confess his crime after a hallucinogenic attack in which the murdered person seems to come back to life. Poe and McCarthy have written variations on their themes—which were not unique to them; others had written about border crossing and confession. But the way Poe and McCarthy developed their stories was unique, through their styles, details, thoughts.

Try writing variations on a theme. And the theme need not be yours. You can get it from another writer's story, the way musicians take each other's themes. Taking a story idea from literature and playing with it does not mean your story will not be original. Musicians never doubt the potential for originality in using variations. "Variations and Fugue on a Theme by Handel," by Johannes Brahms, is a highly original work.

I've found Tolstoy useful in this regard. After reading his story "Luzern," about musicians in Switzerland, I wrote a story about street musicians and painters. The clarity with which he handles his themes encourages me. Of course, while I have learned from him, I can't say that I imitate him. Even if I imitated him, nobody would notice, for his wisdom is not imitable.

Look for the themes that can excite your imagination. Don't ever say, "It's been done." If it's worth doing once, it's worth doing twice. And if it's worth doing twice, it's worth doing thrice. And each time it will be different because "you can't step into the same river twice."

ELEMENTS OF FICTION AS SOURCES FOR STORIES

A piece of fiction can spring forth from almost any element of fiction: setting (your fascination with a place), plot (what happens and how it happens), scene, and so on. Perhaps more than any other element, characterization can generate stories. People are the greatest source of fiction. If you construct a character and dramatize that character's intrigue, you'll have a story, because you'll have to concentrate on several examples of what makes this person who he is. Probably there are more successful stories that are character driven than plot driven.

If your characters come largely from real life, you can make some changes to ensure you write fiction about them, to ensure you are forced to imagine. For example, Steve Yarbrough uses what I describe as "the deportation method." When he finds an interesting character in California, he places her in a Mississippi setting. In the new environment, the Californian changes her lifestyle—she can't go out for cappuccino, doesn't get stuck in traffic, has enough time to read books—and becomes a new character. The original character serves as the starting point for the fictional one. And out of the clash of a character and the new environment, tensions and conflicts arise and plots naturally suggest themselves.

The chapter on character deals further with how characters help you generate stories. If you are especially interested in this element of fiction, explore it. In every chapter in this book, I will look at a particular element of fiction. As you go through each one, be on the lookout for potential stories, and by the time you're through with the book, you may have drafts of a dozen stories and a novel or two well under way.

EXERCISES

1. If you have experienced an unrequited love, write a scene in which your love is requited. But since there is no story if there is no major problem to be solved, imagine some new obstacle for the relationship. Perhaps the lover has recently accepted a new job in a city far away and you cannot afford to quit your

job and move there, at least for now. But you know that if you try to sustain the relationship across many miles, you could lose her. Or perhaps the lover is a drug addict and will stay with you only if you buy her drugs (and you hate drugs), but you can't imagine being without her.

Purpose: To write from an unresolved experience. There's usually enough energy, emotionally, to make a strong story.

Tip: Gradually fictionalize yourself—create a persona, in the first person, who will have your voice and your style of thinking but who will have different biographical facts. Don't write sentimentally. With love it's too easy, and clichéd, to become flowery and to make overstatements. Instead, sharply concentrate on two or three scenes—first the seduction, second the quandary (give me cocaine or I'm leaving) with an argument. It's easy to romanticize something you've failed at, especially unrequited first loves. Give an unromanticized, perhaps satirical or even sordid, version of what the love would have been like if it had worked—just to go against the grain again, and to surprise even yourself.

Check: Are you making good use of the materials? Is the scene playful? Is the seduction seductive enough? If not, come back to this exercise after the chapter on scene and combine this with exercise two there. Or you could rewrite the exercise now; if you have only sketches, you can linger on details, play, be inventive, forget that this romantic situation ever had anything to do with you.

2. Begin to write a story from your own experience. For example, dramatize a social get-together; suppose you visited a family with your family (or alone), enjoyed a meal, and talked. Record conversation, observations, and thoughts in a scene.

Purpose: To write a story from a small idea. Too often, out of a big idea, a small story results because the idea overwhelms you. And frequently, out of a comfortingly small idea, a large story evolves; you relax, and the lowered expectations may release a playful energy in you and surprise you with how frisky and inventive you can become.

Tip: Combine this exercise with number three in the "Description" chapter and with number eight or nine in the "Image and Metaphor" chapter. Use a character other than yourself, someone much shier than you or much more brazen than you as the viewpoint carrier.

Check: After you've written two or three pages, observe what is going on. Find something that holds promise for more development. If you can't find anything that excites you, perhaps you can relish the quietude, the lack of excitement, and see just how subtle and uneventful you can become. Maybe the next exercise, a continuation of this one, will stimulate you to make something out of the nonevent.

3. Start with the same nonevent as in the previous exercise, and evolve another story line that takes off on a tangent. Suppose there was a temptation to do something outrageous, make a pass at the host, walk out of the bathroom naked, something that did not happen. Now make believe it did happen. Go beyond yourself and invent a character who could do something like this. Here, you'll be transforming a mundane event from your experience into a somewhat strange one.

Purpose: To develop a story from a seemingly mundane situation. Once you have a situation—the stage, characters—you might have enough support for a drama to take place, even if you haven't thought out the drama. By working backward in a sense, without an idea but with all the support an idea might use, you might evolve a story line. Worth testing.

Tip: You could write this from a witness point of view; that is, write in the first person, as though you (or your persona) witnessed all the events at the party. The narrator might be the hostess or a guest.

Check: After several pages, see whether you've evolved a problem, a conflict, that engages several characters in a potential escalation. Maybe the plot is about to take root.

4. Research a disease, say a multiple-drug-resistant strain of TB or cirrhosis of the liver, and write a story centered around therapy. Add a second drama to the character's life—for example, on the day she finds out she's got the disease, she gets a proposal for marriage from a person she'd been secrectly in love with for a long time or she gets a great job offer that she now probably won't be able to accept.

Here you'll be able to combine research and your experience, for surely you have visited hospitals, had tests, and so on. And the rest is up to your imagination.

Construct a scene with the character facing her suitor, talking with him, desiring him, and yet evading him, or not evading him. Does she tell him about her disease? Does she choose to kiss him without telling him?

Purpose: To write a story involving disease since disease is one of the most important themes and threats in our lives, and as such, deserves to be one of the central topics in literature. There's no place to hide from disease, not even in fiction.

Tip: Don't dwell only on the details of the disease. Be a bit indirect; foreground another drama in the character's life. And don't let the disease be predictable, even if it's a terminal one.

Considering that this may be an emotionally charged story, the emotion will take care of itself. You needn't say, "She felt sorrowful." Arrange the details around her to convey the sorrow. No need to sentimentalize the passions; passions are stronger than sentiments.

Check: Do you have a setup for a story here? Can you keep going? If not, make sure your character has a project—either getting well or finishing a lifetime hope, such as composing a symphony, against the odds.

5. With the global warming effect as your basis, imagine the glaciers melting and the ocean levels rising, washing off low-lying city fronts. Now, put yourself into this cataclysm, and imagine what would happen if the floods overtook you and your family. Sketch the place and the characters involved; here you may depart from a family self-portrait. Outline the possible events, and choose what seems to be the most promising story line.

Purpose: To write about disaster—a rich source of excitement. Here's a disaster scenario that hasn't been played out too much. Perhaps disasters can be productive for you. They certainly focus the mind: you know what the threat is, who the enemy is, and what the objective is (survival).

Tip: Make sure your characters are believable and interesting, even if that means you must stick with the people you know. Too many disaster plots have underdeveloped characters and poor secondary plots (usually a lame romance or love within a stereotypical family). To support the primary plot—the attempt to escape the cataclysm—the secondary one must be worthwhile too. Could you combine this with exercise four? The character believes he's going to die soon anyhow, so he can afford to be thoroughly altruistic. At the end, it may turn out he's not dying—a new treatment for AIDS, or whatever disease you have chosen, has been developed. That is just one possibility. Don't follow my suggestion unless you feel genuine excitement about what you can do with it. I'm simply trying to focus on a way of thinking that I know is productive for many writers—combining ideas for a couple of stories into one. Conceive a secondary plot of your own to intertwine with the initial story of the global warming effect. The secondary plot may in fact become your primary story, and the disaster scenario will work as an active setting for it. For an example of how to handle this approach, read Don DeLillo's novel *White Noise*. The disaster charges the narrative with tension, but it does not overwhelm the concerns of the main characters, each of whom is involved in other ongoing plots.

Check: Do you think this might work as a story? Jump into a scene where high drama is already occurring, and try to visualize it. Render it in detail and in lines of dialogue. In other words, test the idea in a major scene. Do several major scenes and connect them with transitions, summaries. If your scenes are working, substantiate them with research, and you'll have a serious story under way.

6. The media today is full of information about experiments in cloning. Imagine that cloning human beings is now possible and that your clone is in much better shape than you are—doesn't have the bad knee, is more muscular, is a perfect version of you. Do your version of "the double" theme. Outline what could happen in a story in which you meet your clone.

Purpose: To create your "double" and put him in a story with you. "The double" is a classical theme in which the basic story idea is already given, but treat it as something fresh. Psychologically, this is a stimulating theme—we all have in us doubles that embody our better or worse aspects than what we exhibit in our daily lives. Why not examine yourself in competition with your saintly or demonic side? The benefit of doing this exercise is that you'll create a character with psychological depth, someone at odds with himself, in an essential conflict. In fiction, nearly all external conflicts are hollow if there is no character to internalize them. A divided self generally lends depth to the action. Here, we can take the divided self literally.

Tip: Let the two characters compete, perhaps like Cain and Abel, for wealth or glory or love. If the outline of events doesn't excite you, determine what setting the characters are working in and plan an intense scene in which one of them is getting the honors and the other one is jealous. Write from the first-person point of view of the jealous character. The jealous one needn't be the less perfect character; perhaps it would be more interesting to observe from the viewpoint of the perfect but inexperienced clone. If the earlier dinner party exercises are set up well, could you throw these two characters in? Let them compete in telling jokes or in seduction. Or place this competition within the war situation in exercise eleven in this chapter. You could feature an encounter between a POW and his guard. The two could be startled to recognize themselves in each other.

Check: If you've gotten three pages or so into the story, could you outline some of the action that's going to take place? Or could you simply keep going? If you could do either of these, you have a story. Take it.

7. Outline ideas—situations, characters, potential story lines—for a sports story. If you like to play golf (or tennis, basketball, football, swimming, soccer), develop a story around an intense competition between friends. After the outline, develop at least one scene in the middle of a game. If the game draws you in, keep going and finish a draft.

Purpose: To outline a sports story. Sports are naturally tense when the outcome is uncertain. Tap into that tension for a story.

Tip: Describe a critical moment of extreme concentration from the point of view of one protagonist—his thoughts, breathing, sensations, perceptions. Choose a sport you know well. Of course, don't describe the whole match, blow by blow, but zero in at several crucial points. During a lull in the match, you could give some background of what else is going on in the lives of the friends. Sometimes friendships fall apart because of competition in sports; sometimes, they become stronger. No matter what direction you choose to take, let the match be a war.

Check: Have you conveyed the tension? If you managed to create a moment of uncertainty in a highly detailed, superconscious way, you have a pivot for a story. The rest could lead to this moment and out of it. Of course, there can be several such moments, and several matches, but during this peak tension, you need the most concentration and skill. Can you write the whole story? What's to prevent you?

8. Outline a story about living in a conservative religious community: A character realizes she is an atheist, and she has to break the news to her family and friends, all of whom are fierce believers. Or approach the conflict the other way around: In a community of scientific rationalists, none of whom believe in God, an adolescent, after having a strange, perhaps mystical, experience, declares his faith. Or in a cult setting, perhaps a member suspects that the cult leaders have strange ulterior motives, and she tries to expose these motives. What happens next?

Purpose: To lay the groundwork for a story about ideas. Too few stories these days tackle ideas as the dramatic force in our lives, yet many of us live by ideas. If you like religious and philosophical ideas, perhaps you could write a novel of ideas.

Tip: Here it would be healthy to strike a balance between the discussions of ideas and something else—fear for one's life, the strange behavior of cult members or scientists.

Check: The main concern with this scenario: Can you take off from here? Write several pages. Keep going. Pages are easy. You can always discard them if they don't work, but if you hit the right stride, there's no telling how far you could go.

9. Plan a story of a person's obsession with collecting some-thing—stamps, famous friends, languages, mystical experiences. Let this obsession work against the person's best interests.

Purpose: To use an obsession as the basis for a story. Obsessions, as concretized passions, are highly productive for fiction. The character's focus helps yours.

Tip: Through sensory descriptions, make readers experience the charms of whatever enthralls the protagonist. If you choose mystical experiences or a quest for knowledge, this exercise could combine well with exercise twenty in "Plot."

You could combine a collection of sexual conquests with exercise two from "Scene" as well as exercise ten from "Description." Add to all this a wife discovering a husband's diary (or vice versa), wherein the conquests are catalogued.

Check: Could you imaginatively get into the fascination with an object of desire? If not, choose some objects or experiences that intrigue you and rewrite the exercise.

10. Write several pages that would work as an obituary. It could be a true obituary, at first, of someone you imagine having lived interestingly. Explain the major moments in the person's life, as though you were witnessing what the person did. Change facts, but keep the story in the tone of a homage to someone dead.

Purpose: To write about someone who has died. Death, more than anything else, stamps a biographical story as complete. You can write a definitive biography or use the sentiment of finality to give you a voice of authority and perhaps solemnity.

Tip: You could also write about someone who is alive from the perspective of an obituary, as though the life were finished. Imagine how the life will end. You could write this with dread about a person you love or with malice, to get mean thoughts about someone out of your system.

If this all strikes you as too grave, you might still use the obituary form to write the life story of your horse, cat, dog, python. In telling the pet's life story, you'll of course tell bits of yours, and the interest in the story will have much to do with how well you portray the setting in which the lives take place.

Another possibility is to anchor a narrative around the life of an object that has deteriorated beyond repair: a car, a violin, a pair of shoes, a house, a tree.

Check: Do you have an interesting story? Give it to someone to read and see what she thinks. Sometimes the risk in retelling a life story is that it's easy to rely on narrative more than on scenes. If talking about the character in general has watered down the dramatic potential of your prose, rewrite, and tell the life in a series of scenes. Of course, general narrative can be great too—if substantiated by scenes.

11. Write a story outline that includes one or two evolved scenes. Set the story in a war that intrigues you—Vietnam, Korean, World War I or II, Chechnyan, Persian, Civil. Sketch at least two characters, and put them in a trying situation. The background of something so threatening taking place is bound to add drama to whatever action you have among your characters.

Purpose: To write a war story.

Tip: If you hate battle scenes, you can still set a story in wartime; rather than about a battle, write about someone staying home, hiding from incoming armies. Or write a story in the aftermath of the war; for example, using the fact that the Spanish flu at the end of World War I killed more than twenty million people worldwide, imagine a war veteran's family grappling with the flu. Even if wars might sound distant to an American ear these days, disease doesn't. There'll be enough universal content here to interest anybody. If you prefer to write about disease, why not combine this exercise with number four in this chapter?

Check: How do the outline and the scenes read? Do you have a story under way? If the war sounds too general and distant, perhaps a little bit of research would help, to get the names of guns, ammunition, places. Give many realistic and mundane details—toothbrushes, chocolate bars, texture of a mushroom cap.

12. Begin a story using one of the following sentences: "I found out an astonishing thing about my grandfather, whom I had adored until then" or "How could my grandmother do something like that?" Tell what your narrator has discovered about her grandfather or grandmother and why it's a surprise.

Purpose: To write about surprising behavior. Finding out an unexpected aspect of a person is a great theme for fiction.

Tip: You could relate this scenario to exercise ten. But be sure you bring it close to home. Write like a relative.

Check: Is what readers find out about the character surprising? Do you have a good character portrait to set up the surprise? And will readers be able to understand why, after all, the grandparent did what she did? Substantiating the whole loop, to see a surprising action and to understand it, could make a whole story.

13. Have two characters, a husband and wife with children, disagree about what to do about their beautiful house near a toxic dump. Describe the place where they live in terms of toxins: lead paint, radiation, poor water, air pollution.

Purpose: To write a quiet disaster narrative—not a volcano erupting, but a slower environmental hazard attacking. You can show different ideologies and approaches to living and dying.

Tip: Augment your narrative with the details of what lead paint looks like, how the air smells and feels in a heat wave, and so on.

Check: How does the story sound? If the narrative appears a little flat, you might throw in another element—the husband might be a manager at a nearby nuclear power plant. Or combine this with a murder mystery, where an intentional murder is covered up as an environmental disaster.

CHAPTER TWO

CHARACTER

There is no sport without players. There is no fiction without characters. How you choose and create your characters will to a large extent determine the success of your story. You could start with character sketches and treat each sketch as an exercise. Here you'll find exercises that will help you build your characters. Just as a painter sketches many portraits before venturing to try a complex painting, sketch your characters before you begin a novel, and even while your novel is in progress, you might sketch new characters before you introduce them.

Like a painter, you may get ideas for characters from observation, even from models. You can adapt characters directly from life—you may know fascinating people who would fit in a work of fiction. Import them into your fiction and disguise them—change their features and biographical facts, and transform them so not even they could recognize themselves in your work. There's nothing wrong with using your original fascination with a person to give you energy to create a character, who might, through pages, evolve into a new character, genuinely different from the model you started with.

You can make composite characters from the traits of several people you know: Fuse the looks of two or three people into one striking appearance; add other people's biographical facts, and yet another person's basic psychology, an obsession or passion. As you synthesize these elements from different people, strive to create a new, coherent character, who will not be based on any one person and who will gain a certain autonomy. Be ready to improvise, transform, play, create. This is a highly common method, and you may use a term from physics for it, the *fusion method*.

You can also make several characters out of your bosom, in what can be described as the *fission method*, similar to the splitting of atoms. Out of a tiny atom, a lot of energy can be released. Find some passion in you—which may appear at first to be a minor one—and build a character out of it. You can assign almost any external features to the character, but make your passion become the core and the dynamic force of that character— the spirit that gives him life comes from your insights, your suffering, your longings. No doubt, you have all sorts of obsessions and passions you can work with to create a host of characters who will be different from you yet in some way still be you. For adding external features and biographical facts, you could use some of the exercises in this chapter.

The exercises here will build upon each other and you will cover the same characters from several perspectives—through how they look, move, talk; where and how they work; how they fight, daydream, and so on—so that by the end of the exercises, you will know the characters very well.

MOTIVATION

The main aspect of a character is motivation. What moves him? What's his passion, his desire, his fear? A character without a motive is not a character, properly speaking, in a dramatic sense, but is an element of the setting, static like a piece of furniture.

When you introduce a character, imagine what her motive is. Setting several characters in motion, with conflicting motives, may give you enough momentum for the whole story. You need not worry about plot as much as about getting several characters together with strong motives at cross-purposes. Let the motives in conflict work until a climax, a showdown, occurs, and from there a conclusion will flow.

It's nearly impossible to make a dramatic story with only one character. In nonfiction, it's possible to write a solo character profile, but even then, the profile will work best in the character's interaction with others—at least with the interviewer. In fiction, you need two, preferably three or more, characters for a dynamic story. However, there's a limit to the number of characters that can be profitably employed in a story, and even in a novel. Too many characters with their own motives will make the action disjointed and chaotic. But if many characters have the same motives, they will create a monotony through repetition.

A character does not work in isolation. A wolf in a cage, away from its natural habitat, does not appear to be his natural self— the wolf is without will, has no motive to hunt or roam, and hence does not even look like a wolf but more like a beaten dog. A character in isolation, alone in a room, pretty soon becomes like a wolf in a cage—he becomes solipsistic and depressed. How many interesting stories have you read about highly motivated, exciting, and excited characters who stay alone in a room? So don't spend pages, as some inexperienced writers are wont to do, escorting your lonely character into ever deeper levels of self-consciousness and depression. Instead, take him out to a party or on a date or put him to work at a construction site or send him packing on a trip to some exotic place.

When you introduce a character, you could tell outright what the character wants, but in most cases, it's best to show the motives in action. Show the motives through body language, appearance, action. Make readers see, hear, and occasionally touch and smell and taste your characters. Bring readers close to your characters; make them intimate. Writing is one of the few safe arenas where we can truly get to know people. So don't be shy! Go for the heart—for the passions, the motive force.

EMPHASIS

In this chapter, you'll practice how to portray characters—their looks, their patterns of speech—in interaction with other characters, as they are perceived by others, and as they perceive others.

In describing a character's appearance, emphasize the distinctive, the unique, the striking details. Avoid the usual, and especially avoid expressing the usual in the usual way—namely, avoid clichés. Don't say, "He was tall, dark, and handsome, and his face had regular features." This creates no image for me. You may want to begin a description this way, but add a trait that sticks out, that will contrast with the usual. "He was tall, dark, and handsome, and his face had regular features, except that he missed his left ear and in conversations he always faced you in the right semiprofile." Now, this description still suffers a bit from the clichéd first half, but the odd detail places the character for us, creates an image and an angle from which we can watch him. He becomes dimensional; he steps on the stage according to his flaw. One flaw, one odd trait, and the character becomes a person who moves, who hides, whom I begin to see.

The word *character* stems from the Greek word for cutting grooves, etching. How a person's face is creased or scarred, how a nose is broken, and how one feature relates to other features— these particular details create a character. Show the geography of passions reflected in a person's body; that's what you aim to do, like a landscaper approaching a forest on a mountain slope. You look for the direction the trees take in weathering the storms, noting if their branches still bend even when the winds have passed and how the roots grasp and hug rocks like stringy arms and fingers. You look for how the body bends, with desire, pain; you look for tremor in the hands, thickening in the knuckles.

This is not to say that writing is a cruel act—you look for strength and beauty as well: for serrated muscles on the jaws, for a glitter of pride in the eyes under thick eyelashes, for a seductive gloss on the round curve of a lower lip.

Another word for character is *personality*, which stems from a Latin word for mask. This should give you a hint too. Hardly any masks soften facial features; on the contrary, they strengthen the features—make mouths bigger, noses longer or snubber, cheekbones higher, chins more pointed. Masks depend on exaggeration. Even to catch a realistic image of something, to express it, you have to exaggerate for emphasis. Your reader has to construct an image from what you offer him—and the more striking the features you offer, as a hook, the easier it will be for your reader's imagination to work with it, to hang the rest on the hook—the coat, the hat, the walking stick.

THE TELLING DETAILS

Express your images in details. Don't rely on adjectives to accomplish your task, but rather on nouns. For example, "his dignified appearance" and "her graceful looks" won't accomplish much, unless the adjectives are accompanied by images that corroborate the adjectives. Adjectives express your intention as to how your character should be portrayed. But after your intention, you need the things, the nouns, with their colors and shades, not with abstract qualities. Like a painter, show light, colors. Show people in motion—especially people at work, using their hands, shoulders, feet. Express their characters in how they tackle their hammers, stones, ice, papers, typewriters, phones, forks and knives, and so forth. Make your characters come alive in an interactive way—the way they interact with their setting and their co-workers and their observers.

Now follows the series of exercises that will help you fully develop several characters. You could use the series several times, to create more characters and engage them in conflicts that might generate plots for your stories.

This should be fun. Go, create your characters, meet them, play with them, have a party. After all, they will be highly passionate people with wonderful masks, striking features, the most stimulating people you've ever encountered.

EXERCISES

1. Construct a character from one aspect of your personality (not necessarily the dominant one). Make this trait the main motive force of the character's feelings and thoughts. If you are shy, for example, construct a character who is much more shy than you. This character should be different from you in most other ways—age, occupation, appearance.

Now describe his behavior, in summary, in several social situations, interacting (or avoiding interaction) with several relatives, strangers, his doctor, his therapist, and acquaintances.

Purpose: To practice the fission method for making characters. You personally have all sorts of psychological traits, passions, and insights about these traits. You can make many characters from these insights. No matter how dissimilar from you these characters are outwardly, they will have a part of you in them, and through that part, you will be able to give motivation, understanding, and life to them. You'll be able to identify with them. They will be in some way you, only nobody will know it but you. Using them as masks, you can explore different aspects of your emotions and imagination.

Tip: If you find that your description of the character interacting with others is too external, write in the first person so you can report the character's thoughts freely. To make sure this scene won't be quite autobiographical, make the difference between you and the character substantial—your character might be of the opposite gender, live in a different city, have a different family.

Check: Is your character believable? Can you easily develop more thoughts and create lines of dialogue that will easily flow from the motive trait you've assigned the character?

If the character appears static, rewrite your description—get your character moving, acting, in a dynamic scene where something is taking place. For example, he could stumble and spill a glass of wine into his boss's lap.

2. Choose three people you know and construct a character from them. Combine one person's eyes and nose with another's hair and mouth, and take the rest of the body from the third person. You don't have to copy these traits faithfully—exaggerate them to make them striking.

From among the same (or other) acquaintances, find an interesting personality trait—such as a tendency to be particularly offensive and then profusely apologetic. Think of a person who has an intriguing voice or speech pattern, and make this your new character's way of talking. Now you have enough to go by—place the character in a scene, give him projects, and see what happens.

Purpose: To develop fictional characters you'll be able to visualize and hear, using the fusion method, merging several people's traits into one character. This way of inventing characters is perhaps the most common one these days; mastering the method will certainly help you in writing your fiction.

Tip: Try to integrate the various traits so they form an organic whole. Some seemingly contradictory traits actually might help you to create a rounded character. Suppose you've chosen to match the trait of someone who says offensive things and then apologizes with a quiet voice and formal patterns of speech. That makes for a more interesting tension of personality traits than if someone who is loud and boisterous does this. In a boisterous person, this tendency would be almost predictable, and might amount to a caricature. By combining the unexpected traits, you resort to work, to psychologizing your character. The quiet person may be an introvert who makes awkward forays into extroversion and sociability; he may be shy yet aggressive.

Check: Do you have a picture of a person? Could you draw her? Could you visualize how this person moves? Talks? It's important that you can set the person in motion—write several sentences describing the person undressing and taking a shower. You don't have to make an elaborate scene, but do test your composite creation.

3. This exercise will help you outline your characters. You can use the two characters from exercises one and two or choose ones from stories you have written in the past or are writing now. Complete this basic questionnaire about your characters. You may, if you like, be a bit whimsical. Forget the real people, yourself and others, you may have started from, and freely invent and assign different "facts" about your characters.

Name _____

Gender _____

Age _____

Place of birth _____

Domicile _____

Citizenship _____

Height, weight _____

Eye color _____

Hair quantity and color _____

Unusual facial and bodily features _____

Marital status _____

Parents _____

Children _____

Pets _____

Occupation _____

Education _____

Medical conditions _____

Bathing habits _____

Sleep patterns _____

Favorite clothes _____

Driving habits _____

Organizations _____

Goal (publicly proclaimed) _____

Obsession (whether public or private) _____

Sins _____

Virtues _____

Secret passion _____

Main frustration and obstacle _____

You could include more characteristics if you like. Skip the topics that don't interest you.

Purpose: To create character profiles. If you establish the main external facts about your characters, you will save yourself a lot of time. Whenever I have introduced a main character without assigning him the basic facts of life, I find later that I have to pause, sometimes in the middle of a scene, and wonder, What should I make his occupation be? A painter? A doctor? An insurance agent? Deciding late on such a basic fact often costs me a lot of revision. You can't simply tack on basic facts, such as the character's profession, later. You have to go back, revise, make the addition believable. However, if you know all these facts about your character from the start, you'll integrate the facts in the character's behavior, setting, even appearance. While this may appear to be a fairly mechanical and noncreative exercise, it's certainly a useful one, a good foundation for the rest. Knowing the basics about your character might give you ideas of how to surround her with a setting and people and how to get her into trouble—in other words, to get a story going.

Tip: At this stage, don't worry about much. Fill in the blanks, playfully, have fun. However, assemble fairly realistic sets of traits. Ideally, the traits should not be absolutely predictably harmonious—a happy doctor, with a happy wife, happy children, perfect health, and a degree from Harvard, with goals to improve the world and a secret obsession of helping the rich. Nor should everything be totally out of whack—a billionaire born in a garbage dump outside of Fargo who is an evangelical Christian with a passion for snuff movies and a goal of saving Bosnian orphans and who has fifty children chained to their study desks in the basement. Try to strike the balance between harmony and discord—give enough ordinary facts and perhaps an odd one to create some tension, to intensify her motives.

Check: As you check what you've done, think of what more you could do with this. This should be a seed exercise for others to follow.

As you assemble a character's basic biographical facts, begin to think of where there's potential for a drama in this person's life. Maybe you can imagine a crucial moment in her life when she became what she is now: if she's ill, the moment she contracted a disease; if she's a zealot, the moment of conversion; if she's married, the steps leading to her marriage, and so on.

If you already have a plot outline or a notion of a conflict you're going to work with, do the basic characters' biographical facts fit the story? If not, adjust your characters' biographical facts to suit the story, or adjust the plot to suit the characters. Be flexible and ready to change, and test many ideas until you hit upon something that clicks, something that ignites your imagination with possibilities.

4. Choose one of the characters from the above exercises, and reveal him through several means of communication.

Let readers see a note or a brief letter he has in his desk but has either forgotten to mail or thought better of it.

Dial his phone number, and get his answering machine. What does he sound like? How does he fill the gap between the end of the message and the beep? How does he describe the beep?

Now suppose you have a tape with a message from him from his lover's or best friend's answering machine. He's trying to be pleasant—inviting her for a drink—yet it's clear he's troubled and has a lot on his mind.

Let him write E-mail if that would fit his character.

Purpose: To reveal a character through his communications with others. In whatever we say, write, or mail, we express ourselves, our strategies. Some of us may try to appear extra nice or extra harsh when we have an important goal. At this stage, you are still developing your character, his way of thinking and approaching the world. Letting him speak in various ways will help you to get to know him.

Tip: When your novel (or story) is in progress, you should be comfortable resorting to all sorts of means of communication. Varying the means of communication might help you stay fresh. The multimedia approach to your character can increase the level of realism in your writing—this is, after all, how we get to know many people, not just through conversation, but through message machines, E-mail, letters.

If you are setting your novel in the past, such as during World War II, you might resort to letters. People used to write letters much more than they called on the phone.

Now even if at first you think your character may not be the E-mail type, do let him play with it—you might find that this medium works for him and delights him. E-mail has certainly loosened up many people's communication, including the people you wouldn't expect to enjoy being playful and even silly.

Check: If you find using different modes of communication stimulating for developing ideas, potential story lines, strong voices, and other seminal elements of fiction, complete this exercise again with another character you developed in one of the first three exercises or in the "Voice" chapter. You might think of writing an epistolary story, or an E-mail story, involving these two and other characters.

5. Write this exercise twice: once for each of exercise four's characters.

We want to find your character in her office (or wherever she works). You could write this in the first person, as though you went to her office. You may give us first a sentence or two about the neighborhood and the building where the office is located. Walk into her office even if uninvited. (Don't worry if that seems rude—writers often are rude, in the sense of being nosy.) What do you see in the office? On the desk? Bookshelves? Floor? In the garbage bin? You can tell a lot about a person by how she organizes her work space.

Now let's try to track your second character either at her workplace or, for a change, at a place of leisure. Suppose she spends her afternoons in a coffee shop or a bar. Go to the bar, describe the clientele in several strokes, and describe the table she's sitting at—for the moment she's gone, maybe to the rest room—with her coat, her book, notebook, postcards. Or go to the gym, describe the clientele and the machinery. Look in her locker, find the clothes she wears, how they are arranged.

Purpose: To indirectly introduce the character. You can learn a lot about a person through how he arranges his environment. By listing various objects, you are bound to be concrete, to show, rather than to summarize and generalize. In exercise three, we get to know the character abstractly, and here, concretely, through her possessions and her impact on them.

Tip: Here's your chance to flesh out some of the character's traits. If she's resourceful but disorganized and has too many plans she can't juggle, you can show this in the disarray of her office. If your character is a control freak, you can show that through how perfectly she has arranged her office.

Choose a place that expresses your fictional character best. Some people express themselves best in their hobbies, others at work, and some at home, by how they arrange their gardens.

Check: Go through what you've written. Delete any guiding generalizations you may have used to portray your character through her space—such as, she's messy, anal, obsessive, possessive. Can you, while reading the description, be sure you have revealed this trait? You might give the exercise to a friend and ask her to tell you what trait you've tried to express.

6. Do this exercise once for your first character in exercise five, once for the second.

Describe the character at work, in the above setting. You may do this in the first person, as if you were a client dealing with the character, or in the third person, through the eyes of another person to whose mind you have access as an omniscient narrator.

Describe the character's appearance—her face, hands, body, clothes. How does she move? What's her gait? Posture? Body language? Speed of movement? What are her repetitive motions? Any smells? Perfume? Lotion? Makeup? Any sounds?

Does she have any nervous habits—popping her neck, shaking her leg, sighing, blinking, constantly checking her lipstick lines in a small mirror, grinding her teeth, or any others?

If your character is practicing a craft, such as pottery or piano playing, show us her individual process of doing it. What do the fingers do? How does she handle her tools?

Purpose: To portray characters by what they do and how they do it. A painter is a painter insofar as she lives with her canvas and paints—describe that life, the one that creates not only the product but the character. If you have a novel of passions, say love and revenge, and yet your characters do nothing but love and plot, your novel will appear airy and unconvincing. Sure, in some eighteenth-century novels about aristocrats, that's all the protagonists seemed to do—love, hate, and scheme. But even there, they were described in their leisure, at their balls, their hunts, as the leisure class. Nowadays, since most of us must keep our jobs and hardly any of us can abandon ourselves to extreme passions, bring in work for the sake of realism, believability. Work will be a great background, a medium in which you can create rounded characters who try to balance responsibility and passions.

Tip: If your descriptions seem to be flat and too straightforward, be indirect. For a general impression, can you use a metaphor to describe your character as an animal? In many Native American religions, every person has his animal that expresses his spirit best. Can you find such an animal for your character? Is she a cat, a mosquito, an elephant? If she is thin, has long hands and legs, and wears a silky shirt, she might be a mosquito or a dragonfly.

Check: Are your descriptions sensory enough? Do you give enough colors, sounds, smells, sensations?

If you say she's beautiful, delete that word because it's too general. It may express that you plan to accomplish an impression of beauty but fail to create the impression. Show the beauty through your description.

If you say she's nervous, delete that word. Can we still see that she's nervous, through your description of her nervous tics or troubled breathing?

Are your details striking? It's better to have a few striking details that your reader will easily reconstruct in her mind than a slew of vague, unfocused, and crowded images. Can you find a pivotal detail?

Go back through your exercise and delete whatever descriptions you have that you can't imagine through your senses. Keep the ones that work. If not enough of them work, go back and sharpen the details—two hairs sticking out of her chin, a blue hickey on her bared shoulder, above her thin clavicle. Be concrete.

7. Have the two characters from exercises five and six meet each other. One could interview the other for a job. Or they meet in a car accident. Or they meet at an auction, trying to buy the same piano. Or they flirt in a bar. Or they have the same seat assignment and fight for the seat.

If the characters seem too dissimilar to have anything to do with each other, all the better. Odd couples can be an effective theme. Let them talk. If you did not fully develop their voices in exercise four, do it now. They should sound different from each other, and natural. You may import voices from people you know, the ones you could imitate, like an actor. Don't worry where the exercise is going. The main goal is to let your characters speak, to let them be themselves. If the characters don't sound right, start anew, trying different intonation and diction. This should be mostly a talk scene, like in a play.

Purpose: To test your characters. Do they come off? If they can talk naturally, you've most likely succeeded in creating not only characters but people who'll work for you. Employ them. Give them tasks, jobs. With good characters, the momentum is on your side for making a story.

Tip: If the conversation lacks energy or is a bit aimless, remember what you've chosen for the motivations of your characters. Let them start to express their central motives—psychological dependence, optimism and dreaminess, greed, lust. Engage them in a competing interest—one wants friendship and support, someone to lean on; the other wants her money. Or one wants sex, and the other dreams of creating a better world.

Check: Have your characters hit it off? If they have, keep working with them and develop a story. If the chemistry between these characters isn't great, keep the character you think you have developed more successfully (and either ditch the other one or keep him for another occasion). Rework several previous exercises from this chapter, starting either with exercise one or two (one method may work better for you than the other), and create a character that could interact well with the successful one. Do exercise seven again, with the new character. If you still don't have enough dynamism, use three characters rather than two. Sometimes conversations between two people liven up if the third person shows up and participates.

8. Your characters now know each other well; maybe they are married to each other or they work together. Engage them in a

vehement scene, where they are fighting for something that is crucial to them both—the same job promotion, the same friend's attention, the same lover. Their primary motives should dominate their actions.

Imagine this as a climactic scene in a story. Describe what's going on by all the dramatic means you have—through cinematic description of how the fight looks and through dialogue.

Purpose: To write a climactic scene. What you have been doing so far is a preparation for the big scene, the climax. Now you have everything set up for it; write it. Deliver whatever the action calls for. A successful story usually must have at least one climactic scene in which you give details and render dialogue as though what we are reading is happening on stage right in front of us. The conflict has given rise to a tense fight, and the outcome is uncertain. You may know the outcome, but don't reveal it; can you surprise us with some reversal?

Tip: Show us first what the characters are doing from far away, then zero in on a detail from up close. You might choose an indirect detail, rather than a head-on description of a character's agony. Show a startled sparrow flying off, a snail coiling back into its house. Show then what the characters' feet and hands are doing. As you escalate the action, become more direct, show the lips, the eyes. You could weave these details among the lines of dialogue or lead into the dialogue this way, cinematically. Once you have the dialogue going, interrupt it now and then, with details from odd angles, for the sake of surprise; keep us a bit off balance, don't be predictable. Rather than describing a character's tears, you might resort to showing us a child's lone blue running shoe hanging from a leafless hedge by a muddy shoelace—that'll be a better image of sorrow.

Check: Do you have a good mix of dialogue and description? Do you mix indirect description (concentrating on something outside the characters) with direct methods (showing their bodies, faces)? A balance of methods is more likely to succeed than simply relying on dialogue or description. Is there escalation from tense to frantic? Can you identify the highest point of action?

9. Choose one character from the previous exercises who interests you the most. Write in the first person, and let her sit on an Amtrak train bound for her childhood town. Let her free-associate, remember, think, daydream, perceive through the window. Through stream of consciousness, relate what your character experiences. What's going on in her head?

Purpose: To get to know a character in depth, subjectively, from her perspective. If you feel comfortable constructing her thoughts and perceptions, her consciousness might be your best means of perception for the story. You could write it in the first person. And even if you write in the third, you could focus on her, on what's visible from her angle, with free access to her thoughts and perceptions, whenever you need to deepen your reader's experience of what's going on.

Tip: Mix concrete details from the train with lines of thoughts and with memories. Alternate. For example: "A redtail hawk surfing on rising warm air seems to be floating backward. I'm sure that's an illusion, because we are moving forward faster than he. That's a bit like my thoughts: I think I'm going forward, but my thinking goes backward. Why am I remembering the time when for a bet I licked a frozen pipe? My tongue was supposed to get stuck to the pipe, and it didn't. Is that another hawk or the same one? Are we running in circles? If I had lost, I would have had to kiss Tom. I wanted to. I wonder whether he's married now. I could have pretended that my tongue was stuck and that I couldn't unglue it. Can your tongue get stuck on ice when it's very cold? I doubt it. I doubt even the natural phenomena. No wonder I can't believe the literal biblical interpretations my parents have taught me. Or in love, for that matter. Where's the redtail now? Wow, that was a bump. Do they ever repair the rails? I always loved watching how hawks float on hot air. That's even more graceful than ice-skating. I wish I had kept that up."

In a stream of consciousness, you can weave details from a person's life as her thoughts, and thus provide background information naturally, without needing to resort to exposition.

You may choose to do a complex stream of consciousness or an interior monologue with long and incomplete sentences. However, I think a succession of thoughts and perceptions and memories may be enough strain on the reader as is, so I like to simplify the grammar, use short sentences, to be easy to follow.

Check: Do you get a mixture of thoughts, perceptions, and memories? Give us something from now, let us perceive it, and something from then, let us remember it, and something in general, a thought. Does the stream of consciousness flow? Here you may use a simple trick—keep coming to the same image, as I do to the hawk in the above example. Are your sentences relaxed, flowing one from another? If not, go back and make more connections between them, thematically. Seek a balance between non-sequitur leaps and logical sequence.

10. Experiment with other ways of devising characters.

Work from a snippet of conversation you overheard—perhaps all you remember is the tone of someone's voice, the attitude in it. Take that tone and attitude and simply let the person talk, in a social situation, say with her father or brother. Once you have a page of dialogue, pause and describe the person. More than likely you will have begun to visualize her by this point. Keep going—the body, the dress, the movements. Now more external facts—job, schooling, ambitions, or lack of.

Work with an image. You saw someone who intrigued you at a subway stop or in the streets. Supposed it rained, wind blew and drove the cold rain, everybody flinched and looked miserable, but there he was—walking as though it were sunny, smiling, looking obscenely happy, in a T-shirt. What's his secret?

Work with an idea. Imagine someone who is so virtuous his virtue becomes a vice. Perhaps it's someone who always tells the truth and consequently hurts people: Whoever has cancer, he tells them they have cancer; whoever looks ugly, he tells so. Or someone who is compassionate and worries about everybody, who has grown up in a little town, and is now in New York City. He can't pass by a beggar without giving a quarter. Can you imagine this person's walk through the city on a sunny day? At the same time, he has a family to keep and his income isn't great. How does he resolve his conflict? Maybe from this conflict, you can build the rest of the person. The appearance, the voice, all else may easily follow, once you unleash him in a setting where he can practice his virtue to the point of vice.

Purpose: To discover which methods of character development work best, or seem most natural, for you. Surely you will want to use all of these approaches in your fiction, but you may find yourself drawn more often to one or two of them. Your imagination may react more to visual stimuli than to aural—or vice versa. You will learn about yourself as a writer by examining these different sources for characters.

Tip: If it sounds like fun, mix and match these sources to create a single character. For example, put the snippet of conversation into the mouth of the smiling man at the bus stop.

Check: Have you allowed yourself to experiment, to try methods you have not used much in the past? Again, ask yourself which ones have been most effective.

CHAPTER THREE

PLOT

I t's best to think of the word *plot* as a verb rather than as a noun. Plot is not something you can buy like a recipe (or get ready-made in a book like this, for that matter) and simply apply. Plot is a way of thinking—an activity, a scheming out of a story. You can plot a bank robbery, an assassination, a rescue mission, a commando action in enemy territory. The metaphor works in fiction—to undertake a commando operation in enemy territory, you must know the landscape, the setting; you must know the enemy's habits and your capabilities; you must know the antagonists; and you must have a goal and an idea how to attain it. In fiction, you can plot your stories not only when you face the computer screen but as you drive, walk, wait in lines, go to sleep. You can contemplate the possibilities and further connections. Answering some questions, such as How could it be done? What else could happen? could help you come up with the plan of attack—or defense—in the story.

CHARACTERS' STRUGGLES MAY HELP YOU TO PLOT

To plot a story, it's simplest to have a character with a scheme, and following his scheme, you'll get yours. Find someone in the story who generates events and follow his strategies. What's he after? You don't have to delve into his childhood to make sense of his motives; out of the same childhood traumas, all sorts of personalities may evolve. A character may find some childhood events reasons for his current sentiments, although, of course, he could be a poor self-analyst. In the name of past hurts, whether real or imaginary, people do all sorts of things. Childhood as an arena of a character's subjective rationalizations can be productive. Let the character ascribe causes to his childhood for his present motives, but there's no need for you to make such a temporal and causal leap. Anyhow, what the character does must make some kind of logical sense in his mind—let us see what the character fears and wants. Whatever the reasoning that goes with a protagonist's motives, the motives are the dynamo that generates energy for your fiction.

Your characters must be intriguing enough to pull us into the journey, their story, but not necessarily likable. I think writers have exhausted our poor likable characters. Biographies of Stalin, Charles Manson, Hitler, and Chairman Mao fascinate most people at least as much as the biographies of Gandhi—so much for the argument that your central character has to be likable. One could argue almost the reverse—give us villains. Let us shiver with the dread of evil. Actually, whether the character is likable or not, I think, misses the point of what fascinates us in reading a novel. We need intense characters, whose passions we can get into, thanks to the depth and cogency of writing that takes us into the minds of the characters, whether saints or sinners.

LINEAR VS. NONLINEAR PLOT

Creating a series of causal links is the most prevalent paradigm of plot—one thing leads to another. This chain of events can be told in chronological order, and it can be told in a thematic and logical order, with one event explaining another. The sequence of events need not mimic the actual time sequence in which they took place, but it is arranged to illuminate why and how a character happened to get into problems and out of them.

A good example of a chain-of-events plot can be found in Fyodor Dostoyevsky's *Crime and Punishment*. Raskolnikov, as an impoverished student, wonders how to improve his lot. He has strong motivation, to get out of poverty. As a compassionate idealist, he wants to help many other poor people. He concludes that if he killed and robbed a rich old woman who would die soon anyway, he would have enough means to help many young people. However, he miscalculates. After killing her, he is overcome by guilt and fright. He realizes no human is above life. One human life can't be sacrificed for the happiness of many others. He agonizes over the atrocity of his action and, therefore, turns himself in and gladly goes to Siberia. All the events in the novel seem to stem from the previous ones. The peripheral events become meaningful through the main line of the plot—sights of poverty and child abuse inspire Raskolnikov to get money to help—and the peripheral events support the main plot. The motivation results in the deed. Raskolnikov's miscalculation, as the idealistic hubris and hamartia, brings about his confession and penance.

Events in a novel can be presented in reverse chronology and still be orderly. The more time passes, the farther back into the past the astronomers can look. The better the telescopes, the earlier the picture of the universe we get. We are being hit by older and older light from the stars every night. The story of the universe told by light goes backward. A criminal investigation may go backward—from the murder, via clues, to the culprits, their motives, their schemes years before.

This type of linking of events, whether logical or chronological, is called a *linear plot*, a much maligned term. *Linear plot* is often used as a put-down, the way, for example, *politically correct* is used. The word *linear* implies the lack of excitement, experimentation, novelty. But study one of Picasso's drawings—one or two lines make the dove, quite excitingly. There are many ways lines can move—in a circle, a spiral, a zigzag, and many other shapes. I don't think we need to place value judgments; no matter in what form we plot, we can write well or ill.

What's the alternative to the linear plot? Quantum leaps? Even the leaps could be described in space-time trajectories. Of course, there *are* alternatives to the chain-of-events (linear) story. You can concentrate on a series of snapshots that aren't chronologically or logically connected and explained. Much is left to the reader, who can make connections if she so pleases; the text can be an open read. A description of a nonlinear way to plot comes from the world of painting, as does linear: pointillism. You can create images not in lines but with clusters of points—sentence fragments. *AVA*, by Carole Maso, is written like that, in snippets. A narrative like this might be confusing, so it's important for the sake of readability to write clearly in each fragment, as Maso does. Even an introductory essay to give readers directions could be useful. Maso wrote an introductory essay to go with the first chapter (for publication in *Conjunctions*) about how the narrative came into being. She wrote from fragments she jotted in her notebooks while she traveled. "Among the many voices I had accumulated I began to hear a recurring voice, an intelligence if you will. She was a thirty-nine-year-old woman, confined to a hospital bed and dying, yet extraordinarily free." So now we can read the impressions and images from the standpoint of someone recapturing life before death; it's not so important what happened but how we can experience the passions and moments of beauty.

> Each holiday celebrated with real extravagance. Birthdays. Independence days. Saints' days. Even when we were poor. With verve.
> Come sit in the morning garden for a while.
> Olives hang like earrings in late August.

A perpetual pageant.
A throbbing.
Come quickly.
The light in your eyes.
Precious. Unexpected things.
Mardi Gras: a farewell to the flesh.
[a page later]
August. They sit together on a lawn in New York State in last light—bent, but only slightly.
Come quickly, there are finches at the feeder.
Let me know if you are going.
The small village. I could not stay away. My two dear friends. Always there. Arms outstretched, waiting.
A dazzle of fish.
My hand reaching for a distant, undiscovered planet.
Through water.
Where we never really felt far from the sea.
He kept drawing ladders.
We dressed as the morning star and birds.
He bows his head in shadow. He turns gentle with one touch. In the Café Pourquoi Pas, in the Café de Rien, in the Café Tout Va Bien where we seemed to live then.
We were living a sort of café life.
Let me describe my life here.
You can't believe the fruit!
I'd like to imagine there was music.
Pains in the joints. Dizziness. Some pain.
A certain pulsing.

Here, each sentence forms a moment of experience, an image. Fragments are separated. Just as in a poem, between stanzas, we can pause to contemplate. Part of AVA's narrative strategy is for us to slow down and pay attention to the details. Part of plotting (or antiplotting) here has to do with the fragmentary form, the manner, the spacing.

The poetic moments accumulate and form patterns, and as you read you get the impressions of longing and nostalgia and eros that seem to be the driving force for the composition. Childhood memories, love affairs, travels, beautiful places occur as inklings that express the experience, the emotion.

A pointillist narrative such as *AVA*'s is highly readable. You don't have to worry about following or losing the chain of events. You work with emotions and impressions. In a way, it's easier than a strictly ordered novel. And it can also be unstressful to write—you can be free to concentrate on the detail in a day-dreamy manner. If you love poetic moments and fear the shackles of a chain of events, you might try to write in a pointillist way. Also, if you are hovering between poetry and fiction in your approach, this form of narrative might resolve your dichotomy—in this manner you can narrate *and* poeticize.

This is how Carole Maso describes her approach in writing *AVA* (in the beginning of the novel).

> My most spacious form thus far, it allows in the most joy, the most desire, the most regret. Embraces the most uncertainty.
>
> In an ordinary narrative I hardly have time to say how beautiful you are or that I have missed you or that—come quickly, there are finches at the feeder! In a traditional narrative there is hardly any time to hear the lovely offhand things you say in letters or at the beach or at the moment of desire.

Almost anything goes here. There needn't be separation between writing a narrative and experience, current life. Even the act of writing the novel is a fair subject in the novel. This metafictional element—of assessing writing on the page while writing—can add a dimension of honesty and total engagement of the writer with the narrative.

Nonlinear storytelling usually appears not to be plot driven in the sense of events leading one to another, but you as a writer may be quite strategic in attempting to give us the sensations of a jumpy mind at work or of a character's walk to the farmer's market and back; you could deliberately write a story that works as a slice of life that is nonclimactic and nonepiphanic yet rich with perceptions, images, and wonder.

UNIFYING ELEMENTS

Between being hinged to a causal sequence and being unhinged through being experimental and nonsequential, there are options that can share a bit of both extremes.

If you have several stories that aren't connected but could belong together, you might ground them through a character or even an object. Concentrating on the history of an object as an anchor for a narrative can be quite effective. Annie Proulx uses an accordion in her novel *Accordion Crimes*, to link stories of several immigrant families who otherwise would have little to do with each other. Without the link, the stories would comprise a collection, but the link—the accordion and the music played on it—effectively pulls the stories together.

In a memoirlike story, you can tell several loosely interrelated stories, as, for example, John Updike does, in "Packed Dirt, Churchgoing, a Dying Cat, a Traded Car." There's a central event in these stories: the death of the narrator's father. But the narrator's experience of his father's death doesn't follow any chain of causes and effects. The narrator reminisces about various incidents in his life—a dance with a woman who later holds on to his thumbs as if driving some machinery, the birth of his baby in England, a cat struck by a car, his being bored in the church where his father worked as a deacon, with a furnace humming its devotions. The big events take no precedence over small ones—in a way, the small take precedence over the big.

The story is a series of images deployed as a work of memory, in a contemplative and impressionistic fashion. When tackling a big theme, such as the death of a father, perhaps this indirect method, of concentrating on the details loosely woven, might be an effective choice. You will not lose the emotion; the details will enhance it rather than hide it.

PLOT IN RELATION TO FORMS OF FICTION

There are many possible choices for plotting a piece of fiction, and you might avail yourself of the traditional options. There are many forms of long fiction that have proven themselves as effective and that are still worth trying.

Picaresque novel. You follow, usually in an unreliable first-person point of view, a fool, or a naive person, who goes through strange trials and tribulations, from one social circle to another, and thus exposes the folly of much of the society. Usually, the chapters are episodic, connected primarily through the persona of the fool. The secondary characters who show up in the beginning needn't be there later, unlike in many traditional, tightly plotted stories. If you are interested in this, you might take a look at *Tom Jones,* by Henry Fielding, or *Confessions of Felix Krull, Confidence Man,* by Thomas Mann, and analyze the novels to see how they are structured.

Bildungsroman. We follow the education of one character. Usually you start with childhood or adolescence and follow how the protagonist's relationships with his family and lovers change as a result of his education, not only at a university but in life—army, jail, the arts, and so on.

Family novel. This form follows several characters in a family, sometimes through several generations, against a historical background. *Oldest Living Confederate Widow Tells All,* by

Allan Gurganus, deals with the Civil War as well as the present. Family novels, however, can be difficult for many writers who do not live in extended families and don't have a large-family sensibility. But maybe out of nostalgia for what one hasn't experienced, one could imagine an extended family.

Absurdist novel. To fit the maxim that reality is stranger than fiction, you can have a series of events that are not connected by commonsense logic. This is especially effective when dealing with bureaucracy of one kind or another. Franz Kafka's *The Trial*, in which the protagonist doesn't even know what's he to be tried for, nor how to get to the judge, plays with the legal system. Joseph Heller's *Catch-22*, with many strange events, such as bombing the empty sea, deals with the army bureaucracy. Samuel Beckett's *Malone Dies* toys with most of our basic assumptions, about identity, logic, consciousness, and so on.

Novel of ideas. The excitement here doesn't come from actions or emotions, as in much other fiction, but from ideas. This type of novel usually has a plot of events that supports the exposition of ideas. For example, Jostein Gaarder's novel *Sophie's World: A Novel About the History of Philosophy* is structured as a series of talks about the history of philosophy; a teacher and a student fall in love with each other, but they sublimate it into the excitement of sharing ideas and learning together.

Genre novel. You can combine several traditional shapes of the novel as well as genre novel formulae. Not all genres are formulaic, but usually you can find a basic setup for the events in a ghost story, vampire story, romance, murder mystery, western, adventure, and so on. It is healthy to read the best examples of the genres and to make plot outlines for yourself, to study the formulae. Once you have the formulae, you can play with them, make variations or hybrids. Don DeLillo is the master of this approach. He combines a novel of ideas, an absurdist manner, and a disaster plot in *White Noise* as he examines how American society dysfunctions amidst consumerism and superfluous technology. A chemical plant blows up, and the protagonist, a chair of Hitler studies at an American university, worries that he has contracted cancer. In the meanwhile, we examine how we deal with disease, environment, history, and how absurdly we live in our postindustrial society.

Part of the decision in developing a plot has to do with whether you think you can logically cope with a series of events to make sense out of them, or whether you need to be expressionistic, impressionistic, perhaps surrealistic in your treatment of the subject, which may defy ready logic. Should you tackle the theme directly or indirectly through a series of images? These questions can become formal: What shape should your story assume? Should the narrative be tightly organized and connected, or should it be fragmented? Should the story have the shape of an interview? A series of letters? Diary entries? A memoir? A legal case? A courtroom hearing? A police investigation? A medical case history? A travelogue? A dramatic monologue? A raving? Most of these combined? Should there be a frame (for example, a librarian discovers in obscure archives a correspondence between two persons, and while reading them he decides to join a cult; there could be two parallel plots, one in the reader's life, the other in the letters)? Maybe all the possibilities cramp you before you start. But they should actually liberate you to play and try many things. If you get stuck in one manner, try another.

There's no reason why we actually shouldn't try nearly all the forms in our writing careers, like a composer who creates a sonata for the cello and piano, a piano concerto in C and in F-sharp major, a series of symphonies, each in a different key. Now that's a peculiar thing, that you rarely get a composer to compose two symphonies in the same key. Maybe that could give writers some thought, to try to write each story from a different angle, each novel in a different voice or point of view. Classical composers study musical forms throughout their lives; each symphony is a series of tests, experiments. I think productive writers, too, learn in each piece not only about the world but about the fictional forms and possibilities that each shift in perspective (point of view, voice, and so on) affords. One should rarely see the same thing come out of the same writer, except in formula fiction. You can try all fiction forms even though some people claim that a person has only one story to tell over and over again. Maybe you do have one basic obsession to deal with in your writings, but if you cast it in a different form—and plot it differently—you will write many different stories.

ELEMENTS OF FICTION AND PLOT

All the elements of fiction come into play in plot. Plotting involves synergizing the elements. You are a composer; you determine when to use the timpani, and when the flute, and when the two together.

When is the big question in plotting. What comes first, what last? How do you time and orchestrate various events? In a one-thing-led-to-another kind of story, straightforward chronology may still be the most effective organizational strategy. But in a story that probes subjectively into how a person's mind works, it's probably best to use shifts in time. When you think, you might daydream about the future, remember an event from ten years ago, and perceive something in front of you right now. All these times form a medley, a texture, that demands the weaving in of various moments; in a story with an internal point of view (following a person's thoughts), you have the freedom to be non-chronological in laying out your thoughts and impressions. Same with the pointillist manner.

In planning a criminal action, you need to be devious, surprising, covert. The same applies to writing a story. You don't want to be caught being unobservant, uninventive, dull. Think of what you want to accomplish, what to steal, and how to do it. If you want attention, entertain.

Part of plotting is style, seduction—the manner, rhythms, jokes. Sometimes your word choice should be cheeky, spicy; sometimes your descriptions should be poetic, other times, raw. Shock, provoke, use marvelous information, write interesting sentences—beautiful or crisp. Of course, what you emphasize will depend on your temperament. Devise your style of seduction to keep stealing the reader's attention. Be crafty, charming, thoughtful, but never slow and dull, unless of course, you want to bore the reader.

People sometimes read for the sheer beauty of prose, but to finish reading the whole novel, they need something more—intrigue, tension. Create problems, and make the solutions unpredictable. Be suspenseful by raising questions and attaining the answers gradually, through a series of steps and revelations. Solve problems through action evolved through scenes rather than by simply revealing and telling us what the solution is. Keep raising the stakes.

Somebody's skewed point of view, such as paranoia or extreme greed and envy, may pull together the voice, the details of perception. Or somebody's peculiar voice may convey an attitude and motivation from which you can capture a whole series of events.

In some stories, setting gives birth to plot. You may tell us the story of a place through the buildings, streets, rivers, and peoples there. The setting could organize your story; as you talk about the place, you can tell us about the events that happened there.

I want to emphasize again how all the elements of fiction are interrelated, and starting with one, you may end up using them all. That's comforting. You don't need to have your story completely plotted and outlined scene by scene; start with something strong and urgent, and develop it through voice, imagery, thoughts, scenes. Of course, the way these elements connect, they way they grow and expand and harmonize, that is the central issue in creativity. How do you create? There's no simple answer. I believe that making new and surprising connections in many permutations has much to do with creation. In instructional books like this one, we must separate the various elements to discuss and explore them. But in the actual creative process, the elements are connected—in fact, cannot be separated. Throughout this book, I emphasize how one exercise can be combined with another; while some combinations will not result in anything, others will prove productive, like two chemicals that react to each other.

Two or three chemicals brought together under optimal conditions (right temperature, light, etc.) can result in a strong reaction. Bringing together several elements in your fiction might produce strong reactions if you are willing to play with the natures of the things that you experimentally bring together. You know how a priest behaves in his usual setting, a quiet hamlet. How about in an unusual setting? Let him meet a model in an airplane, or let him envy someone who is apparently more spiritual than himself.

EXERCISES

1. Construct a story as a series of three causally related events, and present each event as a scene. Show a woman who has lived for pleasure alone and who, therefore, compromises her family, fortune, and happiness. Under extreme duress—nearly on her deathbed in a hospital, from drug overdose or disease—she realizes how wrong her life has been. From this central "epiphany," the character decides to change. Either she dies, and the change is only a spiritual one, or she recovers and tries to reverse the damage she has done. Perhaps she succeeds

and becomes happy—maybe it's best not to make that decision now, but in the midst of events as you detail them.

Purpose: To work with a simple chain of events, the core of much traditional storytelling.

Tip: This could be a moral tale, but don't subordinate the telling to the moral. The story shouldn't be simply reducible to an answer to the question, What is the author trying to tell me? If the author is interested in the message primarily, a sermon might be a better form than a story. You can start from a basic moral idea, but accrue life around it, until it overwhelms us the way it overwhelms the character in the story. Let each detail count, let us savor the story at each step. Here you could first develop the character's obsessions and then construct a scene in which the objects of desire are irresistible to her and to us. Later, construct another scene, of collapse. And then another one, of redemption. The story could have these three big scenes to work with. For the obsession, perhaps you could combine "Description" exercise ten with exercise seven from "Image and Metaphor."

Check: How do the three scenes connect with each other? If they don't, make explanatory transitions and construct smaller scenes to elucidate the big ones.

2. Study the character from exercise one in "Character," and make sure you have developed the central motive for his actions, such as extreme avarice or envy. Now put him in a threatening situation because of the motive, and outline three or four possibilities of what can happen next.

Purpose: To work directly from a character and his motive. It's usually easier to develop a plot out of character than character out of plot.

Tip: Once you have a notion of what might happen, write a scene in which the character practices his vice. If you manage to develop a scene in enough detail, you might be pulled into the story and begin to see it, hear it, experience it.

Check: Have you managed to enter the scene? If you have only an outline so far, try to apply it, see how it works, in a direct scene. After that you can tell whether the exercise holds promise to become a viable story. That is, if the scene is interesting and complex enough, you could show us how the character got into the scene and what will happen as a consequence of the scene.

3. Bring the character from exercise two in "Character" in conflict with a person of a diametrically opposed nature. Suppose your character is temperamental and bombastic so that for the sake of a moment of fun or a joke, he tends to offend his friends and later to apologize. Let him be involved with a woman who is polite but firm, who doesn't make friends easily and who doesn't forgive easily. Let him insult her in public just as their relationship is flourishing, and see where that takes them.

Purpose: To work with a basic conflict between two characters. The opposites not only attract but give you a range of possible conflict and action.

Tip: Maybe you can foresee the action, but if not, making the characters act out the potential for events might create the plot for you. Plunge into a scene. Once you've written three or four pages of it, you might see what we need to know to make sense out of it, the background, and where else you can go from the scene.

Check: Can you keep going? Is there a story evolving out of your exercise?

4. Suppose one person from "Character" exercise three joins the army (make her younger if necessary). At first, she's at odds with nearly everybody around her. She forms a friendship with someone, and the two have a brave plan to disable nuclear warheads, or something equally outlandish, in order to save the world or themselves.

Purpose: Develop a conflict-driven plot. Individuals who ally against a large group can generate productive conflict, and once you have a good conflict, the drama should easily follow. Thematically, this could be rich—friendship, romance, faithfulness, betrayal, salvation.

Tip: If armies don't work for you, you could try another group—a basketball team, a rock band, a law firm, an advertising agency, a team of evangelists, a cult, and so on. Follow the conflict to its full potential; don't dodge events.

Check: Do you have a plot here? When angling for plots, you are story hunting. Can you see the action? If not, perhaps a bit of research to gain confidence with the setting will enable you to visualize the action.

5. Form a story as a memoir. Deal with an important event, such as the time your narrator, under severe emotional stress, got diagnosed as insane, although to his mind, he was the sane person and most people around him were insane. Now he's no longer in the asylum, and he remembers the events.

Purpose: To practice outlining stories in various forms. A recollection as a gathering of images may be a gentle way to tell a story.

Tip: Work with images, such as a stamp collection; your character could be a philatelist who exchanges stamps and who is diagnosed when he goes through great lengths to protect his collection. His paranoia could be manifest in his relationship with the stamps. Add some other details from the chapter on images. You can relate the images as retrievers of memories—what was the character doing when he got a particular stamp? If insanity doesn't work for you, you could make a variation on this exercise, as you can indeed on all the exercises to adapt them to your vision. Maybe a character remembers being convicted of forgery, rightly or wrongly.

Check: Do you have interesting images and opinions? If the causality of action, one thing leading to another, is not your primary modus operandi, you need to maintain the reader's interest by the quality of your writing—thoughts, paradoxes, shapely sentences, and maybe absurdities.

6. Write a segment of a loosely structured story—that is, a story with many untied ends and tangents. Let a character think about five things in her life. One could be the importance of bread; another, socks; third, cafés; fourth, knives; fifth, bicycles. Create your own list, randomly and by free-associating if you like. The character's point of view (you could do this in first person) could reveal much about her while describing the objects.

Purpose: To move the story impressionistically.

Tip: Create a lot of images and fleeting scenes, and make a beautiful flow of language to compensate for abandoning a chain of events.

Check: Do you sense a plot here? Do the juxtapositions of different images spark possibilities for you? If so, develop these possibilities further. Push deeper into them. If not, think of a few new thoughts for your list of five and try again.

7. Write several fully developed pages of a story about the death of a mother from her daughter's point of view—either in the first person or in the third, although second person, the daughter addressing her thoughts to the dead mother as "you," might be interesting. Tackle the death indirectly, impressionistically, through a lot of imagery, thoughts, about all sorts of things, during a wake and the funeral.

Purpose: To write about death. Death can be a good occasion to celebrate life, to remember it in its full texture, at its best, worst, and even seemingly irrelevant. Just recently I interviewed a man who had been a soldier defending Sarajevo. I asked him what his favorite memories before the war were, and he said, "All of them. I used to separate memories into good and bad, but now after this terrible war, all of them are beautiful, every little thing I remember I cherish." That's the kind of attitude that death can generate too; even dissonances in a relationship with a beloved dead person may add to the harmony of memories.

Tip: To give us a world, choose a definite setting—for example, a tenement building in Washington Heights and a pharmacy where the mother used to work. Make sure you know the setting.

Check: Do the memories of the mother and the images of various places weave a colorful memoiristic tapestry? Is your writing rich? Are there strong passions that aren't stated but can be felt in the way you nostalgically pet the details? The intensity of the story should be in its strongly woven texture—thoughts, images, emotions.

8. Structure a story as a piece of metafiction. For an example of metafiction, you could take a look at work by John Barth, such as "Lost in the Funhouse" or "On With the Story," whose beginning paragraphs follow.

"In our collective headlong flight toward oblivion [Alice reads], *there are a few among us still, remarkably, who take time out from time to time to read a made-up story. Of that small number, dear present reader, you are one."*

The writer of these lines is another, and a third is the abovementioned Alice, chief character of this story-now-in-progress, whose attention has been caught by the passage that you and she together have just read.

In the story, a writer sits by the antagonist who reads a story about herself. At various points, she has the choice of what can happen to her next in the story, and the writer toys with the possibilities and discusses them. The story engages everybody in fiction—the reader, the writer, the protagonist, in a seeming discussion of how stories are made, among other things.

Write the beginning of a metafictional story. While setting a scene and introducing characters, discuss the options you have, why you make one choice rather than another, and so on. Don't let the discussion kill the narrative, but let it work as a series of asides, or a parallel story. You could use a story you've already written, and write within it a discussion on the choices you made, the nature of fiction, cognitive problems, or whatever interests you in the text.

Purpose: To write a story and at the same time to examine *how* you write a story. Let this be a study, a self-examination, about what you do with your fiction materials. Sometimes, thinking about how to structure a story may be at least as interesting as the story itself. It's worth checking whether that holds true for you, whether bringing in your thoughts about what you are doing yields something liberating and richer for you than traditional fiction in which one excludes the questions of how the writing is done.

Tip: This is a chance for you to play, entertain, to poke fun at the business of writing. For some people, the source of frustration can be a source of much jesting. Writing fiction, to most of us, can be frustrating at times, so why not get some fun out of it?

Check: Do you enjoy the permutations that one scene invites? This could be a healthy habit to acquire: to examine ways in which one event can change through one's imagination and daydreams—an essential technique in making fiction. How does your observing your writing change the writing?

9. Write a story as a diary. A wife finds her husband's secret diaries and is shocked to find he's led a double life. But then, the more she thinks about it, the more she realizes she's been leading a double life herself. So in the margins of his diary, she writes her retrospective diary; she remembers what was going on at the time, and in many ways outdoes him.

Purpose: To create parallel plots and to experiment with narrative forms. This kind of structure stimulates some writers to write dialectically—that is, the dialogue between the parallel events can enhance both story lines.

Tip: If you're not interested in examining a marriage, you could apply the same technique to another kind of relationship, say of a daughter and her father. The daughter discovers her father's diary and learns that he'd been a Nazi officer and that she was adopted from a family who vanished in the concentration camps. Use different voices for the two narrators.

Check: Have you managed to make the narrators sound distinct? Have you concretized moments in the diary? That is, rather than retelling what happened, have you created the substantial details of something that had taken place, even the taste of baklava and the dust from the wings of a monarch butterfly on the tips of your fingers?

10. Let a married and impoverished counselor (or teacher or bus driver) fall in love with expensive wines. He doesn't become a drunk—he can't afford it—but he must have one bottle of wine that costs $100 every evening precisely at eight. He goes into debt, starts a second job, moonlights, steals, just to support the habit.

Purpose: To explore a basic human conflict: pleasure vs. practicality.

Tip: Instead of wine, you could give us some other expensive taste: cocaine, prostitutes, silk shirts, massage. Jump straight into a scene where the character is tempted to backslide into his expensive habit and wonders whether it's worth it. Let the temptation be tremendous, and don't plan ahead his succumbing or not succumbing; report the thoughts of the man in temptation, and let us see the allure of his habit.

Check: Is the decision making tense, suspenseful? Have you focused on enough detail to slow the action for us and to give credence to the power of temptation?

11. Create a conflict, evolving it from exercise fifteen in "Description." A character is seriously ill, but he wants to hide his disease. He works as a healer or has been boastful about his health, and now he can't face the people around him, for he is in need of healing more than anybody he knows. Yet he goes out and does his healer bit. This could be straightforward—a doctor who is ill, but is afraid of losing his practice; or a spiritual leader, who preaches against sex, drugs, and tobacco and himself

is succumbing to AIDS (acquired through sex or drugs) or lung cancer (perhaps from tobacco).

Purpose: To try writing a story of an intense and unrelieved suffering—nobody to lean on, nobody to get sympathy from (not even the reader)—magnified by the character's vanity and keeping up of appearances. Suffering is a great theme; if suffering is relieved quickly through sympathy, support groups, and so on, it may also be diminished. Let's experience a great suffering.

Tip: Put the character into crisis—the healer trembling from weakness as he does the laying on of hands. Report his thoughts in the third-person flexible point of view so we could take a look at him from the outside and then switch into his thoughts and emotions.

Check: Have you got the symptoms of the disease right? You don't need all of them, just a few. Do you believe in the situation, in the scene you are making? If not, concretize the setting, and develop the scene fully, through exterior dialogue and interior monologue.

12. Write a short fable or an animal story with a moral.

Purpose: To write from an animal's perspective. Why not try a story that stems from such a great tradition? We can easily see our lives mirrored in animals; we are animals after all. Checking out some of the essential aspects of being alive, with sympathy for the animals, might give you a fresh perspective on our lives and on animal lives.

Tip: Don't worry much about the moral. But do give the details of how a fox and a cat compete, or a rattlesnake and a crow, or a coyote and a cowboy. The tradition of the fable will even make it acceptable to have the animals talk to each other, but see whether you can do without that so that the fable could work even as a realistic story. Make sure this doesn't turn out simply cute.

Check: Do you have the correct details of how the animals live? Have you developed interesting questions? A suspense? A surprise?

13. Write a scene three times—one event from the standpoint of three persons involved. Who will we as readers believe? You as a writer don't have to decide that we need to believe one person more than another. But tell the same story from different angles so that it will become three different stories that will complement one another.

Purpose: To relate an event from several standpoints. How we interpret what happens is sometimes a story in itself. The person's point of view, which involves the person's motives, slants the perception, and catching this slant is sometimes more interesting than what actually happened.

Tip: It could be something simple like a kid's fight. Two kids report who started the fight. The third sibling gives a version too, but not a disinterested one. Mom now has to decide which story she's going to buy, if any. Hers will be the fourth version. You could construct this as a long scene, with each speaker getting some time to tell what happened, while others may try to interrupt. William Faulkner uses this approach in several of his novels, including *The Sound and the Fury* and *As I Lay Dying*.

Check: Are the interpretations of the same event sufficiently different from one another? Do they contradict or overlap in interesting ways?

14. Develop a variation on this classical tragedy plot outline: A successful, rich, intelligent, and otherwise kind man has

become too ambitious and trespassed the law, or his own limits, and now faces ruin. Give this basic outline more detail. What is the tragic flaw in your character? Where has he overreached?

Purpose: To examine the extremes of fortune—from wealth to poverty. The fall of the mighty is a great theme—consoling to the unmighty and a warning to the mighty.

Tip: Outline the events leading to the fall. If you're reluctant to start embellishing it, you could revert to history. Read about the lives of politicians, scientists, and so on. The fall of Gary Hart, Richard Nixon, Geraldine Ferraro, Napoleon, Benazir Bhutto, Idi Amin, King Saul.

Check: Do you know enough about the place where you've set this story? If you don't, there are two options: (1) research and learn a lot about the history and geography of a place or (2) adapt the story to our times and places you know.

15. Write a plot outline that goes in the reverse order of the previous exercise. Have a poor woman, who apparently has nothing going for her except her intelligence, climb out of utter misery into a great fortune.

Purpose: To examine the extremes of fortune—from poverty to wealth. There's a delight in stories of rising from rags to riches. Most of us would love to. So you'll have a sympathetic audience.

Tip: If the plot strikes you as too straight and linear, you might make it circular. Combine it with the previous exercise; once the woman becomes fortunate and rich, she does not know where to stop and precipitates her ruin. For an example of such swings of fortune, take a look at *Sister Carrie*, by Theodore Dreiser, in which Carrie achieves success while several characters who are powerful early in the novel fall into misfortune.

Check: To see whether the plot outline can live in your imagination and become a story, write a scene, from anywhere in the story, with the heroine doing her thing; for example, you could jump into a scene where through her craft she outsmarts her adversaries.

16. Have a woman think about three unrelated incidents in her life while something else is going on now. Perhaps she is undergoing surgery or going on a date (she's divorced or married). Once you decide what these apparently unrelated incidents are, write approximately a page about each incident and three pages of current action. Then mix: one paragraph of present action, followed by one paragraph of one of the incidents, then present action, then another incident, and so on. Orient the reader enough for each incident, with different names, places, and perhaps even fonts.

Purpose: To tell someone's story through distinct events. This biographic approach is a way to show somebody's life through several pivotal points. Weaving the crucial events in a person's life might give us an intense, textured picture of her experience.

Tip: If you take the date option, you can have a double narrative—one exterior, in the form of dialogue, one interior, in the form of her thoughts and memories.

Check: Once you have about five pages of this, read it. Could this work for you? Can you make a story this way? Do you see some connections in the unrelated incidents? If you feel a bit uncertain about the details in the heroine's life, outline her biography—place of birth, parents, childhood home, school, first job, first boyfriend, major passions, worries—before you redo the exercise.

17. If you have a story in which the moments of experience, impressions are more important—or at least more believable and knowable—than a chain of events, perhaps you could structure the story in a pointillist manner. Jump from one image to another, giving a sentence to each. Keep coming to the same themes, same characters. Maybe this kind of loose structure will free you to reach the experiences that interest you.

Purpose: To use a poetic strategy. Enjoy images. Make beautiful sentences. Experiment. Find what works for you. Maybe this does.

Tip: Connect this exercise with several exercises from "Image and Metaphor." The images don't need to be related directly, but your character's point of view will link them in some way. See how *AVA*, by Carole Maso, works (not just from the fragments I have quoted, but perhaps find the book and read it). You don't need to imitate, but it might be good to see that nearly everything is allowed in fiction.

Check: Does this make an interesting read? Give it to a friend to read and see how she reacts.

18. Write—or at least outline—a science fiction story set in the past. For example, "illuminate" the Great Plague as a biological warfare that an advanced civilization from outer space, or a Pacific island, wages with the world. Or choose any other historical event that intrigues you.

Purpose: To merge history with science fiction. Get used to playing with plot so even if you write highly realistic fiction, you will be comfortable with creating big events. If you already write science fiction set in the future, try the past; here, history can give you much to go by, and breaking out of the usual pattern can stimulate you to imagine freely.

Tip: You can proceed here in several ways. Outline the possibilities—what the civilization that attacks the earth is like, from whose point of view you're going to follow the events (maybe from a serf's or a king's or the Pope's or a knight's or an alien's), and who defeated the invaders and how. Read a couple of history books so you accurately get the details of how people lived in the Middle Ages.

Check: Test whether the outline can work for you by creating a scene somewhere in the middle of the warfare. If you aren't beginning to see this story idea in scenic detail, the idea has not touched the ground yet.

19. Write a science fiction story set in the future. Perhaps tobacco has been thoroughly exterminated as a plant. Several scientists manage to re-create the plant from an old textbook showing the tobacco DNA structures. What happens next? Or, saddened by the decline of music, a dictator orders a team of scientists to re-create Mozart from his DNA. But as Mozart is buried in a pauper's grave, nobody is sure that the corpse is the right one, and the person they grow turns out to be deaf and much more talented in soccer than in music. So they go for Beethoven, and the new Beethoven becomes a punk rocker. Of course, you can come up with many ideas on your own.

Purpose: To plot a story by combining projections about the future with science fiction. Having an idea for a story is still far from having an evolved plot. But it is one way to get into plotting—particularly if you can connect the idea with characters and places.

Tip: Perhaps you could think of a subplot to integrate into the main stream of events. Romance is the usual accompaniment of many fantasy pieces and disaster events, but perhaps a murder mystery or another genre might contribute a productive cross-pollination.

Check: Can you focus to a scene and produce enough detail to feel you've entered the story? Can you get into it?

If your initial drafting of the exercise gets you excited enough to want to write the whole story, read some user-friendly science textbooks in genetics or whatever other field you'll play with. Those will give you a few convincing details.

20. Write one or two outlines for a bildungsroman or a picaresque or a family novel or a novel of ideas.

Purpose: To work toward a novel that fits in a grand tradition.

Tip: To develop a novel of ideas, say religious ideas, you could combine this with "Ideas for Fiction" in exercise eight. Perhaps you could combine the picaresque novel with the novel of ideas and have someone naive and hungry for spiritual enlightenment shop from church to church, and sect to sect, and you can follow his misadventures and, at the same time, seriously analyze various religions.

If your family is interesting, why not write your family novel? You can fictionalize it, change names, exaggerate, but you already have the basic relationships, histories, places, and so on. The family novel could combine with a bildungsroman—an education and maturation curve, perhaps yours.

Check: Can you develop a novel out of your outline? To test how the outline is working, plunge your character into a big scene—for example, in the picaresque novel of ideas, the character is being baptized by full immersion, although he is not quite ready for it. Of course, find your own scene that you can work with, and see how long you can stay with it. If you can sustain several scenes for quite a few pages, what's to prevent you from accumulating a three-hundred page manuscript, a novel?

21. Can you plot an interesting love story? Make it quirky and odd, perhaps a romantic comedy. Choose the characters who fall in love, and describe their first meeting. Once you have a scene where you get the sense of who the characters are, outline the possibilities. What can happen? Find good obstacles for them to overcome.

Purpose: Write a love story, in our postmodern, postindustrialist virtual reality time, and write it in a fresh way.

Tip: Don't be sentimental about all this. The love story could be flat if it happens in isolation from an interesting context. Give the characters something else to do except love each other. Perhaps there's a war going on or the plague or they are trapped in a cult. No matter how serious the context in which the love story is set, humor and irony could certainly help to make this a lively story.

Check: How does your scene sound? Too direct and too lovey-dovey? Rewrite, and give the characters some other urgent tasks, and perhaps enough pride so they would not acknowledge their feelings of love amid the crisis.

CHAPTER FOUR

POINT OF VIEW

F iction has to do at least as much with how people observe and interpret events as with the events themselves. The observation of the event and the event are usually inextricable. The observation of how an atom behaves may influence the atom's behavior; and we don't know, but can only try to infer, how an unobserved atom behaves. Likewise, in fiction we shouldn't be able to know how an unobserved character behaves. (The character has to be observed at least by himself as the simultaneous narrator.) As in a movie, we must be able to follow him and take a look at him from one angle or another, or otherwise we, like judges, have to infer the unobserved behavior from the evidence that's left behind.

What happens is never visible from all the angles at once. We perceive from a certain altitude and distance, and we interpret what is taking place from what we already know or think we know.

In fiction, we usually strive to simulate this specific angle of vision in the point of view we choose. We can shift that point of view, but while we're looking at one scene, or sights and sounds, we are committed to one point of view for the duration of the look. The deeper the look, generally, the better, and for that reason, it's good to stick with one viewpoint for a while before shifting, if we must shift.

My intention here is not to make the point of view issue sound more complicated than it should, but to draw attention to how you can turn it to your advantage if you use it well—make it work for you as an element of freedom rather than against you as a prohibition of what's not allowed. From my experience of reading thousands of students' stories, I could, to paraphrase St. Paul, say that everything is allowed but not everything is to your advantage. So shift the point of view freely and experiment, but after a while assess whether the shifts benefit you.

FIRST PERSON

The most direct option is the first-person point of view that simulates a person narrating her experience and observation.

If you want to tell your story, you can do so without any literary camouflage; in autobiographic fiction, you need not distinguish between you as the author, your persona, and the protagonist (you as the subject of the story). You are not mincing words about it, not screening or masking. Your memory, your voice, your angle of vision make the story. A big part of the story is how you know what happened and to what extent you remember and to what extent you reimagine and change events in your memory.

Many writers have used autobiographic first-person point of view and haven't needed anything else—Henry Miller, Louis-Ferdinand Céline, Harold Brodkey. They found their lives—and particularly their perceptions and thoughts—sufficiently fascinating to keep writing from experience without much disguise. This kind of writing is hard to distinguish from memoirs; and frequently, it's only the writer's awareness of his unreliability in recounting his life that persuades him to declare his autobiographic writing is fiction rather than creative nonfiction. The decision to declare it fiction in itself is a choice of the viewpoint as a fictional tool rather than nonfictional—

and the choice of freedom to grasp at experience for the story rather than an objective precision.

THIRD-PERSON LIMITED AND OBJECTIVE

If you need some protection and privacy in fictionalizing your observations, choose a persona, somebody who is not you but through whom you can perceive actions and problems. Assign different biographical facts—age, occupation, even gender—to this persona, to make sure it's not you. Now choose and construct a voice for the persona. Once you hear how this person would talk, let her talk, be her secretary, turn on the Dictaphone.

If you aren't comfortable writing in a voice that's not yours, and you want distance between you and the materials you write about, choose third-person point of view and use your narrative voice.

In third person, you as a writer and (hidden) narrator behave simply like a friend who knows the character intimately, yet you find no need to talk about yourself. It's your friend's story. Even if it isn't, that's a good paradigm. You've been there, you've observed what your friend did, what she said, how she behaved, how she looked, and you know the background, which you could summarize to another friend. This could be called third-person limited objective point of view. I don't particularly like the words *limited* and *objective*, but they may be useful: limited in the sense that the focus is on the protagonist, not on the whole universe; objective in the sense that she is observed from the outside, not in her mind directly.

If you find being outside of your character's head is a little too distant and the question, What's going through her mind? is too pressing, you can enter her mind and still address her as "she": "As she checked out the sharp edge of her molar with her tongue twisting backward, she wondered whether Vick was a good dentist, and whether she could trust a friend to rummage through her mouth." This will have the subjective features of first-person point of view, but will be told in your voice, using third person.

If you want to show something your character may not know or see about herself, you might stand back now and then and show us from the outside what her folly or brilliance looks like. You'll shift your focus, or psychic distance (in the sense of mental distance). For a couple of paragraphs, you might follow her from the outside: Use the cinematic technique of fading in, then moving closer to observe the details, the shafts of glare from her earring. You might remove your focus and see her from far away in the street, riding a bike, shooting a sparrow. Then you could go directly into her head: "She woke up with the images of the bleeding sparrow. Even as she tried to organize her schedule for the day around the dental appointment, she still saw the red on the gray, the blood on the shivering wing."

OMNISCIENCE

For short stories, the points of view I have mentioned usually suffice, and the same is true of many novels. For a long piece of fiction that covers a lot of ground, you could use what I call the nonperson point of view—omniscience. Here you don't need to simulate the angle of vision. You are like an intelligence service that has collected data from various sources—history books, encyclopedias, spies, reporters—and now is recounting a definitive story about what actually happened in Rwanda in 1995, without constantly supplying the sources. You have moved beyond the data collecting; the story is not about perception and data collection and personal angles of vision, but about a war affecting millions of people. But while, for many pages, you may carry this aloof historian's point of view to create the complete picture of the war, you'd do well even here to focus at least for a while on individuals, their sufferings, expressions, thoughts. You could enter their heads, in the third person or even in the first person. You can shift the perspective and the point of view, from a large historical one to an intensely personal one.

Novels written from the omniscient point of view frequently and for long stretches shift and narrow in focus to a limited and personal point of view. The fact is that the large and distant perspective is not omniscient—it's too distant and sweeping. Hardly any novels manage to maintain the distance and keep their impersonal "cool"; most novels are, after all, intensely personal, so the point of view tends to become personal.

MULTIPLE VIEWPOINTS

If you enter many heads to "report" what people think and feel (whether in third person or in the succession of several first-person accounts), you are using a multiple point of view. The main thing here is to make sure that once you enter a consciousness, you make it worth the trip; show us a lot of what is going on in there and how what's going on outside looks and feels on the inside. Of course, these distinctions (the outside and the inside) are not particularly precise since nearly every observation is a conglomerate of the two, the outside stimuli and the inside perceptions; it's an indivisible continuum.

It's important to choose the angle of vision from which we see enough to understand what is going on but not too much; if we can see everything at once, we might not develop much tension. Tension comes from knowing something and suspecting something we don't know. In that sense, omniscience is diametrically opposed to suspenseful fiction.

SKEPTICAL POINT OF VIEW

Total skepticism, too, is diametrically opposed to suspense, since if nothing is certain, the threat is not certain either. Curiously, you don't hear much about the skeptical point of view, which I think is a legitimate one, especially in absurdist fiction, such as Samuel Beckett's. In this type, the narrator is not sure whether what he sees is true, whether he is sane or not, whether he remembers the facts, whether there are facts. With extreme doubt, you might achieve interesting examinations, toy with epistemological questions, and write funny paradoxes. (Of course, each thought and doubt can have its own plot, but if the doubt is always there, the results of thoughts may be too predictable—questions upon questions.)

Here's an example of a deliberate narrative uncertainty, from Beckett's "Ding-Dong."

> He lived a Beethoven pause, he said, whatever he meant by that. In his anxiety to explain himself, he was liable to come to grief. Nay, this anxiety in itself, or so at least it seemed to me, constituted a break-down in the self-sufficiency. . . .

Here we deal with seeming, likelihood, lack of understanding—"whatever he meant" and "so at least it seemed to me." This sort of skeptical point of view, which depends to a great extent on such words as *maybe* and *perhaps*, is even clearer in Beckett's novel *Watt*.

> And what to me may seem most unlike him, and what to me may seem most like him, may in reality be most like him, most unlike him, for all I can tell. Or perhaps Mr. Knott sends Erskine flying up and down in this way, simply in order to be rid of him if only for a few moments. Or perhaps Erskine, finding the first-floor trying, is obliged to run upstairs every now and then for a breath of the second-floor, and then every now and then downstairs for a breath of the ground-floor, or even garden, just as in certain waters certain fish, in order to support the middle depths, are forced to rise and fall, now to the

surface of the waves and now to the ocean bed. But do
such fish exist? Yes, such fish exist, now.

Beckett clearly jokes—he speculates that there might be a fish
that has to go up to the surface and then down much deeper
than usual, and his character asks, "But do such fish exist?"
"Yes, such fish exist, now," that is, in Beckett's novel, as a joke
of categories and comparisons.

It is difficult to maintain total skepticism throughout a
book, and Beckett varies his angle of knowability to limited
omniscient and back to skepticism. The point of view in which
a character questions everything and is certain of nothing, of
course, can be used in traditional fiction as well, to delve into
the consciousness of someone undergoing extreme stress or
debility or doubt.

In choosing the point of view, you will achieve the best
dramatic results between the extremes, in the modest middle,
which can shift its focus. Even in a suspenseful novel, in a
summary, you can shift to the extremes, maximize your focus
to the omniscient, and then in the most dramatic moments,
when your heroine is undergoing an extreme stress, you could
narrow the focus using the subjective first person, and even
further, to the skeptical point of view, where the character
who is the means of perception does not know what the hell
is going on.

As you read fiction, you can analyze for yourself from what
angle of vision the information apparently comes from and
determine what is effective and what's worth trying beyond
the most traditional patterns. A textbook, especially one that
aims to be primarily an exercise book, is not a substitute for
reading and analyzing fiction. You can learn the technical aspects best from analytical reading. Doing exercises might
sharpen your reading; your reading will, of course, sharpen
your writing.

EXERCISES

1. Retell something that happened to you, in your voice, from your perspective, using "I."

Purpose: To find out whether you express yourself most intensely when you are quite direct, without the artifice of removed points of view, in telling your stories.

Tip: The event you recount could be something highly personal. How about an embarrassing incident that has been bothering you? Or it could be something painful—an illness you've gone through or you've witnessed, a dishonest act you may have done, or a strange experience you've had.

In this approach, you have a chance to wed your voice to the point of view; you are the point of view.

Check: Does this sound like you, or are you simply striking a pose? Reread your story; delete any verbal sequences aimed at sounding particularly chatty and oral or like some other storyteller. Rely on your own wording, and make sure your writing reflects your own sound.

2. Use your first-person voice from exercise one to relate an imagined event as if it happened to you.

Purpose: To personalize or "familiarize" a strange event. Sometimes it's hard to describe something bizarre and to believe in it, to get into it in detail and in thought. First-person point of view, your own way of looking at things, might free you, bring you psychically closer to the event, the possibilities.

Tip: Write a science fiction fantasy set in the past, or any other exercise from the "Ideas for Fiction" and "Plot" chapters that would spur you to write something primarily from imagination.

Your voice and your attitude will help you make it your own show no matter how alien the fantasy.

Check: Are you bringing the bizarre and fantastic home through your voice, your idiosyncrasies? Maybe it's best to ask a friend of yours to read a couple of pages of what you've written. You might orient your friend and give him an outline within which the event, or a scene that you've described, takes place.

3. Use the composite character from "Character" exercise two and make him talk in the first person. Use a voice that is not quite yours but that's not too alien to you—perhaps your brother's or sister's voice, if you can hear it in your head, merged with yours. Now, let the character tell us why she committed an abhorrent deed. Maybe she seduced a neighbor's son, or didn't give medicine to her mother, or overdosed on heroin.

Purpose: To make a "red shift" in your usage of voice, that is, develop other people's voices in a way you can handle, to expand your writing universe.

Tip: After you get the syntax and the diction of this voice going, don't think of where you're getting it. Make sure the story is fictional.

Check: How does it sound? The main thing here is that the voice of the point of view carrier sound convincing. If there is stiff phrasing that sounds more like a pose than like a real person, maybe you could cut the phrasing (unless you aim to show someone posing) and try another way of putting words together that you feel comfortable with.

4. Describe something that happened to a friend of yours, and speak about her in the third person. Don't mention yourself, your friendship, your direct opinions. Follow her, as though on

a stage or in a movie, where you usually are bound to stay outside the character's head.

Purpose: To practice third-person limited and external point
of view. This requires a good deal of discipline, but frees you to
be an observer.

Tip: Talk only about her, but from your intimate knowledge
and perspective, as though you were at her table in the coffee
shop when she broke up with her boyfriend. Visualize a scene,
and describe it with a lot of detail, dialogue. Be free to give us
her background, in the introduction, the kind of stuff one could
read in the newspapers or that one could find in a journalistic
search into her background.

If you don't want to start with a real friend, fictionalize one
and imagine something she did.

Check: Does this work for you? Some people like the limitations
of a third-person external point of view, the observational perspective. Others prefer to have the leeway to enter the character's head
as well as to stay outside, a flexible third-person focused point of
view. No reason why both kinds of approaches shouldn't work
for us, rather than against us. If in this exercise you didn't enjoy
the limits, find another exercise or story that you did in first person
and recast it in this third-person external point of view. How will
your story change? What will you lose? Gain?

5. Keep going with exercise four's event, and enter your
friend's head. Report her thoughts as well as her actions. Forget
it's your friend. Fictionalize or disguise your friend in such a way
that not even she would recognize herself. Change her age, eye
and hair colors, length of hair, occupation, perhaps gender, and
see what happens.

Purpose: To work from a third-person flexible point of view.
This allows you the maximum freedom: You can be descriptive

and cinematic, with your protagonist as observable as an actor; and you can be thoughtful and report your character's impressions and memories.

Tip: In the flexible point of view, you have more freedom than in the external to move backward in time, through reminiscences, and to play around with impressions and thoughts. See what you can do with that.

Check: How is this working? It's a highly useful point of view, so if it didn't work in this exercise, try another one. Maybe alternate your viewpoint by paragraphs—in one paragraph, observe her from the outside in a limited external manner, and then in another, record her impressions, from her perspective, in the subjective manner. That can be a natural movement—to zero in from the outside and gradually get so close you enter the subjective sphere, the thoughts. After we have experienced her thoughts, show her from the outside again.

6. Write the first several pages of a historical novel, using the omniscient point of view focusing on a social movement or era in the past that you lived through or know well. Consider using the punk or hippie movements or even the disco craze.

Purpose: To practice the big-picture point of view—the omniscient. Omniscient sounds intimidating, and it's a powerful theological concept, but the big picture of piecing the story from many sources, and having access to all of them, shouldn't be too unrealistic. After intensive research, interviews, and direct experience, many journalists are able to compile big stories that cover a problem from many angles and perspectives.

Tip: Write about a movement you know best. But don't take a personal angle. Write like a historian for a couple of pages, discussing the possible causes of the movement. After you've established the historical context, you might create a scene set during the Kent State riots or the concert at Woodstock, and you could broaden the perspective by discussing the economic crisis and contemporary wars. Follow several characters in this scene.

Check: How is this point of view working for you? Are you comfortable shifting from the big picture to a scene with a close-up? Why or why not? If the big-picture viewpoint works against the grain of your nature, you might give that viewpoint to one of the characters involved, and let him voice various opinions and interpretations of the historical movement. You will then abandon the authorial omnicient point of view but will be able to use the technique for characterizing someone who has the impression that he understands a lot, and this too could serve you in good stead.

7. Now to illustrate a point about dealing with the peace movement in the sixties, you might choose to follow young American soldiers in the Vietnam War. Shift from the wide perspective in exercise number six to a personal angle, to a small company, and enter the thoughts of one character, who is scared.

Purpose: To deal with a big historical event from a personal perspective. Perhaps you can handle all the questions from this narrowly defined angle, a person's experience. But a lot can be gained from combining the big-picture approach with an intensely subjective experience. Change of focus and point of view sometimes works well in fiction, especially in historical events. If you can juggle point of view in one piece of fiction, perhaps you can write an epic novel.

Tip: For the sake of integrating exercises into chunks that might become stories, or already are stories, let the character involved in a war, or some other big event, be the father of one of your protagonists in another exercise, perhaps exercise six in "Scene." The soldier could worry, "If I get killed, who's going to take care of my son, Jimmy?" Maybe the holiday scene is the character's flashback about being together with his child. Or the scene is a description of the festivity in his kid's letter, which he reads during a break. Or you could branch out into a multiple-point-of-view narrative—and follow for a while what the relative thinks and feels about the war during a patriotic holiday.

Check: How do the different points of view work for you in one narrative? Are you able to maintain the same level of excitement from different angles? The discipline of covering a historical event in a succession of chapters with alternating points of view could pay big dividends.

8. To get a different perspective on the events in which the soldier from exercise seven is involved, write from the point of view of his commander. What does the soldier look like from this man's perspective?

If you are not writing about war and peace movements, you might pursue another global action, perhaps a fight against starvation in Ethiopia through international aid agencies, or an organized protest against logging in the Northwest, or a needle distribution program in New York City and Amsterdam. Follow several characters involved in this large-scale action.

Purpose: To expand the spectrum into a point-of-view framework that could work for a large novel.

Tip: Stick to third person, but now follow the captain of the unit, with a flexible third-person point of view, for a long stretch. Then return to the central character, the soldier, or again to a broad prospective—a summary of where the armies stood at the time, maybe from newspapers—or to third-person omniscient point of view, for a while, before you focus again. Even in a novel written in an omniscient point of view, frequent shifts to the personal perspectives usually help focus the narrative.

Check: How do exercises six, seven and eight work together? If this particular sequence hasn't worked well for you, and if wars don't spark your imagination, perhaps you could deal with some other big social picture theme—an epidemic (AIDS, Ebola, flu), the increasing gap between the rich and the poor in the United States or in Latin America, the collapse of communism, the rise of the Russian mafia, or whatever else strikes you as important enough to ask for a big picture from you.

9. Write a page in a first-person skeptical point of view; that is, your narrator could question not only what is going on but his ability to know what is going on. This could fit well into a piece of fiction that otherwise has a broader viewpoint, perhaps from the historical event sequence. Perhaps the narrator has been shot, or is deathly ill, or has lost his job, or has been abandoned by his family, or is losing his mind.

Purpose: To practice the technique of skepticism. Since point of view has to do with what is knowable and how it is knowable, it's good to practice the extreme perspective of ignorance—in some cases we don't know what is knowable and we rightly feel uncertain. This should be reflected in fiction, at least occasionally, if we are truthful about our knowledge of people and ourselves. Sometimes things we know the least about are the most important ones, and we do worry about them.

Tip: This point of view could combine well with stream of consciousness, in which thoughts, images, memories are brought together without much order to simulate the haphazard movement of materials in a mind that is not pursuing a thought with much discipline or overt purpose.

Check: Have you managed to be a good skeptic? Skepticism is an easy technique. Simply question everything, including your questioning. Present tense might increase the uncertainty, because the tense will give us a sensation that we don't know the resolution. Of course, you might not have the enthusiasm to keep going on for long like this, but even a paragraph of writing in this vein might refresh a narrative that in other sections offers perhaps too much confidence in knowledge about events.

10. Write in first person as a clever four-year-old who has his own way of perceiving the world. The story could be about parental divorce, or Dad's alcoholism, or the quality of presents and toys that Santa Claus brings. Emulate a child's grammar. For help, make a point of listening closely to how children talk.

Purpose: To write from a child's point of view. In a narrative, just as in daily life, it may be refreshing to get a child's perspective on things, to lighten the prose with humor, or make it even harsher, juxtaposing a kid's innocence with an adult's corruption.

Tip: Kids use strange grammar—"bringed," "favoritest," "most giantest." And of course, don't forget the kid's logic. You could combine this with exercise eight in "Scene." Or perhaps in a story where we don't expect it. You might flip through the exercises in various chapters and see whether some exercise that at first doesn't seem a likely candidate for a kid's voice might actually benefit from such a shift of perspective. But if that's too much to burden a child with right away, just get the voice going, for two or three pages; let him talk about wanting to be an astronaut or a forester, or how unfair it is that his dad doesn't buy him toys. Maybe a theme will spring up spontaneously that will suggest the direction in which this could evolve, and whether you could get an acceleration for a story from a combination with another exercise and story idea.

Check: How accurately does your piece capture the thoughts and speech of a child? You don't have to err on the safe side; some kids are precocious and surprising, not just cute.

11. Describe the same event in two different forms. First use the present tense from the perspective of someone in ecstasy, perhaps on drugs or alcohol, getting carried away into doing something of dubious moral quality. This could be third-person subjective: You aren't writing in the voice in the head of that person but in your voice with the elements of the character's thinking; you get into someone else's head but not completely. There's a bit of an analytical reserve that the third-person perspective, even if subjective, allows you.

Then write in the past tense from the same person's point of view but in a different mood, a hangover, a down state. Let him feel sinful, contrite, penitent, and go over each detail of what has happened. You could cast this also as a confession, the man retelling all this to a priest or a psychiatrist.

Purpose: To show a character's varying moods and behavior. A person's point of view is not always the same. There's a subjective, or mood, element to it. Our emotions color the way we perceive other people and events. Things aren't what they seem when we are up, nor when we are down.

Tip: You could have a succession of these forms—elation and sin and no perspective, contrition and wise perspective and promise to sin no more, and elation again, and contrition again. Each time the stakes could be higher. In the end, if the story keeps going, the final backsliding, or resistance to backslide, might be the climax. Let the outcome be uncertain. And perhaps there could be a middle mood—neither impulsive nor contrite—as some kind of compromise angle of the narrator's vision.

Check: Is each perspective persuasive? Are the highs high, described in such a way that we partake of the exhilaration? Are the lows low so that we partake of the depression and the moral reasoning that convinces us of the guilt or that makes us sympathize with the guilt?

12. In the form of a recollection narrative, write one more interpretation of the previous high-low theme. Ten years have passed, and there's new information to cast light on the events. New troubles, much more intense than the old ones, have arisen, or new quietude is taking place. Perhaps the character is now a Zen Buddhist or a Sufi Muslim or a born-again Christian.

Purpose: To examine events after much time has passed. Removal from a scene might give us quite a different perspective. Events can be examined from the perspective of the now, from a bit later, and from much later. The shift in the temporal perspective should cast a different light over the events each time.

Tip: Try to achieve a synthesis of two perspectives, the memory and the present interpretation of it. The event in the past was neither as good as it felt on the nights of doing it nor as bad as it felt in the attack of guilt soon thereafter. It was a turning point, but by now is no more impressive than a sign at a crossroads that has weathered many storms and is all cracked, has lost its color—somewhere far back in the country where one no longer travels.

Check: Does the exercise read more removed from the events than the previous exercise did? If not, use a new tranquil tone, almost a new voice, in retelling the same events. You might deliberately change the vocabulary—even use new terminology, Buddhist, Muslim, or scientific.

13. Write about an event in your family, or an imaginary family, in four different personal perspectives, in a succession of first-person points of view. First from the mother's perspective. Give her a page. Then from the father's perspective. Give him a page. Then from the perspective of two kids. Give each a page.

Purpose: To examine and write from varying viewpoints. The same events will look different to different family members.

Sometimes how a family handles different points of view in itself is the most interesting part of the family life—more interesting than a house burning down. It's limiting to understand only a child's viewpoint or a dad's viewpoint. Giving all the points of view due share of attention might be extremely healthy in family life and in fiction about families.

Tip: This could combine well with "Ideas for Fiction" exercise four. Perhaps the illness affects one or two family members. How do they cope with it? How do the rest of the family members relate to it?

This could also combine with a crime story. One family member is a criminal—perhaps the dad or the oldest kid, or perhaps they all are.

Check: How do you handle different points of view and different voices? If there are too many voices to juggle, you might do most of them in your voice, in the third-person subjective, and maybe one in first person.

14. Using the same voices as in exercise thirteen, let every one of them tell a different story, something that has happened just to that one person, something each thinks the rest of the family do not know.

Purpose: To enrich a piece of fiction by involving characters' secret activities. At the same time the illness or jailing is taking place, there should be something else going on, as there usually is—sports events, bankruptcies, house sales, addictions and so on. One central family concern (the crime or the illness) should be accompanied by other individual concerns, to enlarge and develop the story line.

Tip: Every member has some way of being private and even secretive. So it would be interesting to follow the secrets of the entire family. Only a priest to whom the family confesses, or a therapist, might have access to this information, so perhaps you might bring the narrative together through the fifth person, the priest or the judge.

Check: Can exercises thirteen and fourteen combine into one story? What part has worked best for you? If it's only one person's point of view, perhaps you could write the story only from hers and use the other viewpoints sparsely, only as what the central character imagines they are thinking.

15. Begin writing a crime story from the point of view of a defense lawyer, and then a prosecutor, and then the judge who presides over the trial of an accused person, and finally, the accused. Give each one a page of play time in the exercise.

Purpose: To interpret the same evidence from different angles. Different conclusions can be drawn from the same set of facts depending on one's perspective; it's healthy to examine many possibilities in fiction no less than in law.

Tip: Before you start the exercise, outline the event briefly. What happened? Who did what to whom, where, how? If you don't come up with a plot outline on your own, read your town's newspapers. Don't tell me that today there was no crime story.

This exercise might combine well with the previous two, if you've chosen a crime a family member has committed. Now maybe you could add the legalese voice as well, from exercise nine in "Voice." Simply take the sound you developed there and give it to one of the lawyers, who can talk about the case.

If you've chosen a disease, instead of a crime, you could have a doctor or a psychiatrist for a character, examining the whole family.

Check: Do you have enough legalese—at least a touch—to make the judge's and lawyers' voices and perspectives believable? In case of an illness, do you have the right medical jargon?

16. For an exercise in perspective, describe the same event, a dance party, from four different angles, a paragraph each. In one, the frog's perspective: A tenant is watching a dance through a hole in the ceiling. A bird's perspective: Another tenant is watching the same dance through a crack in the floor. Detached horizontal perspective: Someone standing away from the dance area—in the hallway outside—is observing what is going on. Participant perspective: A dancer reports.

Purpose: To view a scene from different perspectives. It's easy to get stuck in some kind of objective, undefined narrative stance where you are not quite sure from where you are visualizing the events. Perhaps not choosing a definite angle means you will not visualize the events. The shifts in perspective can stimulate your scene making.

Tip: First describe the dance as accurately as you can from the different perspectives. Then redo the descriptions, giving each viewer a different motive. The one from below could be a jealous husband; the one from above could be an irritated tenant who wants to evict the dance host below (or at least wants to go to sleep); the one from the side could be a bored friend; and the participant, a woman who finally feels free from her home.

Check: How did this work? If it was a little too scattered for you to switch not only the perspectives but also the carriers of the points of view, redo the exercise from the viewpoint of one person who investigates the scene from all these perspectives, perhaps a private detective.

CHAPTER FIVE

SETTING I: LANDSCAPE AND CITYSCAPE

Successful fiction attains the depth of insights and knowledge of nonfiction. You need to know the places and times you give us as much as a journalist or a historian or a memoirist does. Show us the places with the authority of a nonfiction writer. Collect the details, the background information, the facts, and present them. This way, you will not only entertain your reader but also inform her, and the reader will recognize that she is seeing something in depth, not only being entertained but learning.

No setting is to be underestimated and dismissed as boring. A drop of water, if you take a careful look at it under the microscope, becomes a fascinating world. What may seem to be a boring town, once you begin to analyze its history, its people, and its stories, may become an amazing place. There's no such thing as a boring setting; there's only a bored observer who has not taken interest in seeing and understanding what he sees. All settings are exotic; go far enough from your hometown, and people will perceive you as exotic or at least unusual. Many young writers indeed despise their hometowns so much that they go far away, to New York, Montana, or wherever, and once they are far away, somehow they end up writing about the place they have escaped, and in some cases, they end up loving their hometowns, because while writing about them, they recall their impressions, intensify them, embellish. Here they are on safe ground; they know their places, or believe they do. As much as you put into a setting, that much, and more, you get out of it. It needn't be your native region, where you grew up or spent most of your life, but sow your seeds in the places you know, and see what happens.

I enjoy reading fiction written more than twenty years ago, because no matter what happens in the story, if it's authentically set, I learn history as well. With time, your story becomes history, in the good sense. And intentionally, you can set your stories a bit back in time—into towns of your adolescence, young adulthood. The removal from the present, what you immediately see around yourself, will stimulate your imagination. You'll be tempted to play with memory, memory will play tricks on you, and soon you'll have the right mixture of the remembered and the imagined to be writing fiction, much more spontaneously than if you write about what you see outside your window right now.

Naturally, don't limit yourself; sow your fiction seeds even in the places you don't know, and see what grows out of the soil. Get to the soil of that place: Visit the place and examine it; talk to the natives; read the local newspapers; study the history; browse in the library, the train station, the churches; bug the ministers, old cops; find oral accounts of what happened in the town. Get some voices to associate with the place. Collect maps.

Stephen Crane wrote *The Red Badge of Courage* about the Civil War thirty years after the war without ever having been a soldier or visiting some of the battle sites. Madison Smartt Bell wrote a novel about Haiti without ever visiting the country. These are exceptions, however, rather than the rule, and they were accomplished through research and imaginative tours de force.

Setting is so important that several genres of writing are based on the types of setting they use, and in each case, research is essential so the details of place and time cohere into a believable whole.

Science fiction. Although setting here is mostly fictional, the writer must imagine and then relate a keen sense of place, a world that the reader can see. And since science fiction evolves to a large extent from our notions of applied science and new technologies, most science fiction writers read a lot about science. Some of them don't hold advanced degrees in mathematics or in any sciences, but they seek literature that presents science in approachable terms. Since what they write should be accessible to most readers, in a way, not being too intricately versed in science almost helps them create a "user-friendly," or "reader-friendly," world.

Westerns. While it may be possible to write a western without knowing much American history and geography, it certainly pays to research. In this genre, the setting is often a character itself. Often, too, setting plays a large role in the plot. To write in this form, you must create a strong sense of place. John Vernon, author of *La Salle*, after we ate dinner, rushed home to read for the third time the journals of Lewis and Clark. He was writing a western novel.

Mysteries. Detective stories and murder mysteries depend to a large extent on how the world of criminal justice and law enforcement works. Courtroom and police department settings must be rendered accurately.

Legal thrillers. John Grisham and Scott Turow, two of the most successful writers in this form, are both former attorneys and bring much expertise to their fiction. Legal fiction dates, of course, way back to Charles Dickens. This form depends on how law functions—courts, jails, law offices. It's not accidental that many lawyers become writers—not only do they write briefs all the time, but they must research, and out of that habit, they easily build settings for fiction.

Medical thrillers. Coma, by Robin Cook, is considered the classic work in this form. You must know—or research—how hospitals work and what technical jargon is used by the medical professionals.

Regional and ethnic fiction. The writer focuses on a region and its culture or on a community, whether he's a native or an immigrant. Again, part of the appeal for the reader is learning about a place and culture that is unique, even exotic.

Most successful fiction must be grounded in a place and a time. Even some contemporary fiction that at first seems to be mostly psychological, such as domestic and family fiction, still is set in the landscape and lawnscape of cities, suburbs, shopping malls, offices, and country clubs, and though you may not include long descriptions of the setting, the setting makes such fiction possible.

HOW DO YOU CREATE A SETTING?

It's best to give descriptions of your setting while the action is taking place, in bits and pieces, rather than in pages of history. As you follow your protagonist in his walk to his office, say he's a doctor, you could give us from his perspective the smells, sounds, images of a hospital, and then you could engage the doctor in the place through his memories of what happened in a certain room. Or you can follow a mother and daughter to a classroom at a university, where the daughter is a professor and mother a student. Along the way, you can give us a picture of a corridor with students sitting on the floor in various positions.

You must bring us into a place so that we can see it. That's crucial for the writer's concentration—to see and hear what is going on as it happens. You convince yourself that the action is visible so you can stick attentively to being here and now rather than diluting your attention to what could be later or earlier or in general. And of course, the concrete details of the setting are important for the reader, to help her imagine the world you're creating, or translating from your memory.

Here's an example of how to weave character, landscape, and action, from Louis L'Amour's *Hondo*.

> When he struck the match he held it well back in the foliage of the juniper, keeping the flare invisible. He drew deep on the cigarette, returning his attention to the terrain. . . . A few lost, cotton-ball bunches of cloud shifted in a brassy sky, leaving rare islands of shadow upon the desert's face.
>
> Nothing moved. It was a far, lost land, a land of beige-gray silences and distance where the eye reached out farther and farther to lose itself finally against the sky, and where the only movement was the lazy swing of a remote buzzard.
>
> His eyes wandered along the ridge. To his right there was a shallow saddle, the logical place to cross a ridge to avoid being skylined. Logical, but obvious. It was the place an Apache would watch.

L'Amour creates suspense while giving us the setting from the perspective of his protagonist; the setting not only helps us get into the story, it also helps us experience the character's mood (tension, vigilance). Describing the setting as a specific place at a specific time creates the dramatic potential; if L'Amour simply described how the southwestern landscape looks every summer, he'd create no suspense. His fiction would be reduced to a travelogue.

When working with a setting, you involve most of the elements of your fiction: You perceive the place from a certain character's point of view (or from the omniscient point of view), and thus, you might do it in the character's voice; you also summon all your descriptive powers, angles of light, shadow play; you apply your syntactical skills, to weave in various aspects of the setting. Even dialogue can portray a setting—the characters may be talking about what they see around them, even if only in passing; by how they talk, their diction, accents, they evoke the atmosphere of a place.

To use a simple metaphor: If you want to plant a tree, you want to find the soil you know to be good, where the tree will sink its roots and suck out the juices of the earth. If you leave the tree suspended in the air, in your pickup truck, it will die. Don't suspend your characters and plot ideas in the air. Plant them in places that can nourish your characters with opportunities for action and involvement, and your prose with chances for some painterly work—lyrical passages of cityscapes and landscapes.

A good setting can do a fair amount of work for you—it will remind you of what can happen in it; it will draw you into scenes.

EXERCISES

1. Walk through a forest and describe what it feels like; portray the sights, scents, sounds, textures, earth, trees, animal presences, tracks. If you've had a strange experience in a forest, make a story out of it, and augment it with the perceptions from your recent walks.

Another option is to use your concrete perceptions to support a story you write mostly from your imagination. Adapt some of your perceptions from a walk in the woods to give to a character in either exercise ten or eleven from "Scene."

Or set a fable in the forest. Combine this exercise with number twelve from "Plot."

Purpose: To explore settings for your fiction. Forests are wonderful places. You will need a diversity of landscape for the sake of variety, especially in a novel. Keep your characters moving, explore the world with them.

Tip: If you can't paint a forest objectively, do it subjectively. Bring yourself into it; talk about yourself as much as about the forest. Recall your sylvan memories. Express yourself in how you deal with your impressions. Here's an example of how to paint a forest, from Mikhail Iossel's short story "Every Hunter Wants to Know" (from the point of view of a boy).

> It was getting light. The moss under my feet was streaked by the sun. It was dry, despite the recent rain. Something rustled behind my back: a hare or a fox, or a snake. Birds were beginning to test their voices overhead. To my left was a thick aspen . . . covered with black spots like a hyena. Its minute leaves shivered as though in fever. . . . I took another look at the tree and saw that I had been mistaken. It was a birch, the dear soul of Russia. When I touched it, its bark felt like onion peels. A sudden gust of wind set its leaves in motion. Then everything settled back into silence. I didn't know how much time had passed.

Iossel paints the woods for us in sound, touch, vision—and intensifies the image with flashes of comparisons ("like a hyena," "as though in fever"). He doesn't identify what he hears precisely but leaves us wondering; he keeps guessing what sorts of trees he sees. In the story, the boy gets lost for a while, and this guessing game together with the strong impressions of the woods, contributes to our feeling his being lost. The lostness is perfectly expressed.

Check: Do you bring us into the woods along with you? Do we breathe with you? Sniff the breath of fallen foliage? Recall the taste of wild mushrooms? No matter how private and personal your walk in the woods, once you write about it, you must express yourself in such a way that you'll create an impression, the way your foot does in wet soil.

2. Visit a farm, with a field or a pasture—maybe near the forest from the previous exercise—and describe the experience so vividly that you make us experience it too.

Purpose: To cover a variety of settings.

Tip: A farm has its history. No harm in giving us some, but not at the expense of our being able to see the farm as it is now. You could compare the farm as it used to be to how it is now.

If you don't know the history, you could do a subjective portrait of the farm from the standpoint of a lady who has never been to a farm but who has decided she would love to live in the country. Write in the first person as though you were the lady. Don't ridicule her; try to deal with the setting honestly and intensely. Imagine her experience and give it full play.

Another option: Bring a person you sketch in "Ideas" exercise twelve, someone who struck you at first as admirable, and show him doing something despicable in the farm setting; or show someone who struck you at first as highly despicable doing a great deed.

Check: No matter what approach you've taken, we should get a sensation of being there. Do you list enough substances— hay bales, cow pies, horseflies? If the description is a bit static, bring in farmers and their machinery at work.

3. Visit the ocean in a boat or on a ship or simply at a beach, and describe your perceptions. (If you are landlocked, try a lake or a river.) What are the waves like? The sun? The wind? The bathers? The passing ships? Go into the water. What does it feel like? (If you live on the Pacific coast, you are exempt from

entering the cold water; you can write this part from imagination.) If you don't feel like going out to gather impressions for your assignment, work from memory.

Purpose: To try many settings. The ocean has generated a genre of its own: seafaring. Though this genre was more popular in the nineteenth century than it is today, the sea still can capture the imaginations of readers. Even if you aren't an oceanic person, you could give this setting a try. Oceans cover two-thirds of our global surface. You can surely write a couple of pages about them.

Tip: If landscape without people leaves you cold, describe your encounter with a person who belongs to the landscape—a sailor, a fisherman, a lifeguard—and weave details about the setting into the encounter. Maybe you talk, maybe you only observe. But show, for example, a craggy-faced fisherman as he anchors his boat amidst shrieks of hungry seagulls while waves slap the mossy dock.

Once you have created the setting on the page, see whether you can use it in a piece of fiction you have been working on. If you can't beneficially use this in your work in progress, try the following approach.

Generate a story—lead with this description into the disaster narrative about flooding as a consequence of the global warming effect, from "Ideas for Stories" exercise five.

Or set a hunting or fishing scene in the ocean. For examples, take a look at the whale-hunting scenes in the latter parts of *Moby Dick*, by Herman Melville, and the fishing scenes in *The Old Man and the Sea*, by Ernest Hemingway.

Or create a story of survival. "The Open Boat," by Stephen Crane, could show you the possibilities here.

Check: Where is the salt in your description? Be sure you provide plenty of substances that comprise the scene.

4. Describe a hill or mountain from afar within a stretch of landscape, from your feet all the way up as far as you see, from your point of view, without constructing a persona. Describe the place at a striking time—in rainy weather or after the sun has set, to capture a mood. You might do the same landscape at different times, to see how your perception of it changes.

Purpose: To catalogue your perceptions of a place. Observe it, listen to it, see whether it begins to whisper suggestions to you, suggestions for a mood, even a plot.

Tip: As I write this, the sun has set in Wyoming, at UCross, near Sheridan. I see that where it has set, the sky is glowing. In this dry air, with sharp visibility, the contrast between the land and the sky is stark; the hills look black. The farther I look away from the west, the darker the sky is, and in the east, the bleached grassy hills appear to fluoresce. In the east, I can make out crevices in the hill, a line of meager bushes; some slopes evanesce silvery blond hues in the moonlight; the moon is a semicircle. The creek bend gleams soundlessly. A breeze, which carries the smell of hay, ruffles the leaves on big cottonwoods, and now and then, there's a glimmer of light reflecting off the leaves flipping in the breeze. A bird cries deep, closer and closer. I don't know what bird it is; maybe it's an owl of the sort I'm not familiar with.

I am probably not doing a great job observing and writing down my observations—but I am doing the job. What frequently happens in a description is that you run into a question, an intrigue. Here, finding out what kind of bird makes the call could easily be paralleled to some anticipated event that could happen in the landscape; for example, a visit by a fascinating stranger, in the spirit of a western.

Check: Do you describe enough of your view? If not, tell us more, even if it seems ordinary. You don't have to strain to describe nuances—for invoking the smell of hay or of cut grass it may be superfluous to pile adjectives, *pungent, moist,* and so on. We have all smelled many things, and just mentioning a smell should trigger our sensory recollections.

Do you raise questions? When you observe, you can't always be sure what you see. A sensation of looking for something can enliven a description. You might even rewrite the exercise, looking for a lost cat or a lost child in the land.

5. Climb a mountain or a big hill. Describe the ascent, your effort, your perceptions. What animals do you see? What plants? How does it feel up there? How do you breathe? What do you hear? What do you think? Describe all this from the standpoint of a fugitive. Then rewrite the exercise from the standpoint of the pursuer.

Purpose: To merge a strong physical experience (exertion in climbing) with a spectacular landscape. This will achieve an intense page. This should be the equivalent of a car chase in a movie, except that it won't be clichéd, so it will be fresher.

Tip: You needn't give us a scientific account of the flora and fauna—don't sound like a biologist unless you take on the persona of one—but it might actually help to use a reference book, such as *Birds of North America, Wildflowers of North America.* From those you might garner some interesting details and facts. Combine these with an interested character—a man in love, who finds in everything around him an affirmation of that love. (If that turns out to be corny, try the yang side of it—the man in hate, who sees the inimical nature of everything around him.) Try using a character you created in the "Character" chapter here. This will give you a chance to develop the character more fully.

I didn't plan to practice this exercise, but just yesterday I went hiking toward the Cloudy Peak in the Big Horn Mountains in Wyoming. Since it was summer with not a cloud in sight, I didn't bring much—just a sweatshirt. After a four-hour hike, at Misty Moon Lake, I got chilled by a strong wind. It rained. On my way down, I was passing another lake when suddenly a strong murmur arose from it and grew loud. I had never heard such a loud rain. I wondered whether the canyonlike setting there, with two cliffs rising on the sides of the lake, augmented the sound, which it no doubt did. I stopped and stared at the water. The cloud above the lake looked torn, with strands falling into the lake. In chilly air, I could see so clearly that I could make out individual drops as they slowly slanted toward the water. *Wow,* I thought, *this hiking business really heightens your senses. How is it possible to see the rain so clearly?* But the cloud moved on, and soon it began to rain on the high shore where I was. Things moved around me, hopped here and there. I wondered whether they were grasshoppers, but would they be out in the rain? Then I realized what it was: hail. Soon it began to pelt me. I put my bag over my head and rushed along. I was at least two hours away from my car in the base camp, the path was wet and slippery, even the rocks were, my sneakers were soaked, my shirt was soaked, and the wind made me feel quite cold. The hail accumulated and didn't melt; there were different sizes so that it looked like hail and sleet mixed together. I had visited winter and was rushing back to summer, and my legs were sore, and I was exhausted. I had to keep going, I couldn't stop. I felt pursued by the mountain.

That's a rough description of a landscape, from my perspective. I could embellish it, exaggerate it, and certainly use it in fiction. I give it here as an example of how I'd do the assignment.

Once you have described a landscape (here or in exercise four), recast it from the point of view of a person in one of your pieces of fiction. This may sound artificial, and it is, but no harm in that since writing stories is a creation of artifacts. I have found various nature descriptions that have proved quite useful in this regard; sooner or later, I can adapt them for a story, to enrich and intensify scenes.

Or generate a story. Combine this setting with "Plot" exercise two. Your stingy character could live in a cabin in the mountains, avoiding spending money he has accumulated. Bring him into conflict with land surveyors, former spouses, or hikers, who, he imagines, are after his money. You can also combine this with "Plot" exercise five and write from the perspective of the recluse in the hills.

Check: Have you shown us the mountain? Do we get the sensation of sticking our fingernails into the soil, grasping the tree roots, or something similar? If you lay the land concretely enough, the rest will come easily.

6. Observe your hometown, or a town you know well, from an airplane. If you can't view it from above, get an aerial picture, or pretend you have one. Describe the landscape—the rivers, hills, creeks, highways, streets.

Purpose: To master urban design. If you have a clear picture of a town where you set your action, you might more easily develop ideas for events, combining them to create a plot. The more elements there are, the more permutations possible. You can take your characters, in the course of a novel, on a tour— through hospitals, jails, parks, taverns.

Tip: You could use a map to organize your picture. If you don't have a map—all the better. Make one, no matter how inaccurately. Create your own town, an expression of you and your imagination.

Once you have designed the town, contemplate the stories you could set in it. An urban design is almost like a multiple plot outline—offering a wealth of possibilities. Make at least three plot outlines of the events that belong to this town.

What spot, what street corner in the town reminds you of an event most strongly? Relate the event, as a story, with scenes, embedded in the town. Perhaps you have several stories here, maybe a novel. Use either real-life characters from the town or one or two you have developed in "Character" exercises.

Check: Can you think of what you omitted? Why did you exclude it? Put it in. Do you have all the cemeteries? Where is the most beautiful building? How about the ugliest? The most boring?

7. Describe the sounds you hear next to the river (or the ocean) in a city at night or in mist. Mention what you see, but rely mostly on what you hear. Sounds can frequently blend into one another and be mistaken for one another; cats sound like babies, a river like a gurgling drunk—so try to exploit that aspect of the river to create an eerie mood.

Purpose: To set a scene through sounds. While sight is the primary mode of perception in description, sound may be the most evocative precisely because it does not give you a picture but suggests it, leaves it to imagination.

Tip: For ways you can use sounds to create a picture, look at the example from "The Danube," by Pavao Pavlicic.

> It's terrifying to stand in the mist on a high riverbank when floes begin to travel and you can't see the water or the huge floes. From below you hear their clashing and grinding against one another, you hear their rattle, squeals, screams, wails, and shrieks, as though some beasts on the verge of extinction—tyrannosauri and brontosauri—fight bloodthirstily, gurgling, trying to bite each other's head off.

Sounds can lead into what you imagine. Since you don't see much through the mist, you can imagine wildly. What do the sounds remind you of? Make likenesses, metaphors, and play.

Can you use this angle of perception in one of your stories? How about in a war story? A guard—perhaps the draftee from "Plot" exercise four—could grow progressively more and more terrified as he stands on the riverbank. You could also combine this with a crime story, "Point of View" exercise thirteen; the accused person could recall an event that you could perhaps fit into this setting.

Check: Is your description steeped in sounds? Do you suggest and imagine strange possibilities, hallucinate, "hear voices"? If not, rewrite to do so—let the river talk to you, exaggerate, spook us, if you can. Describe the river at night.

8. Go into the street. Sit on a bench, if there is one. Observe but don't take notes. Strive to remember what you see. A chess player can play a game all in his head; a writer gains a lot if he can take mental notes and remember them. Once you get home, record your mental notes.

What did you hear? You might close your eyes and list the sounds that reached you. If you can't identify the source of the sound, describe it.

What did you see? List, and if you saw something striking, describe it in detail.

What did you smell?

Did you feel anything on your skin? Did you touch anything? Walls? A table? Did you slide your bare foot over the fountain marble? Describe these textures.

Purpose: To master street life. This is absolutely essential for most kinds of fiction.

Tip: Bring your reader into the street. Pull him by the ear. Tickle his nose with a wisp of smoke. This is where you win your reader; show him the aspects of a place he may not know, through what he does know—his own body, in a highly sensory way. Culture and tourism, after all, are sensual experiences. Intricacies of harmony in a symphony may conspire to give one goose bumps, through an appeal to one's senses; tonal perceptions may tumble together into a strong and distinct sensation so that one may covertly not only be in touch with but also physically and spiritually love the world through the experience of everything coming together. Seduce your reader through the senses.

Check: Have you depicted the sensations of the street? What bodily sense have you omitted? Why? If you were detached in your description of the street, you might try rewriting it from the standpoint of a starving woman, a lustful adolescent, an old thief.

9. Describe a baseball or football stadium in the town. Take us into the stands while the game is in progress.

Purpose: To reveal characters through settting. Setting is a medium, like clay for a sculptor, in which you can express your characters. Setting is also an ultimate body language of your characters—they communicate through it. As you describe the stadium, you also express the father and son seated there—their relationship to each other, their bodies, their admiration for what bodies can do—better than if they were nowhere, better than through abstractions.

Tip: If the game itself doesn't give rise to good descriptions, write from the perspective of a father teaching his son the allure—and the basic rules—of the sport. (Or a man teaching a foreigner what the game is about.) If big ballparks hold no allure for you, and your description could be static, describe a tennis court or a running track as a participant, in the persona of a father teaching his son.

Here's an example of a foreigner's perspective on baseball (that is, mine, before I learned the rules of the game, a while back).

> The radiant grass was so soothing that it did not disturb me that apparently nothing was happening on the field. After half an hour of watching a guy tightening his ass, sticking out a gleaming thick stick, and others now and then running a bit, I was tired of the warm-up, and asked people around me when the game would begin."Begin? It's been going on for hours," said a fat man in green pants and sized me up and down. Finally, the man with the bat swung it, and I feared that he'd blow away the head of his squatting compatriot. The bat struck, the whole audience screamed with horror, so that I feared that the squatter's head must be flying. Tacky organ music shrieked, and the large billboard flashed: Go! Go!

If you don't get a story going out of this exercise, try combining the assignment with "Ideas for Fiction" exercise seven. The scene in the stands could precede the high point in a game.

Check: Can we visualize the stadium or the court from the description? No matter how important the relationship of father and son, the arena is your foreground, the relationship a background. Foregrounding the background, and backgrounding the foreground is a good reversal of focus that might give you fresh views of both.

10. Describe the action in a big construction site—construction workers, cement mixers, cranes, excavators, and so on.

Purpose: To use active settings. A construction site, as a place of basic, loud, and crude creation, could lend some energy to your prose.

Tip: Children are fascinated by construction sites. Why shouldn't adults be? You could take a look at a children's book about construction and write with marvel at how things work. Obviously, it's easy to shrink away from the noise and dust, but try to see the bright side.

There are possibilities for action here too. I remember, in Croatia, construction workers expanding a power plant found three corpses immured in the plant chimney. Obviously, just that image could start off a murder mystery.

Check: Have you portrayed the energy of the place in all its rude glory? Make sure you have the squealing, the crunching of iron and cement, and the boomed clanking of empty dump truck beds, or similar. If construction hasn't worked for you here, try destruction—cranes pounding a building with big wrecking balls.

11. Depict a cemetery from the standpoint of a woman who, for the first time in ten years, visits her lover's tombstone. Even if her emotions are strong, don't express them in global terms "she was overcome with sorrow," but show expressions of the emotion in what she sees, how she sees it—birds, plants, ants, other tombs, mourners.

Purpose: To use emotion-evoking settings. The power of emotional associations in cemeteries is great; tap into it. Cemeteries can enhance even a joyous event, give depth to the joy, by evoking a dimension of sorrow for contrast.

Tip: Since the power here is so great, simply describe, without embellishing the emotion. If you'd like, use a character you created in an earlier exercise, perhaps one you have shown in a different emotional state. This could help you show your character's wide range of feelings and perceptions, her complexity.

Check: Is your description interesting? Engaging? Maybe posing questions might help: Why does that old brown tombstone have a picture of a finger pointing upward? Is that a sign of a sect? How come that slab of stone is broken in half? Your character's distraction and perception of various things might add a dimension of spaciness and disorientation, and thus enhance her sensation of being lost.

12. Relate the experience of being at a public swimming pool. Where is the pool? What do you see when you walk into the pool area? How do you enter the water? What does it feel like? How do you feel about your body in the bathing suit? When you get out, where do you lie down?

A variation on this exercise: Visit a skating rink.

Purpose: To use an energy-filled setting. Here's another useful setting. If you accomplish nothing else, you can at least make your protagonists self-conscious about their bodies.

Tip: Swimmers and sunbathers are all part of the scene. Sketch them as well, in passing. As with the other exercises in this chapter, try to place a character from an earlier chapter into this setting. Don't worry about how well the character fits the setting. If the character is out of place, so much the better. This will add tension to the description.

Check: Is the piece vivid? Are there any unusual details—something you haven't seen done elsewhere? There should be at least a couple of fresh details.

13. Take us on a ride, from the center of the city, say a parking lot in front of the courthouse, through downtown into an old section of the town, then into the slums, and into suburbia.

Purpose: To develop another urban scene. This is another look at the city; for diversity of presentation it's good to cover various aspects of the city.

Tip: A ride like this could be instrumental to your story—*The Bonfire of the Vanities*, a novel by Tom Wolfe, evolves out of a description of such a trip through New York City. Here's an abbreviated version of this exercise.

> Viewed from a train going north, the morphology of Rome is easy to describe. In the center: ruins. Then a circle of firm buildings. After this, again ruins or build-ings about to become ruins: mortar falling off, roofs missing, shaggy trees growing out of walls, shooting their roots through cracks.

Check: Do you give us a picture we can visualize? Is there a story you are writing that could use this description?

14. Write several pages of three kinds of setting-driven stories: a western, a medical thriller, a science fiction story (or a nature adventure story). Don't worry if you are using stereotypes.

Purpose: To practice making setting the major player in your fiction.

Tip: For fun, transpose some of the stereotypes of a western into a science fiction setting. Or of a medical thriller into a western.

Check: Read it several days after writing it. If you are enter-tained by the piece, keep going. No harm in writing another story or a novel.

CHAPTER SIX

SETTING II: INTERIOR DESIGN

I n movies, before each scene, one must write EXT. or INT. to indicate whether the action is taking place outdoors or indoors. Although movies and fiction are different it's always good to be aware of where your characters are—even so basically, whether outside or inside, and the inside is at least as important as the outside.

We are on some level descendents of sea creatures and reptiles, and we have an atavistic need for a shell—ideally, we'd carry our homes on our backs to withdraw into them when danger arises. We build our homes; we find our lairs; we organize our offices. We express ourselves by how we extend our personal space and how we mark it, defend it—whether we gladly share it or jealously protect it. On the shared boundary of the outside and the inside, a lot can be said about a person. When you hear a noise in your yard, do you joyfully spring to your feet, expecting company or a mailcarrier with Christmas presents, or do you bolt the doors and peer through a hole, ready to run into the basement to get your shotgun?

Just as you can use a setting to describe a character, you can use characters to describe a setting. Crowds of people at the train station or Greyhound bus terminal, passengers in an airplane—if you show them, briefly, what they wear, what they sound like, what atmosphere they create, you are establishing the setting.

Of course, if you zero in and begin to analyze someone's psychology, you are making a transition to character. Setting and character need not be separated; the two elements, ideally, should merge with the plot in an organic whole, or a synthetic whole, if you prefer, in such a way that you don't see where one material connects with another because they are so essentially intertwined.

What do I mean? Here's an example, from John Steinbeck's preface to *Tortilla Flat*.

> This is the story of Danny and of Danny's friends and of Danny's house. It is a story of how these three became one thing, so that in Tortilla Flat if you speak of Danny's house you do not mean a structure of wood flaked with old whitewash, overgrown with an ancient untrimmed rose of Castile. No, when you speak of Danny's house you are understood to mean a unit of which the parts are men, from which came sweetness and joy, philanthropy and, in the end, a mystic sorrow.

In a setting fittingly selected and evolved into its own world, most of the elements of your fiction should blend together. Your characters come into conflict with each other not only in the setting, but sometimes because of it—fighting for territory, inheritance, personal space, houses, lovers (who in turn are intertwined with the places they live and how they do their dishes).

Just as with people, in a setting you look for character, uniqueness, oddities, something that distinguishes it from other places. You look for the mark people have left, for the embellishment they have placed there. So how do you find places with character?

Many towns are alike—chain grocery stores, chain gas stations, chain shopping malls, chain nearly everything, but not quite everything. You can select places with local character and flavor—county offices, churches, small shops, unusual streets.

Here you might be a bit artificial even. Go out of your way to find intriguing locations, the way movie people mercilessly hunt for their sets. Get into various interiors where history has left traces, inscribed stories. Describe these places and they may begin to speak to you, give you their stories and ideas for your stories.

When you establish a setting, don't give us what we expect. Surprise us. Something we expect to be unpleasant might become delightful, and vice versa. For example, Junichiro Tanizaki in "In Praise of Shadows" gives us a surprisingly lyrical description of going to the bathroom in a Japanese garden outhouse. Here you also have an example of how landscape and interiors merge into one, in more senses than one.

> . . . there one can listen with such a sense of intimacy to the raindrops falling from the eaves and the trees, seeping into the earth as they wash over the base of a stone lantern and freshen the moss about the stepping stones. And the toilet is the perfect place to listen to the chirping of insects or the song of birds, to view the moon, or to enjoy any of those poignant moments that mark the change of the seasons. Here, I suspect, is where haiku poets over the ages have come by a great many of their ideas.

USING THE EXERCISES

Most of the exercises for this chapter will be set in various rooms of a house. We are born in a room, we will most likely die in a room, and we live mostly at home, with families, or alone. Interior settings may not be as glorious as the great outdoors, but your command of them will allow for glorious prose. (If you live outdoors and spend most of your time hunting bears, skip this chapter.)

Almost any kind of story will take you into several rooms. Here, you will create an arsenal of interior design that you could use, transpose, and adapt in your fiction. This is the arena of most fiction.

Choose a building. It might help to have a plan of the building, as does Umberto Eco, who gives us first the plan of the abbey where the action takes place in his bestselling novel *The Name of the Rose*. Of course, you don't need to actually draw a plan, but you must be able to visualize coherently the spaces in which the action is taking place.

So pay attention to these exercises. It depends on you to make them exciting. Be playful, look for odd details, have fun. Perhaps there's an architect in you, waiting to play. Here's your chance. You don't need math, or hammers here; just imagination, memory, words.

EXERCISES

In exercises one to seven, I offer you an eclectic approach, to recall the most remarkable backyard and rooms from different places you have lived or visited in your life. You could do them each once, covering many houses. And when you locate a house that fascinates you most, redo all the exercises describing the different aspects and rooms of that house. If you already have a house in mind (maybe the house of your youth), you could forgo the eclectic approach and zero in on a thorough portrayal of the house, which the exercises will invite you to do.

Use the exercises as a mill. When you have an important house in a story—whether now or months from now—run it through the mill. Describe it thoroughly. Free-associate at each corner. Let your characters sleep, work, shower, cook, dine, and play in various rooms. You will get many ideas for your stories.

1. In two or three pages, describe an interesting backyard. Does it have walls? Hedges? What can you see from it? What

does it look like from the outside? What objects do you find there? What can you hear and smell there? What is its history?

Purpose: To study a backyard and all its story possibilities. A backyard is a peculiar space; it is located outside, yet it's usually fenced off into its own interiority. A backyard is a great transition in space between the street and the house, public and private space. A backyard naturally has an intensity. It's a place where many stories collide, as often happens in border regions between countries.

Tip: If you can't easily recall a notable backyard and you don't know someone else's in detail, describe in detail the backyard of your childhood. This exercise, which I assigned to myself some fifteen years ago, kept me busy so long I wrote nearly a book-length manuscript, out of which I developed several short stories.

The place where you explored the world freshly, where you possibly spent thousands of hours should give you much to write about. This is your original place, even more thoroughly than your hometown is. Out of this ground, you should be able to write some autobiographical fiction. Recall the walls, tools, toys, sand, grass, sheds, garages, animals, friends. What kind of games did you play? Did anybody get hurt?

Check: Has this exercise got you excited? If so, forget it's an exercise and let yourself be carried away with it. Maybe you'll write a memoir, maybe a family history, maybe a short story, or maybe you'll just write and worry later what shape, form, and genre this is going to take.

On the other hand, if you haven't had backyards, or are loath to describe yours, invent one and match it with an interesting character. No matter what backyard you've described, make sure you mention enough things, objects. You simply insert a list of items in a somewhat unpredictable order.

2. Describe two bathrooms.

Tell about the most intriguing private bathroom you've ever seen. Describe the tiles. Was there a window? What could you see through it? Was there a bathtub or a shower? Was it luxurious or spartan, tidy or messy?

Next, describe a strange public bathroom and an unwelcome communication in it.

Purpose: To tune in to the bathroom as a possible setting in your fiction. This is perhaps the least explored room in a house. Yet here we get in touch with our bodies, evaluate how we live, how we eat, how we make love. It's a thoughtful place that should stimulate some thoughtful writing.

Tip: It's easy to portray a bathroom as disgusting. Work against the grain; make it appear glorious, sensuous. Describe the bathroom from the perspective of a person who has undergone a major crisis and is now relaxing here.

Check: Do you give us the sound and look of water, the hot water and cold enamel against your skin, or something else we could imagine easily? Can you develop a scene here for a story, but nothing as dramatic and clichéd as a shower curtain murder? Or in the exercises on plot and scene, could you bring part of the action here? Perhaps a character from an earlier exercise can come here to think.

3. Describe a living room. First focus on several objects: the table, a love seat, a chair, a clock, a phone. Describe their ages, materials, sizes, textures, feel, smells. Imagine an event that has happened around each object. Describe this from the standpoint of a suspicious investigator, as though you were writing a detective novel (maybe you are), or from the standpoint of a jealous lover, if you are writing a romance.

Or describe the same objects from the standpoint of a character from exercise one or two in "Character."

There are a lot of options. If options only make you hesitate, simply write about a character who feels uncomfortable in the living room. Why is he uncomfortable?

Purpose: To write concretely, through objects. Show your characters in how they live, in their private, yet somewhat public, space.

Tip: The imaginations of your characters work through the images they conjure when confronted with things. Mentioned things (nouns) create associations in the minds of your characters, which you can report. These associations can reveal their motives—fears and desires. So a cherry-wood chair may invoke in a lover's mind an image of a fleshy thigh lurking in a shadow under a trembling draft-lifted skirt—even though the slippery chair is now empty.

Check: Did you include enough images to project a living room? What has worked for you here and what hasn't? Delete what doesn't accomplish anything for you, and play further with what does.

4. Depict a basement—with a den or without—that you remember vividly. No need to invent one; I'm sure you've seen one. Work with it, get it ready to move into your fiction. Again, rather than make it appear disgusting or simply creepy, bring a sense of wonder and mystery to it. (Even if you want it to be creepy, it's good to approach it from an angle other than the obvious creepdom.)

Purpose: To discover the wonders of a basement. A basement is a great space, with the potential for secrecy, hiding, a kind of fallout shelter, at least in a psychological sense. You could accomplish a good character portrait of someone who likes his underground privacy.

Tip: In a basement, the light, temperature, moisture, smells all attain an intensity of earthiness. Rely on the sensory details.

Check: Maybe you could start a story from the basement and work up? Ralph Ellison wrote his classic novel, *Invisible Man*, by starting with a man in the basement with his lightbulbs.

5. What's the most amazing attic you've been to? What was the ceiling like? Where was the light coming from? Who was there? What was going on? Did you have a view from the attic? Describe it.

Purpose: To envision an attic in your story. Just like the basement, the attic holds many possibilities for character and plot development. So rummage through attics, in the attic of your mind, and you will be rewarded.

Tip: Maybe you could combine this with a city street exercise—from the window, you could see a bit of the street over a roof—and involve the elements of a landscape exercise. Now, add one or two peculiar characters. Let them scheme, and see what happens. When they leave the attic, where do they go?

Check: Have you captured the atmosphere of the attic? Do the special qualities of the place inspire you further? Do they suggest a story?

6. Describe a striking kitchen. Picture the stove. Utensils. Cutting boards. Garbage. What does it feel like to cook here? Stop by. Prepare at least an omelet.

Purpose: To explore the kitchen's potential as a fiction setting. Kitchens are magnetic places, as almost any party demonstrates.

They are rarely intimidatingly pretentious. There's the cold mama, the refrigerator, ready to buzz out some milk for you; and in more permissive moods, beer and wine. And there's the warm grandma, the old stove, with her eyes glowing, steaming coffee and tea. A lot of essential living and relating takes place in the kitchen. Cook your stories in one, sunny-side up.

Tip: Don't. There are no waiters here. Seriously, play with foods, have a food fest. Have two friends cook together—a health food freak and an old-fashioned gourmet.

Check: Read through and free-associate. Where's the potential for developing a story? If the exercise has been a bit flat and you haven't hit upon an idea for a story, rewrite the exercise: A member of the family has just been buried. The funeral is over, and the party has gravitated from the living room, or the reception room, into the kitchen. What are they eating, drinking? Whom are they talking to? What is the mood?

7. Describe a bedroom in detail.

Purpose: To explore bedroom settings. We sleep a third of our lives. Some of us make love here; most of us were conceived here, some will die here. Here we dream, worry. So for verisimilitude of your stories, this is an essential space.

Tip: What are the curtains like? Does the night-light bother you? Where's it coming from? What are the noises you hear? Odors you smell? What are the sheets like? Where are your characters' clothes? What do they sleep in? You could index all this and be ready to be playful and imaginative at any turn.

Check: Can you find a story here? If none comes, bring a couple from the funeral party in here. If this doesn't spark any drama in the bedroom, there are other exercises you could merge into this one; for example, the couple (or triple) from exercise thirteen or fourteen could end up here.

8. Looking at the street from "Setting I" exercise eight, imagine an event and where it happened in a particular building—in a post office, a bank, or some other office. Write in the first person, pretending to be a character from one of your exercises, so you can vividly identify with what he sees.

Walk into the building. Describe what you see. If you know some of the building's history, include some of these details in a summary outline and move on. Climb the stairs, open the door, enter the corridor. What are the smells? Mildew? Varnish? Rust? Enter an office and wait.

Purpose: To establish the setting through the senses. Sensory images are the best channels into the past; they give substance to what otherwise is highly ephemeral. You convince yourself and your reader that something has happened if a part of it is still lingering in your nose, on your lips, in your shoe, in your ear.

Tip: The event needn't be a big one, such as a murder or anything glamorous. You could connect the place with an ostensibly minor event—your character was caught stealing sneakers, or he discovered his father having an affair, or he had his first cigarette; a gang of ten-year-olds tried to rob a bank, with sticks for guns.

Check: Review the exercise and find a moment that works for you. Can you concentrate on it further and build a story?

9. Take your character into a shop on the same street—a car repair shop, a small bookstore, a pharmacy, a boutique. Let your character have a pressing need, which the personnel ignore. Through details, make us feel we're in the shop too.

Purpose: To examine fresh and unusual settings in your fiction. Shops are interesting—and frequently aggravating—places. Here you combine unusual-looking rooms with basic needs; your character is not an idle observer. He's desperate, he has motives. The conflict between the character's desire to receive prompt service and a clerk's desire to ignore the customer can give you good tension.

Tip: Potentially, this could become a subplot in a story. How does your character satisfy his need? That's the basic question most stories try to answer. You could combine this with option B of exercise nine in "Description."

Check: As you read this, do you have the impression you are in the shop? Have you evoked the sense and the sensations of the place through details and lists of concrete things?

If your shop isn't convincing enough, combine this exercise with number five in "Description." Now the customer will watch the tool you describe with not only fascination but impatience. An option for added excitement: In the middle of all this, another person appears, a person whom the character does not want to see.

10. Describe an emergency room from the viewpoint of an anxious patient who has been injured but is conscious enough to look around and perceive. Describe the clerks, nurses, doctors, patients.

Describe the same clinic from the viewpoint of a doctor encountering the patient.

Purpose: To use a threatening yet highly realistic setting, since threat can generate tension, conflict, and plot. Unfortunately, sooner or later most of us visit emergency rooms. These are the moments of heightened awareness of our bodies, mortality. Describing what goes on there in detail should be useful in your fiction. You can suspend the action, slip into a stream of consciousness to achieve slow motion; you can give us a character's thoughts, hopes, new insights into what matters in his life. How you perceive the emergency room depends on what your role in it is so this is a good point-of-view exercise too.

Tip: Provide the sensory details. You could combine this exercise with "Point of View" exercise nine and "Character" exercise nine. Bring one of your characters here, for a reckoning.

Check: Read through. Do you have an idea how the patient suffered the injury or became ill? Follow the possibilities. You might write a story about it, and this will be a crisis scene. What can happen later?

11. Draw a floor plan of the rooms of your high school or college or church, as though you were an architect. Now that you have a map, take us on a tour, pretending to be guiding a friend or a relative to give us a personal angle.

Purpose: To evolve and construct more hunting grounds for stories or novel chapters.

Tip: Tell us where something happened. Recall a real event with its texture, and worry about disguises later. Pay attention to how things were back then: Do you remember the fashions? What did people wear? What kind of hairstyles were popular? Jewelry? What did they drink, smoke? What music did they listen to? How did they talk? Did you kiss anybody on the premises? Do tell. Get or give a black eye? How was your baptism or catechism or other religious rite of passage?

Check: Don't check right away. Keep going. If you hit upon something that begs to be expanded, go ahead; try to move from this exercise into the story.

12. Describe a gym, with all the torture machines for stretching and pressing. But include people in your description. You could describe them, and the machines, from the standpoint of one of your characters.

Purpose: To continue to vary your settings. Unlike in theater, where it takes a lot of effort to construct a new stage, in fiction you can easily visit quite a few stages, and in the course of a novel, you will benefit from the variety of settings. And here's your chance to describe your character's physique.

Tip: What are the treadmill people doing? How about the bench press people? How are they dressed? What are their muscles like? Are they looking at themselves in the mirror? At their eyes? Their abs? Are they trying to flirt?

Check: For atmosphere, make sure you include smells, sounds, the sensation of effort. You might combine this with exercise fifteen in "Description."

13. Describe a restaurant you know well—the look and the smell of the place. Describe the waiters, the customers, the sounds and the lighting of the place. Now take two of your characters here for a meal. Perhaps you have already set a scene with these characters somewhere else. Move them here as an experiment.

Purpose: To use a popular and versatile setting—a restaurant. Restaurants are a good place to meet, a neutral territory, great background for special occasions, dates, business, in real life and in fiction.

Tip: As in the description of a family dinner, you can express a lot indirectly. Create an atmosphere—bring in the musicians, odd couples, pretentious waiters.
A variation on this exercise: a bar.

Check: How does the place look? Would it improve if it had more shadows? Where can you sneak them in? How about small details, such as somebody making a wine glass sing with his fingertip on the rim?

14. Now imagine two characters seducing each other in the same restaurant. Describe how they behave, eat, drink, relate to the waiters. Let them talk too, but rely more on the description of how they talk, gesticulate, move in their chairs—on body language.

Purpose: To exploit the setting; to use it as a stage. After all, it's a public kitchen and dining room put together. Private kitchens have energy to them; even public ones do. See whether you can cook and serve your story here.

Tip: If this was too straightforward for you and you couldn't develop much excitement, introduce another element. A person who is deeply in debt to one of the characters appears at the next table, and the character and the debtor could argue about their debt, or even enter a fight. See where that leads. Maybe this could call for rewriting the exercise and recasting it in a western mode.

Check: So that this scene makes sense, be sure your writing is erotic, that the descriptions are sensual, that they engage our sensory imagination in a delicious way, through the beauty of your sentences, word combinations, and images. However, if you can't summon up the erotic jazz, you aren't alone; I always fail at that, and I even wrote an article, "Why I Can't Write Erotica," for which, when I read it aloud, I get a lot of laughs. So I would be tempted to turn this exercise into a parody of erotica. Maybe that's an option. Of course, if you can do it well without parodying anything, congratulations.

15. Be an architect for a while, and design a house of your dreams (or nightmares). Sketch it with a pencil. Then write about the house as though it were finished. What are the floors made of? How are the rooms shaped? Where do you spend time in the house? Now imagine that your favorite person in the world has just moved in with you or has been visiting you for a week. What part of the house do you compete for?

Purpose: To indulge in a daydream, a sketchable one.

Tip: You might combine this with a science fiction setting or plot. Or you could try to do a variation of the classic story "Fisherman's Wife." So you'd have a conflict, let your favorite person have different tastes from you.

Check: Has the writing picked up its momentum? If not, to make the fabulous place believable and concrete enough for you, give it mundane problems—a dripping faucet that drives you insane at night, mosquitoes, cockroaches. Everything else is almost perfect, but those cockroaches—they are perfect. Nothing kills them.

Are you having fun? Play. Make permutations. Be silly. Not on command, of course.

16. Take a sensitive and finicky character and send him on a grimy journey, to the most interesting place, and let him be threatened—or let him imagine that he is—by some of the passengers in a train, bus, ship, plane, taxi.

Purpose: To deal with the interior of a public transportation vehicle. Many strange and incompatible, disparate and desperate characters come together here.

Tip: Take three characters who have as little in common as you can think of—make them idiosyncratic, and place them in the same cab or in the same row of seats. As you raise the sense of danger, intersperse the action with the details of the travel—sights of waterfalls, sounds of coyotes, smells of burning garbage, or whatever—from your memory and imagination.

Check: No matter what, do we have the sensation of travel? If the incompatibility of characters dissolves the possibility for a good event for you, let them surprisingly get together and surmount their differences in a moment of crisis, say when faced with a religious cult of cannibals in Montana, or something similar.

CHAPTER SEVEN

BEGINNING AND DEVELOPING

A story is like a party: You don't want to arrive too early or too late. If you get there early, you'll appear nerdish and too eager, while waiting for the excitement. If you come late, you'll miss the best drinks, and the most interesting people might be tied up.

Begin the story once there's a story already going on—something happening. In some cases, you might want to jump right into the climactic situation; in others, you start with a crisis that will lead into the climax.

What you have as an opening in the final draft needn't be the same as the opening that gets you writing the story. To begin a story, look for what triggers your fingers best, where you get excited to write. Start with that. Later, you can choose whatever scene that'll introduce the reader to the characters and their conflicts best.

Some writers work best from strong images—things that can pull them into a world imaginatively.

Mark Winegardner, author of *The Veracruz Blues*, says that he opens his stories with a pair of seemingly disparate images. He once heard of a man obsessed with shooting rats in his barn. He thought that would make a good opening, but he could not do much with it, until he coupled it with another anecdote, about a man who entrusts his fourteen-year-old daughter with paying the bills. Mark opened the story with a farmer and his daughter standing on the porch and talking about their debts, while their landlord shoots rats in the barn. The story took off from there.

DECIDING WHERE TO BEGIN

You can begin a story from almost any temporal point in it— the last event, the first event, the middle event. It's similar to drawing a portrait: You might start with an outline of a person's shape, or zero in on his eyes, or hands, or ears, and from these find the way to the rest of the person.

No matter where you start a piece of fiction, you probably want to intrigue the reader. Set up some expectations, raise questions. And if you can, dazzle the reader with something, a paradox, a series of images. In fact, even more important than dazzling the reader is dazzling yourself—get the sensation of magic, feel that strange and wonderful sounds and sights are taking place in your fiction. Look at what Angela Carter does in her short story "Master."

> After he discovered that his vocation was to kill animals, the pursuit of it took him far away from temperate weather until, in time, the insatiable suns of Africa eroded the pupils of his eyes, bleached his hair and tanned his skin until he no longer looked the thing he had been but its systematic negative; he became the white hunter, victim of an exile which is the imitation of death, a willed bereavement.

Carter surprises us right away. It strikes us as odd that someone's calling is to kill animals. When I read it, I immediately wondered—How could this be? Who could this guy be? Then, the image of the hunter who spends his time in the sun, as his own photographic negative, gives us a beautiful and entertaining picture. It is also a useful one: The negative portrays a man's perverted love of death. I don't know whether Carter wrote this opening close to the beginning of writing the story, but passages like this one in the beginning could get one excited and thrilled to write.

Since a story is like a good party, the opening has much to do with how to get to the location where it's going on. You first need to know where it is, what part of town, and when you enter the party space, you take a brief look at what's there, the dance, the smoke, the balloons, and the host, who introduces you to people. Once you meet people, you might single out the ones who strike you as most interesting and talk to them.

It's effective to invite the reader to the setting where the story is taking place. For example, Anne Tyler practically leads us by the ear (in a pleasant way) to the setting of *Saint Maybe*.

> On Waverly Street, everybody knew everybody else. It was only one short block, after all—a narrow strip of patched and repatched pavement, bracketed between a high stone cemetery wall at one end and the commercial clutter of Govans Road at the other. The trees were elderly males with lumpy, bulbous trunks. The squat clapboard houses seemed mostly front porch.
>
> And each house had its own particular role to play. Number Nine, for instance, was foreign. A constantly shifting assortment of Middle Eastern graduate students came and went, attending classes at Johns Hopkins, and the scent of exotic spices drifted from their kitchen every evening at suppertime. Number Six was referred to as the newlyweds', although the Crains had been married two years now and were beginning to look a bit worn around the edges. And Number Eight was the Bedloe family.

We are drawn into a story about the Bedloe family. We walk down the street, to see it, smell it, before we enter the house.

Tyler pulls us in, as if to say, look, it's fun in this place—we have an odd assortment of characters and spices here. Come on in!

USING—AND MOVING BEYOND—THE BEGINNING

Some people work well from the beginnings—all they need is a good beginning and the rest takes care of itself. Worth checking whether it works for you. It needn't work in every instance, but if it does occasionally, great.

Because the issue of how and where to begin a story overlaps with the issue of finding the story, this chapter overlaps with "Ideas for Fiction." If you have an idea for a story or a novel, attack it from the right angle, from the beginning. The novel, of course, could take a lot of preparation—jotting of character sketches, places, ideas, thinking—but maybe that can come in the stream of your writing. As you go, you see what you need to research or what you will need to sketch. Perhaps it's best to treat a novel as a long story, or a series of stories that are tightly connected by the same cast of characters. In a story, if you attempt to cast light on every motive for an action, you might cover so much ground that a novel will evolve.

Many writers need only a good beginning to get themselves started on a story or novel, and many writers find it easy to write beginnings but hard to continue—every beginning is easy, every continuation hard.

Partly this is the stage where you need courage, to leap ahead into the unknown. Trust yourself to come up with something, to keep coming up with the strains of stories and dialogue that ask for more. No matter how tenuous your fiction feels at first, if you put faith in your characters and their dialogues and struggles, the story will come. And if it doesn't, perhaps it's time to try another story, one in which the momentum forward can be easier to gain. Your plot outline needn't look like the classic plot graph—an uphill battle. In fact, after a good opening, you might have the most speed to charge right ahead, delighted at the potential, opportunities, twists and turns of phrase and event.

And if you still get stuck, you might ask, What can help me? Who can help me? Do I need to know someone special, a great teacher, editor? Do I need connections to get anywhere in my writing?

My answer to the question about literary contacts and connections: Every writer needs connections. I don't mean people in power. I mean connections between scenes, images, ideas. Connect. Combine. That may sound glib on my part, but I certainly believe that making connections among images, characters, scenes, and events is the key to literary creativity. Even some things that don't seem to belong together—that actually don't belong together—might prove combustible materials when placed together. (Once you have an energetic story going, you are the king—you don't need anybody, just your own attention. And as for connections in the literary world, they'll be easy to make, once you have great stories to sell.)

I think that for moving beyond one scene—especially the opening one—the exercises in this book can be useful. Pair a beginning you write from this chapter's exercises with an odd character, a strange predicament, odd dialogue, and see what possibilities arise from the combinations. Brainstorm. This kind of connection making can enhance your imagination.

In the transition between the opening scene and the rest of the story, you needn't be brilliant and fascinating, as you were in the opening. You'll be brilliant again in the climax or somewhere else. For now, be content to make sure we know your protagonists and we understand—or are intrigued by—the strange things they're doing on page two. In a lull, make sure we haven't missed the introductions, the characters, the place, the problem. As you keep explaining, you can see what other scenes you need. A plot outline may arise.

In some stories, you can follow the first scene in stride, in a forward momentum; in others, you might need to backtrack to show us how we got to the predicament of the opening page. No matter what you do, whether you go a bit backward, or forward, put energy and trust into what you're doing now. You can always shorten long explanations in revision. Don't be afraid to overwrite. How did we get here? And where do we go from here? Of course, you go to an even bigger problem—a bigger mess, more complications, that'll give you enough work to do for a whole novel, or at least a story.

EXERCISES

1. Write the opening page of a party in progress, to extend the metaphor of the story as a party. You might recall the strangest party you ever went to, and see whether you can fictionalize it. What did you expect when you went to the party? What did you see when you opened the door?

Purpose: To start immediately with a scene. In a party, you have a place and people—potential actors in your story.

Tip: Choose an unusual image you remember or can invent; this will catch the reader's attention. To enhance the strangeness, write in the first-person point of view, not necessarily yours.

You could combine this with exercise three in "Dialogue" or exercise one or three in "Setting I."

To enhance the opening, get your character into trouble quickly.

Check: Do we have the music, the description of the dance? Interesting people? Are there questions raised? Do we want to find out what happens next? If not, bring your narrator into a strange quandary or introduce a character who is doing something strange or troublesome.

2. Start a story with a question, a decision that will be in the crux of the story: "Should I turn him in?" This could open the exercise of the encounter between a guard and the POW. Or, "Should I confess this morning?"

Purpose: To begin a story with an intriguing problem. If we know right away what we are going to look for in the story, our reading will be organized, like a search. Moreover, a question that is not immediately answered creates suspense.

Tip: Once you introduce the question, you need to explain what's involved, so you'll backtrack into the setup of the problem.

You could combine this opening with "Scene" exercise twelve.

Check: Does the opening work with the POW (or prisoner) scene? What more do you need to bridge the opening questions and summaries with the event?

3. Begin an illness story. How does the character recognize the symptoms? You could write a scene from her point of view, about how she discovers her symptoms.

Purpose: To begin with a crisis—and diagnosis of a serious illness is certainly a crisis. Now there's much to do.

Tip: If you write from a family member's perspective, you could start with something like this: "We didn't take her complaints about chest pains seriously. She had complained too much years ago, and we had all taken her for a hypochondriac, which no doubt, she was, but even hypochondriacs get ill, and sometimes gravely ill."

To augment this exercise, you could also rely on some images of physical sensations, from "Image and Metaphor" exercises six and eleven. Adapt them to the illness you're writing about.

Or perhaps you could combine this one with exercise four in "Ideas for Fiction" or exercise fifteen in "Description."

If you don't know what one is supposed to feel in the course of the disease, read about the disease, research.

Check: As we read, do we get the sensations of illness? The senses have to be engaged. And if we're following the illness from the patient's point of view, do we get the thoughts, the worries that are part of the experience?

4. Open a story with a miraculous event. It could turn out to be an illusion, but it'll start us dreaming with you. It could be a natural miracle, a meteorite shower, a comet, a forest fire on the horizon, an earthquake, a tornado touchdown. Or a technological miracle—a nuclear explosion. Write from the point of view of a person caught in the event—at least observing.

Purpose: To open with a bang—or almost a big bang. This can impart energy to your fiction.

Tip: If you've lived through an earthquake, tornado or other extreme natural occurrence, try to remember what you were doing before and during this event. Just write about it, and then think of whether you could fictionalize this.

See whether you can use any of the miracles or cataclysmic events as an opening for a story—for example, in "Ideas for Fiction" exercise eight. Or in a story about running away from home. Or choose a perspective from one of the point-of-view exercises to render this major event. If, for example, you experienced a tornado or an earthquake with members of your family, combine this exercise with number thirteen from "Point of View," relating the event from a variety of perspectives.

Check: Are the descriptions vivid, engaging, beautiful? Strive to make them stunning.

5. Begin a story with a scene of public humiliation, from the point of view of the humiliated person. Think of something truly embarrassing.

Purpose: To kick off your fiction with emotion. Humiliation can be a source of strength—desire for revenge or withdrawal or ambition for a comeback in glory. The opening like this will immediately give you the passions, the pain of a character, and hence, a strong motive force. There should be a lot of potential for further development here.

Tip: This scene and narrative with injurious action could combine well with exercise ten in "Dialogue." Give life to the cliché "add insult to injury."

Check: Can we follow what is taking place and what's humiliating about it? If not, make sure you introduce the characters and the context for their insult fest.

6. How would you continue the following opening? I have taken it from "The Star Café," a story by Mary Caponegro: "Carol heard a noise as she undressed for bed; it frightened her— she'd actually been half undressing for bed and half searching for the book she had intended to read in bed. . . ."

Purpose: To begin a story with a threat of danger. What is the source of the noise? Try to make it unusual.

Tip: Later, once you are in the story, strike the beginning and make another one that is completely different from Caponegro's. Often the opening line that sparks a story can be cut—*should* be cut—as the story develops and involves new complexities.

Unfortunately, we sometimes fall in love with our opening line and cannot perceive when it is no longer necessary. We keep the line simply because it has always been there and now seems organic to the story. With this exercise, retaining the line is not an option.

Check: Is the source of the noise interesting? Surprising? Have you created an unusual danger that will sustain tension throughout the story? If so, keep going. If you're not happy with what you've written, try to decide why you don't like it. Are your descriptions suspenseful? Give us vivid images, but in such a way that we don't know exactly what is about to happen, and who is out there. Caponegro's opening is not specific—a noise could be any kind of sound. Describe the sound. "It frightened her." Show the fright in the way Carol behaves, thinks, and imagines. The opening sentence can be a general plan for you to develop a specific scene.

7. Open a story with a couple of scenes—a father discovers that his thirteen-year-old daughter is missing. Did she run away? Was she kidnapped? Was he responsible? What's to be done next?

Purpose: To open with a problem so the story will have something to solve.

Tip: Before evolving the scene in which the daughter is missing, introduce us to the father and the daughter in a summary and/or a scene so we know who we are going to be looking for, whom we are missing. What distracts the father so he doesn't notice at once that his daughter has disappeared?

Check: How does the opening read? If you're happy with it, keep going. If you aren't, make sure your writing is the best it can be—that you pull us in the setting where the father and daughter are, let us feel the streets, the threat of the city through our senses. Also, consider using characters from earlier exercises. Can you take the father and daughter from any of the family exercises in other chapters? Or can you combine this with number nine in "Ideas for Fiction"? Perhaps some obsession has distracted the father.

8. Open with dialogue. Jump right into the middle of a quarrel, with several lines of accusations of infidelity or insensitivity.

Purpose: To start a story with speech. A dialogue means you must introduce at least two characters, in their own words, by how they talk. A quarrel has a conflict. Accusations raise questions that need to be answered. If you set up a scene here, you already have the elements you need for a story.

Tip: Be sure you know a little bit about the characters before you have them talk. Perhaps you could extend the scene from exercise eight in "Character." Has the competition led to the infidelity or insensitivity? Or you could combine this exercise with the first part of number ten in "Character" or with number fourteen in "Setting II."

Check: Does the dialogue have a life—can it keep going?

9. Throw another party. Let a character go to the wrong party. She got the address wrong but has realized this only now, on page three. By now it's too late. What is going on in the wrong party? This could be stranger than the party in exercise one.

Purpose: To start with a confusion—something that leads to trouble or something to clear up—which can be productive.

Tip: Perhaps instead of arriving at a wedding, your protagonist is attending a wake; or instead of a wake, she's visiting a wedding; or instead of a prayer meeting, she's attending the annual nudist colony fund-raiser. To add excitement, choose a character from an earlier exercise who would feel very much out of place at this party.

Check: Are the confusions at first puzzling not only your character but also your readers? Is there something comic occurring here? There could be—misunderstanding and confusion are the basic sources of humor.

10. Open with the summary of a story. Tell what the story is going to be about and who's in it, in the most straightforward terms. Sometimes storytelling can start the old-fashioned way, with the telling that'll raise questions, ask for explanations; the details will come in as the evidence of what we are talking about.

Purpose: To begin with a summary that works as a contract with the reader. The commitment may help you delve into the story. Later, if your opening strikes you as too prosaic, you can strike it. However, there's sometimes pleasure, comfort, and wisdom in a summary that conveys the problems to be dealt with. It's a standard technique of essay writing. Crossing between essay and fiction techniques is good for both types of writing.

Tip: Make sure the summary is interesting—that you offer intriguing thoughts or paradoxes or insights that aren't too obvious. Perhaps you could combine this summary with the third part of exercise ten in "Character." A summary beginning could fit well with a philosophical story.

Check: Does your summary make a promise to become a good story? Are there conflicts and problems that will engage the characters?

11. Open the story with a negative summary, meaning you should tell what it's not going to be about. Then, after a paragraph or two, tell what it is going to be about.

Purpose: To set up a contrast between what could have happened and what did happen. This might add dimension to your story.

Tip: Columbus never sailed around the world, and he never reached India. These negatives are important to his story of how he came to the Americas. Can you construct a story with expectations that were not met but which led to something else that is equally or more interesting? Consider combining this exercise with one from "Setting I." Tell us what we will not see in the landscape, what we will not find in the forest, then tell us what we will see.

Check: Is your opening intriguing, playful? The negatives expressed—do they prepare us well for the positives?

12. Start the story in a startling way—not just with the hook, but with the dagger. Be bombastic or shocking. You might use something you've seen or read about that has shocked you, such as a parent abandoning her child in a dumpster. Be bold. Risk melodrama.

Purpose: To try to concoct an outrageous opening.

Tip: What has startled you or shocked you most? What has surprised you? How? Why? Perhaps you can set up a similar surprise for us. John Cheever opens his classic story "The Country Husband" with a character suffering through—and surviving—a plane crash. Though Cheever weaves humor into the startling details, he creates a powerful opening.

Check: Test the opening on your friends—what do they say? Do they look surprised when they read? I know, there's hardly anything more irritating than to be scrutinized for reactions while you read—but for a page, your friends might bear this.

13. Write the first several pages of a picaresque novel, which should feature a goofy protagonist who undergoes a series of comic misadventures. Perhaps you have created such a character in another exercise. If so, use him here. Or you could rework an outline from one of the exercises in the plot chapter. There we discuss storytelling traditions such as the bildungsroman. The picaresque is another great tradition.

Purpose: To attempt a mood and a mode of this traditional kind of novel, which can be joyful to read and, I believe, joyful to write.

Tip: Try to get the character into all kinds of situations, high and low. Perhaps he can start out in a cheeseburger joint or in a liquor store as a salesclerk, work as a celebrity limo driver, then as Henry Kissinger's butler, and later, let him be promoted beyond his capabilities, as an ambassador to the United Nations or to a new country. Maintain a cheerful and playful attitude in the novel. Humor, satire, silliness—these are your friends in writing this kind of work.

Check: Read what you've written. Is it fun? If so, try to keep going. Don't worry about where you're headed with this piece.

14. Vladimir Nabokov begins his novel *Ada* with the following line: " 'All happy families are more or less dissimilar; all unhappy ones are more or less alike,' says a great Russian writer in the beginning of a famous novel. . . ."
Obviously Nabokov has reversed the famous opening to Tolstoy's *Anna Karenina.* Now, without using this first sentence, introduce us to a unique and happy family.

Purpose: To jump into a family novel. How families work is one of the fecund themes of literature.

Tip: Surround the happy family with unhappy families who are monotonous (everybody has the same kind of disease, therapy, and so on). If you persevere with the story, try to make the story as happy as can be without being corny. If happiness, however, becomes monotonous, be prepared to switch into a tragedy.

Now, for the opening of the happy family saga, choose a scene in which we feel how joyful the family is—perhaps this could combine well with the dinner scene exercise from chapter one, or with a family car trip, or a wedding, or a funeral, or going to church and listening to sermons.

Check: Is your scene effective? Is there enough energy? If not, you might start with some specific crisis—an eviction or layoff. Or perhaps happy families aren't for you. Maybe an unhappy one is worth trying after all.

15. Find five openings of famous short stories or novels that you can make a variation on, the way Nabokov did with *Anna Karenina* in the example above.

Purpose: To tune into an energy and logic that you can get a bounce out of—and into your own work. You don't start in the empty space from zero; you react. In tennis, hitting a ball that already has good pace on it can produce more power than hitting a slow ball would. Use some of the energy you find in literature—react to it, attack, and provide your own twist.

Tip: Once you have written the changed opening, make a good connection with places, characters, images—perhaps from this series of exercises, or from a project in progress.

Check: Find one opening that invites you to continue it most easily. In which one do you see what can happen next? Now write and see how far you can get—maybe you have the whole story. If your energy lessens, try another opening.

16. Work from exercise three in "Setting II." A character feels uncomfortable in a living room he is visiting. Why is he uncomfortable? Sharpen and revise the old exercise to make it into a crisp beginning with an intrigue.

Purpose: To start writing with a suspense—the mood of uncertainty, dark atmosphere, suggestion of danger.

Tip: Write from the character's third-person subjective point of view. How does the room look from his perspective? How does he analyze what he sees? There could be a sporadic dialogue with the host, with an interior monologue that would reveal the character's perceptions, thoughts, fears.

Check: Have you coordinated the details of the living room with the character's thoughts and the dialogue so that the opening paragraphs read smoothly? If not, rewrite. There's enough time for everything. You can patiently describe. As long as you raise a realistic possibility of a threat, you'll provide enough tension not to have to rush. In fact, the suspense lets you suspend the action—to give us the interior monologue, which will intensify the sensation of fear and suspense. There's no suspense without slowing down and waiting for the threat to burst into action.

17. Start with a scene from exercise ten in "Setting I." Revise that exercise to make it sharp, and bring into that emergency room a character who has suffered a strange injury—at home or work.

Purpose: To start with a crisis—one way to make sure you have a crisis in a story. Sometimes one can have a good character and an interesting setting but no story because there's no conflict to lead into a crisis.

Tip: While we are in the emergency room, introduce us to the character. Where's he from? What's he into? What was he doing when the crisis took place? And after you have completed the scene, it shouldn't be hard to keep going with the story. There are enough questions now to pursue. What or who injured him? How? Why? This could start a whole chain of actions and reactions, and the emergency room visit could be the beginning as well as the end of the story—or it could be one of the climaxes, with which we open to backtrack and familiarize ourselves with what has come before it and which will lead us into a bigger climax.

Check: Do you convey to us the sensations of being in an emergency room? Is there tension? Uncertainty as to the outcome of the visit? Dramatize the scene to make us feel the panic and the fear, with the character.

18. Write a two-paragraph opening. Write in first person as an imaginary witness. First describe a firm and respectable character in one paragraph. Then in another, show this character act "out of character"—that is, let him behave completely contrary to his ordinary image.

Purpose: To open with a surprise. When we surprise and act in an unpredicted fashion we can make a good story. In contemporary fiction workshop fashions, there's too much emphasis on character consistency—He wouldn't do that, would he? is a pat criticism that has spread like a computer virus and that derails many a playful writer. Well, maybe he would do just that. Character consistency frequently has more to do with our pigeonholing people with certain traits than with what people are like—frequently inconsistent, unstable, impulsive, and so on. The notion of character is a convenience for the observer—to simplify—rather than for the observed. Before you do something, do you say to yourself, Wait a minute. What am I supposed to be like? Am I a melancholy passive sort of person? So then, let me sulk and do nothing about it. But an observer who has formed a prejudice about you might expect you to behave passively, aggressively, or whatever. Almost all "character traits" amount to foregone conclusions—it's good to spite and challenge the narrow notions of character.

Tip: Establish the expectations to break them. The contrast between expectations and the action will give much energy to your scene. This could be a story about the fall of an idol—a mayor, a politician, a minister—or about the rise of a criminal or a sinner. Or about an exceptional day in a life of a seemingly constant character.

Check: Have you realized the contrast between what the character is supposed to be like and how he behaves?

19. When were you most puzzled, amazed? Can you recall a particular moment of perplexity? Describe it in detail, and use it as a story opening. Why did the puzzlement arise?

Purpose: To present a puzzle right in the beginning, which can lead the readers (and the writer) into the story with a focus. We now have something to find out; we are curious.

Tip: In order to fictionalize this initial situation, after you have written it in the first-person point of view, rewrite it in the third-person subjective point of view, exaggerate it, and be open to a different solution from the one that held true in your real-life situation.

Check: Is the initial situation puzzling indeed? Is there a paradox, or something hardly believable, going on? Now after describing the puzzlement, have you left enough unresolved to keep us reading into the next scene?

CHAPTER EIGHT

SCENE

Whether you can make a scene out of a story idea is a litmus test that shows whether there's life in the idea. Same with plot: to see how your plot is to build, and whether it can work, you can construct a scene with the major players in conflict. If you enjoy making scenes, the other elements of fiction should naturally fall into place.

Scene is a description of an action, or a series of motions, that progresses in a chronological and spatial continuum. You can jump back and forth in time as much as you like when you narrate an event in general—giving summary, background, analysis, thoughts—but once you begin to show us exactly what you mean, what and how something happened, you are bound to respect the time sequence. (Of course, you could make asides that'll deviate from the sequence—character's thoughts about something that happened earlier—but they'll be grafted to the tree of chronology.) Which is not to say you must be shackled by chronology.

In a scene, rarely do you have to represent realistically the amount of time something takes. Besides, some people speed-read, others savor each word and syncopation, so the relativity of perception in your readers makes it impossible to be mimetic as far as the duration of an action is concerned. A lovemaking scene could take a whole evening but could be described in less than a page, which takes a minute to read. A shooting could occur in several seconds but fill several pages.

WHAT YOU NEED TO CREATE GOOD SCENES

Flow with the details, grasp them, expand them, overwrite. You'll edit later. In your early drafts, include images, twisted words, anything to keep the illusion of the scene going and growing, moving, shifting, bursting with energy. If your whole novel takes place as one scene, all the better. It's better to err in the direction of dwelling in a scene than summarizing. A major scene is your here and now; this is where you need to let go, experience the moment to the fullest, with its drama, pain, pleasure, music.

To create a scene, you need characters and settings. You usually need a command of dialogue and individual voices. Each of these elements is addressed in another chapter, but here you can pull them all together.

Don't let the prospect of pulling together many elements in a scene intimidate you. In a way, once you have a scene going, it's the easiest kind of writing to do—there's a natural dynamism there. One image triggers another, a punch requires a counterpunch, a line asks for another line, a question for an answer, an assertion for a contradiction. Here your pieces move, pick up momentum, and sometimes it's difficult to stop them.

The sentences at first don't have to be all that descriptive and pretty. You can rewrite later, if you've taken care of the major blows, major lines of dialogue. After you have the lines, you might intersperse body language to augment them, locate them, space them, anchor them. Or after you know the event—a happening—you might enrich it by bringing more dialogue, more subtlety. There are different ways of constructing a scene, and although most of your writing skills should come to the fore here, you can keep coming back, chiseling, adding, changing. No reason to be anxious. On the contrary—be joyful, exuberant.

Be not only a *Homo sapiens*, a conscious human being, but even more importantly, a *Homo ludens*, a player. For creation, the attitude of having fun, horsing around, kidding is most productive. Many good scenes are written almost unconsciously, through play. You don't have to be superintelligent to write well—but I think you need to be free and playful. Allow odd and bizarre ideas to come to the page. You can always delete them later if they are non sequiturs or are unsuitable. If you achieve a state of mind in which you can surprise yourself, tell yourself something you haven't heard, or known, you're in the full swing; you have released your creative demons, who talk to you, as though they were a different person. I don't mean that you have to be possessed, but there may be something akin to possession here, and for that, it's helpful not to worry, not to strain. Let your free associations construct a net, a mesh, to catch the fish in the streams of your consciousness.

ELEMENTS OF SCENE

One simple trick to help you concentrate on writing a scene at a specific time in a specific location is to state, right away, something like this: 10 A.M., NYC Athletic Club, Jim and John. If you know when, where, and who, you could probably jump in, and if not, add one more element: what. What are they competing for? What are they in conflict about?

When you read novels, watch for scenes that work particularly well. Analyze them. What do you like in them? Can you do something similar? If it's all right in tennis to imitate a good stroke, why not in writing? You will still end up doing it your way.

I'll give you a scene from my story "Hats and Veils." In Zürich, an exile from Bosnia, Vadim, and his daughter, Sonya, are going to a commercial district so he can buy her a violin. See how the action evolves chronologically, but at the same time, Vadim's thoughts follow their own chronology.

They climbed onto the bus together. There were several elderly people; a dozen high-school students; a leathery adolescent with green hair and a ring piercing his lip; and two young women, with black lipstick, in mink coats and torn fishnet stockings. . . .

"Could we go sailing?" Sonya asked in German, looking at the bouncing sailboats among the choppy waves of the lake. He did not answer because he was busy with his reveries.

He remembered how when Sonya was thirteen months old, she had loved fish. Whenever she saw a drawing of a fish, she'd silently open and close her mouth. When he showed her a red starfish picture—and said, "Starfish!"—her finger tried to trace the mouth, and not finding it, got confused, stopped on the picture of a submarine rock. She put her tiny forefinger back in her fist, and stared at Vadim openmouthed, as though confronted with the concept of a lie for the first time. Later, on a moonless night with a breeze murmuring through pines, when he pointed to the sky and said "Stars!" she opened and closed her mouth happily, and turned to him to show him how well she was doing. She'd learned to accept all kinds of fishes, in their variety, even those that did not have mouths and that swam in the sky at night.

"*Sag mal,*" Sonya began again. Tell me . . .

"*Mozda kasnije,*" he said in Bosnian. "Maybe later, after I teach you how to ski. Would you like that?"

"Hush!" Sonya put her forefinger on her lips, and said in English, while blushing, "Somebody might hear you!"

As he stared at her red face uncomprehendingly, she whispered in Bosnian, apparently thinking that he was not capable of understanding other languages. "Keep quiet, people will hear you."

"So? That's what speech is for!" he said.

She turned her head away and bit her lips.

So that's it. She's ashamed of me. She's afraid of being identified as Bosnian. I'm a Bosnian peasant, and she's a Swiss lady. My child, my best friend, is a foreigner to me.

This scene leads to a revelation. Chronologically, we follow father and daughter on the bus, on a short ride. We deviate into the past reveries a little to prepare us for the present, which is the mainstream of the scene. The reveries, with their images of stars and starfish, enhance the man's nostalgia and dreaminess, out of which he is jolted in the conversation with Sonya, when he realizes that she, though he has and is going to sacrifice a lot for her, is actually ashamed of him, and ashamed to be a foreigner.

EXERCISES

We have already developed a lot of locations and characters, so bring them together and let them clash about something, give them a conflict, no matter how banal. People often fight about banal things and have spectacular fights.

1. Develop a nature adventure scene—a rafting trip at its most intense, mountain climbing, swimming (and drowning), or a skiing accident. Describe the sensations of the trip, the effort, the danger shared by two or three people whose relationship will change as a consequence of what has gone on under pressure.

Purpose: To air out your characters. Perhaps they needn't stay in apartments and cities all the time. An elemental setting can refresh the way you portray the interaction between your characters. (Of course, if your characters are mostly in the wild, you might do the reverse, and take them into a city, which might assume the elemental properties of threat and beauty.)

Tip: Combine this with exercise five from "Setting I." You might also want to combine this with exercise fifteen in "Dialogue."

Check: Have you pulled readers into the trip so they have the sensation they are taking it? Some details, but not too many, relating to the technique of skiing (rafting, climbing, etc.) should help. Several nature images—a raven flying with a stolen egg or something as quick as that—could do much to bring us into the setting. Is the threat believable, evolved gradually, and kept in suspense for enough time to give tension to what's going on?

2. Write a lovemaking scene between two people who at first don't seem to be well matched at all. Put them in a strange place—a dump site, a jail, a hospital waiting room. Create an odd circumstance—earthquake, eclipse, fire, nuclear radiation accident. Aim for an erotic effect, through descriptions, images.

Purpose: Should there be any? Some pointless sex is in order, at least in fiction. If nothing else, it could get your characters in trouble, and trouble is nearly always good in fiction. Or it could prevent your characters from getting out of trouble.

Tip: Be indirect in trying to achieve an erotic effect. No need for blatant appellations or clichés.

You could use "Description" exercise two here, for a scene taking place before or after the lovemaking. Recast the description to fit here.

Consider using "Image and Metaphor" exercise two. Especially if you describe a sensation one wouldn't expect during lovemaking, the effect might be refreshing. Some sensations from "Image and Metaphor" exercise eleven could contribute to the sensuality of your scene here.

Check: Give your scene to a friend and see whether he finds the writing erotic, or at least funny or beautiful or disgusting or horrifying—some strong effect.

3. Blow by blow, describe a slaying with a large knife, or with a gun, a bomb, a car.

Purpose: To write a murder scene. Even if you don't write murder stories, sooner or later there might be a murder in your fiction, if you follow the conflicts and tensions to an extreme. It's good to be ready when you get there.

Tip: You could combine this with a Greek myth or a biblical story. Of course, Oedipus has been killed enough times, so find another paradigm. Perhaps Moses killing the Egyptian guard could serve as the starting point. You could modernize the story and have a man under military occupation kill a soldier, or a POW kill a guard, or a guard a POW.

For how to handle the details, you might look at the example by Richard Selzer, from "The Knife," included in "Description" exercise five. You could use this murder as the shocking opening for exercise twelve in "Beginning and Developing." Combine them and see what happens. Or perhaps there are characters from earlier exercises whose conflict has reached the point of physical violence. Put them here.

Check: If the scene works, it could be one of a story's climaxes. Maybe to explain how you got to this point, you could backtrack, and then the question, Where does it go from here? could carry the story far, as far as the promised land, a finished story.

4. Create a quiet war scene. Perhaps soldiers are going to sleep in a tent. They awake and make their beds in a rush. Follow

them from the point of view of a soldier who wants action, who wants the glory of combat, and who has an attack of insomnia, then, as he readies for battle, fear.

Purpose: To vary your rhythms when writing about war. War is not continuous excitement. Most of it is continuous boredom. Before and after the combat scenes, for the change of pace and for setting up the suspense, it's good to have a lull.

Tip: Slow needn't mean dull. Here, the interest in the scene could come from thoughts, strange conversations, odd details, memories, hallucinations. You might combine this with the previous exercise, perhaps preceding the murder (say of a POW). Or combine this with "Description" exercise six; play with shadows to enhance the soldier's imagination and fear.

For a fine example of soldiers in a quiet moment, read Ernest Hemingway's story "Now I Lay Me." In it he drifts between one soldier's attempts to stay awake—to avoid nightmares—and the sounds of the night around the soldiers.

Check: In a slow scene especially, the writing needs to be crafty, to maintain the reader's interest—and the writer's interest. As you read, do you find enough interesting thoughts? Some insights? Paradoxes? Bizarre images?

5. Write about an encounter between a POW and his guard. The guard recognizes something of himself in the soldier. A sympathy evolves and complicates the guard's life. Write from the point of view of the person who has more power—the guard. However, if psychologically the prisoner has more power, you might choose his viewpoint.

Purpose: To develop an unlikely relationship between two characters. A forced, regulated relationship that apparently leaves hardly any room for a spontaneous relationship and free will might actually be a great setting for a relationship to evolve against the odds. In fiction, working against the odds can be effective; an obstacle, a challenge, a problem are all plots in the making.

Tip: If you're not interested in wars, translate the exercise into another encounter—between a guard and a prisoner or a student and his teacher in a school that is like a combat zone.

Check: Has the scene accomplished a meaningful encounter? Do we have the sense of the guard and the POW—do we see them? Hear them?

6. Use a holiday scene—Fourth of July fireworks, Columbus Day parade, Christmas shopping—as backdrop for another action. Describe the floats, the fireworks, or the fanfare common to another holiday, in striking detail.

Purpose: To use a big public event as a background to a personal drama. This can give dimension to the personal drama and is a good juxtaposition to master.

Tip: Write from the point of view of someone undergoing a personal tragedy, say a man who has just found out he has cancer and who is grappling with how to break the news to his wife. Or a woman who has found out that the child she's pregnant with has Down's syndrome: She has to break the news to her husband; she wonders whether to go through an abortion late in her term. Or a patient and family members are participating in a deathbed scene in a hospital.

You could link this scene with exercise one in "Plot." The holiday backdrop could make her experience all the more poignant.

Use a moment or two from "Image and Metaphor" exercise six to augment the experience here.

Check: Is the scene original enough? Does it include details that are odd, that are unexpected? Let the scene be unusual, even though we deal with a usual holiday.

7. Set a scene in the kitchen. Amidst cooking of an elaborate meal, two people enjoy the harmony of working together, then there's a falling-out and coming back together.

Purpose: To use food to enhance a scene. Food is expressive; it's like clay for a sculptor. Taste buds are generally a neglected sense of perception in fiction; it's refreshing when you get a chance to taste what is going on.

Tip: The conflict that two people have elsewhere can be mirrored in food, sometimes quite simply. For example, one person likes to use a lot of hot pepper, which tastes hot but disguises and distorts the flavor of mild food. The other one wants only paprika, which looks hot but is mild and deep.

Combine this assignment with "Image and Metaphor" exercise eight to get us close to the food here. Or use it to continue exercise six in "Setting II." Or use this scene to extend and develop any of the exercises in which two characters are in conflict.

Check: Do we smell and taste enough of the food? If not, perhaps you could follow a recipe in a cookbook. Perhaps some of the quarrel could focus on different ways to interpret the recipe. There have been many quarrels stemming from various exegetic possibilities in the ultimate book of peace, the Bible, so why not a few disagreements in how to read a cookbook?

8. Imagine a primal scene in which parents are making love and they realize their four-year-old is watching them. Write from the perspective of the mother and then from the perspective of the child.

Purpose: To involve one of the basic psychological events in a scene. Why not use it, sooner or later, in your fiction?

Tip: Make this a special event for the parents—they are discovering the joys of sex for the first time in a long while. Make the scenes erotic through the detail. From the four-year-old's perspective, make the scene a bit odd; the parents are bouncing on the bed just as he likes to do, so he joins in and bounces too, or thinks they are fighting and is terrified. Perhaps the parental explanation that they are only fighting terrifies him even more than some kind of direct explanation would.

Several of the multiple-perspective point-of-view exercises would connect with this one, would offer a useful strategy for developing a sensitive scene. If you developed an engaging voice for a four-year-old in exercise ten in "Point of View," you could use it here.

Check: Is the scene interesting? If not, perhaps one more event, such as a pet bird or cat flying out the window amidst all this, might create the needed commotion.

9. Describe somebody dying slowly, in the bedroom. Relatives gather and wait for the last words, and at the same time they scheme and have conflicts, unholy thoughts about the will.

Purpose: To write a death scene. Such primary stuff that permeates many of us with dread can give depth to your fiction, if you slow down and concentrate on the death. Even superficial details will add a dimension.

Tip: Render the scene from three different points of view. First, the dying person's. Obviously, this will take imagination, unless you've died and come back to life. Here's your exploration of what it might be like—the light at the end of the tunnel, or not.

Then observe the event as someone deeply attached to the person dying.

Then observe it from the viewpoint of someone who never cared much for the person dying.

You could incorporate all the points of view into the dying man's—the other two working as his speculative flashes, figuring out with unusual lucidity, such as can precede death, everybody's motives.

This could be connected with the disease series of exercises, which starts in "Ideas for Fiction." And you could further develop the story if you connect it with number seven in "Plot." You could set the story in the bathroom, living room, and bedroom you have described in "Setting II" exercises two, three, and seven. Naturally, be free to change what you have done in the exercises to adapt it for this one.

With all these connections, you have enough materials to visualize a story and develop it as several scenes.

Check: Is the writing melodramatic and sentimental? I think the facts themselves, if given in enough detail, could arouse sadness, without the need to drum up how sad dying is.

10. Write a persecution scene. Perhaps your character has a sensation of being followed, and he is not wrong. A variation: Your character is following someone who gets scared although the pursuer's intentions are good, or who doesn't get scared although the pursuer's intentions are evil.

Purpose: To work from a basic nightmare. Many people's dreams feature flight and persecution. This is a deep-seated anxiety. Why not write about it? You will capture many readers' attention. They'll know what you are talking about.

Tip: Use a lot of hallucinogenic images. A shadow cast by a nighthawk flying beneath a streetlamp could be mistaken for a hand swinging from behind your narrator. Don't tell for a while whether he gets caught; keep the suspense building.

Combine this assignment with "Image and Metaphor" exercise twelve. Almost everything the character in flight sees could become something else; to a fleeing man, metaphors occur not as figures of speech but as terrifying possibilities. Or you could combine this one with exercise five in "Setting I."

Check: Have you conjured several scary images? That is far more important than to say your narrator is terrified. Are all the senses engaged?

11. In a hunting scene, include a temptation to change the aim from a deer to one of the hunters. Even if you detest hunting, this might be a good scene. Who says you must write only about things that don't bother you?

Purpose: To build the potential for danger in a scene. In a competitive friendship, hunting could give a great opportunity to escalate conflict and danger.

Tip: Integrate this with exercise one in "Setting I." You could also bring the unreciprocal lovers here from "Dialogue" exercise sixteen, and either the beloved or the unloved could get irritated with the other and consider shooting him. If you hate hunting, try to withhold your judgment; describe hunting from the point of view of an intelligent hunter, following his excitement and his attempts to get in touch with his primal self. If you love hunting, try to see the other side; follow this from the viewpoint of a witness of the killing, who shudders at the cruelty involved.

To develop the story further, combine it with "Plot" exercise twelve. The hunters could tell each other a fable, or even better, what happens in the hunt with dogs and hunted animals could reach the level of a fable, as does William Faulkner's story "The Bear."

Check: Do we have the excitement of the chase? The uncertainty of whether the animal will be shot? The tension? The details—green briar thorns catching your hair, a mushroom bursting under your boot—should help us experience the forest.

12. For a betrayal scene, do the classical Judas kiss scene variation, or the Unabomber's brother turning in the Unabomber, or a member of a sect turning in a leader after realizing how much the leader exploits his followers. There could be a just betrayal and an unjust one—two options.

Purpose: To involve betrayal in a story. Faithfulness and betrayal are among the biggest themes in fiction, religion, and life, and certainly worth exploring further. What should one be faithful to? Principles? Safety of many people, even at the expense of one close person ("You are dear to me, but Rome is dearer!")? What if the close person is the wrongdoer? What if she only appears to be?

Tip: Reveal the betrayal from the point of view of the betrayer, and concentrate on his thoughts and actions and perceptions preceding the turning-in. Let it be a decision: to turn in or not to turn in, with wavering, pros and cons. Perhaps in the middle of the turning-in, he gets scared and wants to turn back, but it's too late.

You could combine this with exercise five in this chapter. Despite the friendship that has evolved, the guard, out of a sense of duty or a struggle to keep his job, is tempted to turn in the POW's scheme for escape, or confessions of crimes, which turn out to be too horrific to keep silent about.

If wars and jails don't interest you, you could combine this assignment with "Plot" exercise nine.

Check: Is this suspenseful enough? To make it suspenseful, perhaps you could introduce a great threat for the betrayer. Now his perspective could be that of an unreliable narrator who has been brainwashed in a sect, and despite the insight into how brainwashed he is, and how he needs liberation, he has the anxieties he has been conditioned to have.

13. Portray an act of true heroism in a dramatic scene. Someone who is not expected to be a hero, perhaps who has until this point been a villain or an antagonist, in a moment of insight, a conversion, does something truly noble, to save his enemy, the protagonist. At the same time, for contrast, you might have a parallel surprise in the other direction: A brave, virtuous protagonist does something vile.

Purpose: To add a twist to your story. The good stay good, the bad stay bad is the modus operandi of fairy tales and much fiction, but this can be too static and uninteresting on the moral level. Probe further into morality. At any moment people have the capability to do good or to do evil.

Tip: You could combine this assignment with exercise twelve in "Voice."

Check: If the total reversal of roles seems too neat, too geometric and rational, not lifelike, rewrite in such a way that you reach a point of entanglement where the virtuous have vices and the vicious have virtues, but none are clearly good or evil. Nobody goes to heaven or hell—everybody stays on earth.

14. Write a humorous scene, with misunderstanding as the source of the ludicrousness.

Purpose: To use misunderstanding to evolve humor. Test out that basic technique and milk it.

Tip: I have heard an example about how misunderstanding can be turned into humor from James Still, author of *River of*

Earth: A man from the country follows directions to a motel in a large city. Instead of finding the motel, he ends up in a jail, but refuses to be convinced the place is not a motel. Seeing the policemen only reinforces his belief that since he's in a big and dangerous city, he's in a fine and well-protected establishment for sleeping. He's upset when told that his name is not on the reservation list.

You could create a misunderstanding of a similar sort—a man imagining he's a house sitter, while the house owner actually wants him to be a butler; a woman thinking she is hired as a manager while she is actually hired as a typist.

You could combine this exercise with a seduction scene from exercises two or eight in this chapter. Let there actually be no seduction, but one person might misread the interaction.

Check: Is the scene funny? If not, try several others, and keep the misunderstanding going, and joke with it.

15. Support exercise six in "Ideas for Fiction" by making a fully evolved scene. There you were asked to imagine yourself encountering your clone. Here, fictionalize and create a persona that's not you; be free to imagine. In this scene, the narrator competes with his double. Write in first-person point of view.

Purpose: To get the dramatic potential out of the story idea about competing with your clone.

Tip: Let the narrator be jealous: The clone is outdoing him, and it's time to stop the humiliation. The narrator could do something extreme, or he could take the clone aside and talk with him. The clone is like the narrator in all respects except he doesn't have a biography, a life, and the narrator tells about his life, trying to make the clone envious.

Check: Do you have a dramatic encounter? Good dialogue? The clone needn't sound like Dan Rather. In a rewrite, enliven his conversation. If the clone idea doesn't work for you, rewrite the scene as a competition between two very similar people, perhaps twins.

16. Use a story idea you have developed throughout this book—maybe you've already worked out the setting, the players, and their conflicts. Now jump straight ahead into the most intense thing that could happen as a consequence of this conflict, and write your high-point scene—accusation, counteraccusation, action, reaction, and perhaps a revelation.

Purpose: To write a climax scene. This is a sine qua non in most storytelling. You gear your pieces for this summit. You have hiked for a long time, now you want to step on the top and see where you've been and where you will go.

Tip: If the events aren't focused enough to get the full intensity of a climax scene, leave it in a rough draft, and return to this exercise when you've developed a conflict elsewhere—in a story you're working on or in a series of exercises you have connected.

Check: Is the pacing slow enough for the details of the drama? If something big is happening, it's a good idea to decelerate, exchange lines of dialogue, give many images, details, descriptions.

CHAPTER NINE

DIALOGUE

Ⅰn fiction you are free to write any way that pleases you, and
if you don't want to write dialogue, it doesn't mean you
can't write great fiction. Some writers—for example—fear
dialogue and yet write fine stories. There should be no tyranny
of what is required to write fiction. But there's certainly no reason to fear dialogue; you probably spend much of your time
conversing. Putting conversations on the page and playing with
them should be quite simple. And, although it's possible to write
without much dialogue, good dialogue-writing skills make the
task easier.

Dialogue can accomplish almost everything you need in a
piece of fiction. Characters' voices create a sense of personality.
The attitudes in your characters' ways of speech can create an
impression of what their bodies are doing. Dialects augment the
setting. How characters negotiate and quarrel can give us crises.
Big scenes are usually made mostly of dialogue, and big scenes
are where the story primarily takes place. In scenes, you concretize an event naturally, and you show what people are like without needing to resort to generalizations about them.

To learn to structure a dialogue, it's best to pick up a novel
with effective dialogue. See what happens there, how the lines
are tagged, etc. While you write, if it makes you feel spontaneous
and helps you concentrate on what's said, skip quotation marks

and dialogue tags. Later, you can separate speakers, by paragraphs and dialogue tags and so on. How you format the dialogue should be your last worry; that's a technicality you can master by imitating the technique in a good novel.

BALANCED DIALOGUE

It's important to strike a balance between total realism—with repetitions, false starts, sentence fragments, even word fragments, as in a faithfully transcribed taped conversation—and idealism, with everybody talking in complete sentences, correctly and always to the point. For the sake of making the conversation sound natural, fragment some sentences and jumble the word order occasionally, as many people do when groping for what to say or when in a rush.

It's also important to vary sentence lengths. In order to make their dialogues brisk, too many writers have long exchanges of one-liners (or half-liners). Sometimes, a terse conversation like that works, but too often people write in this hyperminimalistic mode because they have been led to believe that in brevity lies wit and energy. True, it does, in a well-placed brief line, but not in a constant barrage of four- or five-word quips. A good quip, as a speedy response to something that is slow, works, partly because of the change of rhythm. If there's nothing to cut into, the constant brevity will be as monotonous in rhythm as fat multi-liners are. If the point is to have silent and strong types, why have dialogue at all? If talky types, well, let them talk.

It's healthy to avoid the other extreme, of people exchanging treatises and sermons, in chunks of monologues by different speakers in place of dialogue. Sometimes, for the sake of parody, in describing an encounter of academic nerds, this might work. In real life you do get talkers who can carry on and who are hard to interrupt—and this could be reflected in the dialogue too, whenever appropriate, but in moderation. It's rare that someone who talks your ears off remains entertaining for long; you don't want to bore your reader simply for the sake of realism.

Dialogue length should fit the subject. Thomas Mann and Saul Bellow in their novels of ideas let characters speak sometimes for pages at a time, and that fits the purpose.

No matter what, your dialogue should be interesting. If the dialogue is functional but dreadfully boring, add some spark. If you can't, cut it and summarize it, then move on to where the action is more compelling.

A dialogue needn't be brimming with wit to be interesting. If everybody talks like Oscar Wilde, you will write a comedy, a farce—which is all fine, if you plan to. You won't have characters, but a bunch of comedians. If you want to write a tragedy or any kind of suspenseful story, you needn't indulge every whim to be witty. Skip some jokes—in suspenseful moments—but don't skip them otherwise. It's great to have wit, humor, and above all, liveliness, unpredictability. Let the characters say something surprising—not only to surprise each other but even you. In your fiction you needn't have outrageous things happen to make exciting prose, but it's healthy to have your characters say outrageous things now and then. Even if you violate some kind of character consistency with joking, the gambit is worth it.

Most effective dialogues use a good deal of variation. Some speakers might say ten sentences in a row, giving a minispeech, following it with one-liners, and two- or three-sentence long statements, questions, and so on. Of course, there are exceptions to this too, and if you find a good reason to have a dialogue made of one-liners, fine, why not?

DIALECTS

One question in dialogue—and in voice—is how to use dialects. If you know a region well, you are blessed. Don't hide your knowledge; play with it. Lee Smith, the author of *Oral History*, has adroitly used her Appalachian background. She recorded people's stories, transcribed them, and adapted them in her novel. This is what she says about it (in an interview for the *Novel and Short Story Writer's Market*).

> My intent was really to document that culture, with all its stories and lore and songs. Because like every other very isolated regional culture in this country, it's passing. . . . *Oral History* was the first thing I wrote which involved a great deal of research and taking notes and taping. And I kept thinking, "This can't be fair. These are great stories, but I didn't make them up."

Neither did she have to make up the way people talk. The title, *Oral History*, acknowledges her appreciation for the oral tradition. Tradition means you are passing along something that is not only yours. If you are as open about it as Smith is about her ethnographic technique, of collecting people's stories, this is certainly legitimate. There's always space left for originality. Her originality is in how she juggles many different idiosyncratic ways of speech and connects many anecdotes in one narrative. Moreover, in her narrative parts, and in the monologues, she has a great knack for detail.

Here is a brief dialogue from *Oral History*.

> "They's something else," he said.
> "They's always something else," I said. "Well, let's hear it. What is it?" I asked.
> "She's gonner have a baby," Almarine says. He cries down into his hands.
> "Good God in heaven," I say. "It won't be no baby like none of us-uns ever seed, I'll tell you that. You get rid of her, Almarine," what I told him, "afore you get you a passel of witch-children up there."
> Almarine stood up. I'll swear it was the prettiest day, full June, bees a-buzzing and butterflies flitting all over

the creek. Queen Anne's lace ever place you look. Almarine rubbed at his eyes like he couldn't see.

"I come back here a free man," he says. "I served my time. I growed up here, Granny."

"I knowed you," I says.

"I love this holler," he says.

"That's so," I told him.

"I ain't a-going to lose it," he says. Then he looks down at me and grins. Despite of him being so thin, he looks like himself now in the face, around the eyes. "I won't have no witch-children in my holler," Almarine says. "I don't know what come over me," he says.

"Holp a old woman up," I says, and Almarine done so.

Then he puts his hands on his sticking-out hipbones and laughs so loud it comes back from the rocky clifts.

Smith gives readers a sense of the dialect without overburdening them with unusual spelling. The dialect gives the sense of place, and she augments this by the description of the land, deftly placed in and around the dialogue. The narrator herself has a dialect voice.

You can do direct research the way Smith did, or rely on your ears, or see what she and other good regional writers do to give us the spirit and the flavor of dialects. After you write something in dialect, read it aloud to see whether it sounds right. If unusual spelling gets in the way, do a minimum of it, and instead rely more on word choice and grammar. In writing, you can hardly ever get every sound nuance; that's for the tape recorder. As with erotica, suggestion works better than full reproduction.

EXERCISES

1. Write a couple of pages of dialogue between two liars trying to outdo each other. They start with mild exaggerations and gradually shift to outrageous boasting.

Purpose: To use lying as a method for generating your fiction. How people lie to each other is fascinating, frequently amusing, and sometimes tragic. You can accomplish a lot if you remember your characters could lie. Fiction is a lot like lying, and maybe it's best to let the speakers in your fiction do the lying.

Tip: Let the speakers try to impress each other. They can imagine that it takes a lot to accomplish this goal. This could combine with the exercise in which the pretentious people talk to each other, number five in this chapter. Or place this pair of liars in one of the settings from your exercises in "Setting II." Or, if you already have a plot going, can you use a competition between liars for comic relief?

Check: Are there interesting and amusing lies? Preposterous statements? Boasts?

2. Write a couple of pages of dialogue between two truth tellers. The confessions that surface are so astonishing and humiliating that the two characters go at each other with guns and knives at the end of the evening.

Purpose: To use the elusiveness of truth as a source of fiction. The quest for truth motivates much fiction—we write imagined lies to find out what the truth of our experience is. But we aren't always strong enough to take the bare truth. Our inability to take the truth certainly can make good stories and good scenes with dialogue.

Tip: This exercise could be combined with number fourteen in this chapter. Part of the celebration could be self-congratulatory—the characters are lauding each other on how honest they've been with each other—but while celebrating, they become too honest. You could handle the exercises separately or in unison. If separately, see later on how they could be combined.

Or you could use your skeptical character from number nine in "Point of View" in this dialogue. Though the other character is being truthful, the skeptic does not believe what is said.

Check: Are the revelations shocking? If not, are the characters involved too sensitive and unduly moralistic? Either direction is fine, but it's good to be aware of what the characters are doing, and to keep the authorial distance from them. Let the characters moralize, but if we have an impulse to, maybe we should write tracts. (Of course, I may be contradicting myself, if this sounds like fiction writing ethics. I don't mean to preach.)

3. Write a dialogue of a couple of pages in which one person tries to seduce another. Make the seducer a fairly unlikely candidate for the role.

Purpose: To give strong motivation to your characters, and thus intensify their speech. A dialogue that is motive driven is easier to write than a dialogue that has no apparent mission behind it. The stronger the reason for someone's talking, the more likely it is that you can drive the dialogue meaningfully.

Tip: This could take place in a restaurant as an augmentation of exercise fourteen in "Setting II." Or it could fit into the mountain climbing adventure, number one in "Scene." Seductions (or attempts at seduction) can occur almost anywhere, so do pick a setting from an earlier exercise in either of the setting chapters or one you're using in an ongoing story or novel.

Check: How does the dialogue sound? Read it aloud. Do the participants sound like living individuals? Different from each other? And is what's going on sufficiently veiled? Transparent seduction is no seduction but a proposition. As an alternative, if the seduction didn't work, you might as well try a blatant and unexpected proposition. What conversation ensues after the proposition? Is the direct approach successful?

4. Involve three people in several gossip exchanges. In the first scene, A and B gossip about C; in the second, C and A about B; in the third, C and B about A. And then all three talk together, pretending they don't know anything about what they've said to (or about) each other.

Purpose: To use gossip, one of the basic story sources, as the modus operandi of a story.

Tip: This could take place among college roommates. They could invent lies or, at least, exaggerations, about each other. This could combine well with the duel of liars assignment in exercise one or a story written out of a strong emotion—jealousy, envy, lust.

Check: Gossip is not always an innocuous pastime. There could be some serious consequences to telling tales. After you've completed two or three pages of gossip, do some dangers suggest themselves? Maybe those dangers could give you enough drive and imagination for a story.

5. Write an imaginary conversation among the three most pretentious people you know or imagine. The people could pretend to have socialized with several famous people whom they apparently don't know.

Purpose: To expose pretension and falsehood, which has traditionally been one of the tasks of fiction. There's no less need of such exposure now.

Tip: Try to nail down the voice of each pretender. Here it's important to capture the attitude as much as the content of what's being said. Sometimes the manner itself, as a posture, is the most irritating and entertaining part. This exercise could be wed to the seduction dialogue in number three. One of the conversationalists could be a naive and conceited egomaniac, easy to flatter.

It would be appropriate to give minispeeches rather than one-line exchanges, although, for the sake of rhythm, the one-liners could work, as put-downs, comebacks, and so on, amidst the long presentations.

Check: Is this dialogue entertaining? Pretensions are a good subject for a comedy, or at least a satire. You could import those liars from exercise one to this situation or place them at the party scene developed in several of the exercises in "Beginning and Developing."

6. Create a scene in which several members of an immigrant family argue about money.

Purpose: To show struggles involving money. Money is one of the most dynamic forces not only for the economy but also for fiction. Struggle about money easily focuses your analysis of families, friendships, social relationships, and so on. How money in America works could be a source of much confusion and strife in an impoverished immigrant family.

Tip: Occasionally use foreign vocabulary to give flavor to the immigrant dialect of English. The younger members speak English better than their native tongues, and they push for the conversation to be in English. Part of the argument taking place could be about the language. Naturally, jobs and dignity in the workplace could be other themes to handle here.

Check: How is the dialogue working? If it isn't, analyze it. Perhaps you don't have the characters down yet. Maybe you're working with stereotypes of an immigrant group. Make the immigrants idiosyncratic and diametrically opposed to what a stereotype might predict. Maybe there's no central event around which the talk about money revolves. They could talk about teeth—no dental plan.

7. Construct dialogue that takes place between someone famous and a sycophant who is overjoyed to meet his idol. After a while the two get over the barrier that fame has imposed upon the conversation, and pretty soon they begin to envy each other—the famous one envies the freedom of nonfame—and decide to give each other a tour of their daily routines.

Purpose: To explore the idea of fame, our big cultural obsession. Since we pay so much attention to the media, media is part of our lives; you have an opportunity to play with the energy that you spend on paying attention to the famous.

Tip: Let the famous person be different from what you'd expect. Let the sycophant have his own reasons for escaping his identity, and let him be not just an airhead but otherwise a reasonable person.

Check: Do the two participants sound different from each other? Not that they must: The sycophant could try to sound like the idol; maybe he has adopted the speech patterns.

8. Write a couple of pages of a conversation between Lucifer and an archangel. Both are taking a break from their jobs, incognito, in Las Vegas, or are taking a Club Med vacation. They are comparing their jobs, their dental plans, and their retirement packages.

Purpose: To write a comic dialogue and a piece of fantasy.

Tip: A variation on this exercise, a bit more down-to-earth, would be an encounter between the Pope (not necessarily from our era) and a suicide bomber (or the Pope's failed assassin), or Gandhi and Stalin, discussing their pursuits of peaceful existences.

Check: Are there funny lines here? Are there unusual takes on these personalities? Have you created idiosyncratic voices for them so they won't sound the way you'd expect them to? Surprise us. Consider using one of the settings you've already developed, either interior or exterior, as the stage for this unlikely meeting.

9. Write two or three pages of a dinner conversation. Intersperse the descriptions of the activities around the table and the body language of the diners with the dialogue. You might choose two characters from a piece of fiction you're currently writing, or even characters from different stories.

Purpose: To use dinnertime as a conversation starter. Dinner is a good reflection on how we live, what we do, what we are up to; the context of dinner can help your dialogue immensely. Here you already have a reservoir of body language, manners, and images.

Tip: Expand exercise three from "Description." Of course, be free to find any permutation of exercises—characters, places— that might work for you.

Check: Do you have an interesting dialogue? No matter what your purpose in having a dialogue, it should be interesting, engaging. Many people, after all, during dinner, want to be entertaining—perhaps they tell jokes or boast or confide or interrogate or quarrel.

10. Recall an insulting conversation you've had or imagine one, perhaps using characters you've already created, and use it to create a scene.

Purpose: To use insults to create conflict. Insults give you a conflict off the bat. There's dynamism here: Why is the insult taking place? What's the motivation? What's the response? Revenge? Submission? And if submission, is it subterfuge before revenge?

Tip: Perhaps you could write a brief summary describing the person having the delightful conversation with you. Introduce yourself in the third person, and disguise both yourself and your partner in insults so that hardly anybody would recognize you. Write in the third-person point of view, and don't take sides. This may be hard, but don't root for yourself.

If nothing else, you should get some good fiction mileage out of the unpleasant experience.

This could involve the characters from "Voice" exercises seven and eight encountering each other at a party. The insults could all be an invention of the self-conscious person, or they could be an accurate observation. Even this issue, to what extent something has been meant to be insulting and to what extent it is interpreted as insulting, is a matter of point of view. You might rewrite the scene from the insultor's viewpoint so we find out whether he meant the insults. Many insults are a result of a failure of communication—and an aggressive attempt to correct the failure.

Check: Do the insults sound insulting? Are there good dialogue exchanges? Insults are sometimes a work of wit or clever cynicism, and a stupidly done insult demeans the insulter more than the intended insultee.

11. Create a scene in which one character flatters another. Don't reveal the ulterior motive for the flattery right away. Let

the person being flattered be so vain as not to notice the ulterior motive even once it becomes obvious. This could be a different approach to exercises seven or eight from this chapter.

Purpose: To use a character's ulterior motives as the driving force of a dialogue. Energetic dialogue always relies on a strong motivation; otherwise, it is simply aimless chatter. Different motives require different methods of communication. Selfish, manipulative motives go well with flattery. See what you can do with such a motivated dialogue.

Tip: This could combine well with the seduction dialogue in exercise three. Or, if you are tired of seduction, you might try sales or evangelism. After a great conversation, the flattered person is disappointed to find out that it was the soul the flatterer was after or it was the commission he was after. To sharpen the disappointment, you could write this from the point of view of the person who is being flattered, in the first person.

Check: Is the flattery skillful? Is the conversation interesting? Could the conversation evolve into a story? What possible plot outlines can you think of that could evolve from the conversation?

12. Write a dialogue in a dialect. There are three speakers who may be gossiping, telling jokes, or talking about cutting down trees in a forest or about salvation and damnation.

Purpose: To practice writing dialect, a highly important skill for writing fiction grounded in a place.

Tip: To distinguish speakers easily, you could have one talk in standard English and the other two in dialect, one more strongly than the other. Don't use a lot of strange spellings to suggest how words are spoken; rely more on syntax and diction to achieve the effect of dialect. Only alter spelling if the sound is particularly odd and different from what we'd expect.

This exercise could be combined with number seventeen in "Voice" in that the dialect could be grating, even annoying, to the listener. And surely you have already sketched a setting where this conversation could occur.

Check: How accurate is your representation of dialect? Have you been constrained by not being absolutely sure of your knowledge of the dialect? If so, you could rewrite without having to be as accurate as an ethnographer. Individual variations allow for deviations from the common form of dialect. For example, a German immigrant living on a Navajo reservation might have a peculiar Navajo version of English. Or a Navajo who's been stationed in South Korea for years might have his own variant of English.

13. Write a dialogue in which two people argue intensely about something, and in the middle of the quarrel let them discover that they are both wrong. There had been some misunderstanding that in the quarrel got exposed and settled. Then write the dialogue of the reconciliation.

Purpose: To write dialogue that ends with a change of heart. A twist in how the events unfold creates dynamism—a triumph of understanding over strife. Revelation or epiphany is one of the standard resolutions in fiction. The revelation needn't be internal; it could come out in dialogue.

Tip: The archetypal story of reconciliation comes from the Bible. Jacob, who has tricked Esau, meets Esau. Jacob is scared, and the two reconcile. The twist of forgiveness is the climax of one of the first touching stories in the Bible.

This exercise could lead you to an ending of a story, especially one that has been fraught with conflict and misunderstanding between two characters. You could fuse this exercise with various ones from the character, plot, and point-of-view chapters in which two or more characters are at odds—the family, the lovers, the soldiers at war. Or you could try this exercise on a story you've written but have not completed. This may be the ending you've been lacking. Of course, stories don't have to end in reconciliation, but sometimes this ending can give a story a satisfying sense of conclusion.

Check: Does the reconciliation grow naturally out of the conflict? If it seems forced or occurs too easily, your reader will not believe it.

14. Write a discovery dialogue. Two people are celebrating their good relationship, and in the middle of the memory fest, a piece of information surfaces and totally upsets one partner so that a furious quarrel ensues.

Purpose: To introduce a plot twist. Stories are frequently about what we do with new insights. Such twists (as in this and the previous exercise) are essential for the sensation of unpredictability, adventure, exploration, self-knowledge.

Tip: Even if there's no discovery of something essentially different and new, the possibility of a discovery could keep the story going. In science, even the research that refutes a hypothesis it was supposed to support is important. Such research eliminates one possibility and saves a lot of labor to other researchers. In stories, too, proving an expectation was wrong could be an important revelation. Suppose a jealous husband hires a detective to follow his wife who disappears for a couple of hours every day. He discovers she has rented a cubicle in the library to write a novel. So there's some kind of discovery here—that the supposition about cheating is wrong. (Of course, once the wife's novel gets published, with a ridiculously jealous husband as the antagonist, the husband might not be pleased after all.)

As with the previous exercise, you can combine this one with many of the earlier exercises involving two people in conflict. It connects especially well with several of the plot exercises, providing a possible resolution for conflicts you have already established.

Check: Is the scene suspenseful so we don't know whether the suspicions are right or not until the end?

15. Sitting in a restaurant or café, a woman needs to tell the man with her that she is ending their love affair. Write a dialogue in the present tense from the woman's point of view either in the first person or in the third-person subjective.

Purpose: To write a scene with a task that organizes the details. You might use it as an occasion to write a story backward; from this final scene, you would go into the history of the relationship.

Tip: Mix the woman's thoughts and perceptions into the reported dialogue, between the spoken exchanges, so we'd have a parallel interior monologue and an exterior dialogue. Combine this with "Setting II" exercises thirteen and fourteen. Set the scene in a restaurant, where the couple at the next table are seducing each other. The two actions progress in reverse: one leading into an affair, another out of it.

Check: Is this working? If not, rewrite, not as the end of a love affair but of a hate affair. Two people who had hated each other until now are forced to meet, and they discover that they fascinate each other, that the hatred was a kind of love in disguise.

16. Write a scene featuring a woman who is so much in love that she doesn't notice how exploited she is. In this scene she

appears with her exploiter, serving him faithfully—until she realizes what is going on.

Purpose: To use a mismatch as the theme for a story. A perfect match is corny; it takes care of itself. But a mismatch has potential for comedy or tragedy—a story.

Tip: Maybe just as we get used to the love being unreciprocated, there's a surprise: He sleeps with her, and for a while it seems they are in love. Maybe they are, or maybe the guy realizes that sleeping together is the only way he can keep the manipulation going. You can reverse the genders, naturally. This could combine with exercise one in "Sources of Fiction." Or perhaps it provides a new twist to exercise seven in this chapter. In this scenario, the two are married.

Check: Are the scenes taunting enough? Is there enough suspense and uncertainty? Humor?

17. Write the dialogue of a public confrontation scene. Use the two characters from exercises seven and eight in "Voice." Write from the point of view of the self-conscious one. Perhaps you could use the restaurant setting from "Setting II" exercise thirteen.

Purpose: To work with a psychological contrast for good dynamism as a source of energy for making a scene.

Tip: Evolve the setup you have in "Voice" exercises seven and eight into a thoroughly developed scene involving a conflict between an exhibitionist and a shy person.

Check: Is the scene all it can be? Rewrite to evolve the scene without thinking about getting a story out of this, just for the sake of seeing how much you can do in one scene, with description, thoughts, asides, dialogue, action. Later, if you have good moments here, you can delete the ones that don't impress you and make a story out of the ones that do. Sometimes thinking you are not making a story but only a sketch helps a writer relax and concentrate on details playfully.

CHAPTER TEN

VOICE

Y ou don't have to strain to have an original voice. Write often, and a certain pattern, color of sound, rhythm, shape of sentences, and diction will emerge. Linguists took it as a challenge to discover who the anonymous author of *Primary Colors* was, and by analyzing many texts, they identified that the novel's syntax and diction corresponded to the texts of Joe Klein, a journalist, and so the linguists solved the mystery. Klein didn't strain to sound different from other writers—if anything, he tried to sound generic—but he sounded different. His signature sound, his voice, stayed with him.

There are some things you can do to strengthen your voice. Fine-tune your sentences to convey precisely and clearly what you want to say. Find words that are expressive, that are to the point, that evoke, that focus what you want to say.

Once you complete a draft, it helps to read it aloud to yourself and, even better, to a friend so you can feel in your throat what you've written. If your words taste right, keep them; if they don't, reconsider them, choose new ones. Your physical voice will tell you where your writing voice has struck a false note and where it has hit the right pitch. Trust yourself. This strategy also can help you to pace your fiction; you'll feel the passages that are too slow or too quick, and like a composer, you'll be able to time your allegros and adagios so the allegros don't slip away too quickly and the adagios too slowly.

If you love speaking more than writing and you want to capture your speaking voice, use a tape recorder and later transcribe and revise. Many writers find it convenient or simply more effective to work this way. I think that pretty soon the difference between the spoken voice and the written voice will disappear, owing to technology. The keyboard will probably become an outdated technological device; computers will transcribe our speech and we'll simply talk—back to the oral culture. (Instead of from carpal tunnel syndrome, writers will suffer from laryngitis.) If anything, voice will become an even more important aspect of fiction than it is now.

YOUR CHARACTERS' VOICES

Besides having your own voice, you must create characters with their own voices. Like an ethnographer, you could study regional voices and dialects, collect regionalisms to give color to the voices of your characters.

In *Little Big Man*, Thomas Berger convincingly creates a voice of someone barely literate who wants to sound literate.

> Whenever he wasn't raving he would fall into the dumps and barely answer when he was spoke to, and at his meals he was single-minded as an animal in filling his belly. Before he got religion he was a barber, and even afterward he cut the hair of us kids, and I tell you if the spirit come over him at such a time it was indeed a scaring experience: he would holler and jump and like as not take a piece of your neck flesh with his scissor just as soon as he would hair.

"When he was spoke to" uses the past tense rather than the participle for a passive, which is a colloquial way of talking in mid-America. And then the usage of the participle "come" rather than the past tense "came" furthers this regional sound. "Scissor" in singular rather than "pair of scissors" sounds unusual, as does "scaring" instead of "scary." There are enough slightly odd word shapes here to create a voice.

But no matter what voice you choose to construct, it will have a bit of you, the rhythm of your thought, just as the above excerpt has the characteristic Berger cleverness and humor. Naturally, you needn't abandon your wit, your spitefulness, your temperament if you assume someone else's persona and voice as long as you create the illusion of the character's being an independent speaker. If an actor reads your dialogue, it should sound authentic, not only because of the actor's skill, but because you have from your ear created a voice. In the Bible a new character, Eve, is made out of a rib. In your stories, you'll do best if your new character's voice is created out of your ear. Perhaps a phrase sticks out in your head, and you can let it keep speaking.

Part of the strength in a voice comes from having a point to make, from disagreeing. If you agree, whatever you agree with has been said before and isn't yours. If you disagree, you articulate your position and put forth something of yourself.

EXERCISES

1. Speaking into a tape recorder, recount an incident—something scary or bizarre—that happened to you, speaking freely, as though talking to your friends. Get carried away, exaggerate, invent, give yourself license to go into fiction. If you are at your best when you drink coffee, drink coffee before this; if you enjoy telling stories to your friends when you have a glass of wine, get a glass of wine. In fact, you could actually talk to your spouse or partner or friends, but do the exercise alone if that's more comfortable. Then transcribe.

Purpose: To determine whether you like your natural sound when transcribed on the page. Some people write as they speak, and when you read them, you can hear their voices, if you know them. For some, this works wonderfully; for others, it doesn't. It's worth taking time to evaluate how much your writing benefits from using your spoken speech patterns. You don't need to make up your mind after just one exercise.

Tip: When you transcribe, edit your speech. Remove repetitions and "warm-up" phrases—"of course," "as I was saying"—which are almost unavoidable in speech. Don't transcribe all "uh's" and other hesitation sounds.

Get rid of most phrases that are aimed at sounding spontaneous—"now get this," "as I was saying," "you know." These phrases have been overused in fiction, and in many cases they sound cheap and phony. Find more unusual speech patterns, and get spontaneity out of dialect or wit.

Check: Do you like what you've written? Ask some of your friends to compare your speech transcriptions with your other kinds of writing and to tell which kind of writing they prefer. You might like only some things that work in your speech. Attempt to isolate these and apply them consciously in your written style.

2. Recount the same or another event without tape recording. Write it directly, with all the freedom that writing gives you—concentration on details, careful word choice, and so on. Try to emulate only the best aspects of speaking—spontaneity, momentary inspiration, directness. Avoid the worst—repetition, inexact word choice.

Purpose: To compare what you get here with what you got in the previous exercise. Which reads better? Perhaps you could combine the advantages of both: the naturalness of the spoken word and the precision of the written word.

Tip: Here, you have time to zero in and play with the wording. You might lose a bit of your spoken sound but gain opportunities for acrobatic moves that you can control on the page, without fearing that they'll slip out of control. Here you can experiment with syntax, see how long you can keep a sentence going, how many dependent clauses you can juggle gracefully, how many different metaphors you can construct, and so on. In writing, you have time to deploy your best word choices in various permutations.

Speak your first draft, write and revise, with the freedom to dwell on key words for minutes, even hours if you have time to spare, to nail the mot juste. You might work the other way around. First write, then read aloud and revise into the tape recorder, then transcribe. That would take patience, but the result could be worth it: an easy flow of words.

Check: Do you like what you've written? If not, try the same technique with another incident; for example, tell a story of an illness. If you still don't like the results, perhaps you should strive not to sound like your easygoing self, but wrench sentences out of your self with craft and work. Of course, it's easier to be a natural writer but not necessarily better. Sometimes carefully written and planned sentences sound better.

3. In first-person point of view relate a fictional event, with all the freedom to make asides and express thoughts and opinions and perceptions that first person allows. Give your voice to a fictional character, your persona, and sound your conflicts, concerns, and thoughts. You can imagine what it would be like to be in somebody else's position.

Purpose: To use the strength of your voice in your fiction. Writing fiction suppresses many people's voices because they feel they should not be autobiographic in any sense, that they should not be themselves. Such an attitude is frequently more a hindrance than a help. It's wonderful and sometimes liberating to be able to develop a voice very different from yours, but it is also quite liberating to use the freedom and immediacy of your voice. Don't let any writing ideology silence you.

Tip: Imagine someone physically and in many other ways different from you who has your voice, your way of thinking. You might even write the variation on the double in this way: The double is not your physical clone but a mental one, somebody like you in another body, competing with you in an uncanny way.

At any rate, place your character into a problematic situation. Perhaps he has unintentionally hurt his brother and now has to deal with the accusation of having tried to murder him. Or maybe he has been caught stealing. If possible, use this exercise to develop an event you've written about in an earlier exercise. The exercises in "Ideas for Fiction," "Plot," and "Scene" should be particularly appropriate for combining with this exercise. The first-person perspective could give you new insight into the event.

Check: How does it feel doing this? It should be a natural way to write. If the exercise hasn't worked well, perhaps it's because you haven't found the right event. Choose a different one, again using material you've developed in an earlier exercise.

4. From third-person point of view and in your voice, recount an event you imagine happening to you. Third person might help you defamiliarize the event if it's something that hits close to home, but don't defamiliarize the voice.

Purpose: To take an external view of yourself and transform much of yourself into a fictional character. If writing autobiographical fiction in a confessional mode might be embarrassing for you, third person will give you distance and disguise.

Tip: Treat the character as someone other than yourself: Criticize, expose weaknesses and vanities, make fun of the fictionalized you; or go the other way, and lionize, exaggerate.

Even if your chosen character becomes transformed into someone quite unlike you, when you concentrate on her perspective and thoughts, freely use your diction, your thoughts. Now and then, for flavor, use a word you might not use, but one your character, considering her background and evolved personal idiosyncrasies, would use. As with the previous exercise, try to find a combination with an earlier exercise or from a sequence of exercises you've been developing.

Check: After you've written a couple of pages, examine what you've done. Does it sound good? This should be one of the easiest ways to write fiction. You don't have to twist backward to find some kind of different way of building sentences. Naturally, you can polish what you write this way, in your voice, and play with it in revision, deleting unnecessary words, replacing some with stronger ones, and so on.

If this exercise hasn't been particularly effective, you might try it again, with a different set of variables, different events.

5. Again using your own voice and writing in third person, relate an event involving a fictional character who is as different from you as you can imagine.

Purpose: To try to bridge the distance between you and a very different character through your voice.

Tip: Use a flexible third-person point of view; that is, describe the character from the outside and summarize his background, motives, milieu in your voice; and then enter the character's head, his thoughts, which could be different from yours, but do present them attentively. This should be an exercise in empathy in which the third-person point of view is yours; you as both the writer and the narrator honestly imagine and analyze the person in question. Bring the person into trouble, and let her choose a course of action that you know you wouldn't choose. Make her reasoning convincing, though, using the best arguing power and your most convincing voice. Maybe you could even open the exercise with something like this: "Joan did something that I would never do. . . ." Then present it.

Check: How is it going? Have you hit a stride imagining the action? If not, you could try it again and combine this with exercises five and twelve in "Scene."

6. If you know a foreign language, construct a voice of an immigrant who mixes English and that language. Imagine what it would be like to be that immigrant. (Maybe it's easy; maybe you are an immigrant.) Put her in a situation in which people around her consider her a bit slow and stupid, while in fact, she is far from that.

Purpose: To develop a foreigner's voice in English. Languages influence each other; it's fascinating to see the different versions of English you can get in different immigrant communities. Bringing a bilingual framework to your fiction might make you playful with the language, especially if you can parody someone's voice.

Tip: You could write this predominantly in English, but perhaps as much as a third could be in Spanish or some other language that is familiar to most readers. But if your native language is too uncommon for you to rely on your readers' knowledge of some vocabulary (as is the case with my native Croatian), use foreign words sparingly, for the flavor, and when you use them first, give a translation in parentheses or a footnote rather than assume your reader will love figuring out what the words mean.

You could use one of the characters from the immigrant family in exercise six in "Dialogue."

Check: Is what you've come up with readable? Does it flow? It should, unless, of course, your intention is that it shouldn't. Do the foreign words blend? If you eliminate the foreign words, do the sentences sound better or worse?

7. Sometimes a psychological trait has a lot to do with a person's voice. For example, a bashful, highly self-conscious person might express himself cautiously, using a lot of "if's" and "maybe's." Even the thoughts of such a person would have their voice. Construct a highly sensitive, insightful character, using a voice of self-consciousness. Bring the character to a party where he has a crush on a woman who he thinks ignores him, and show us what the character's speech and thoughts sound like. Let there be a dichotomy in how he tries to appear and what he feels.

Purpose: To create a bashful person's voice. There's perhaps no better medium in which to analyze psychology and societal cruelties than a fragile, bashful person's perspective. The bashful person may perceive and imagine more threats than there are. If you keep imagining new possible threats, no matter how absurd they are, you'll move the action. Threat is a great dynamic force in generating fiction.

Tip: Write in the third-person point of view, freely describing what the character is doing, with a silent running commentary of his thoughts. For example: "He gripped the cup of coffee with both hands and brought it to his lips, and gulped so that his Adam's apple bobbed up. Furtively he looked around, and when it seemed that nobody was watching, he put the cup down. And he thought, *Good thing that I don't have to hold the cup anymore. I don't know whether I could stand controlling my tremor—did I drink too much coffee? Why should my hands be affected by my anxiety? Let me loosen up. Can I? Probably not. Has she looked at me? She must think it's weird that I'm sitting here by myself, all bent up over the cup of coffee, hesitant like a cat with a crayfish.*"

Check: Have you managed to speak convincingly from another person's experience? Have you rendered the self-consciousness in a situation from the inside rather than from the outside, in such a way we can feel with the character and understand his reasoning and his way of perception or misperception?

8. In a variation on the theme from exercise seven, create a scene using a voice of a highly extroverted, exhibitionistic, and cocky person. Here you needn't switch to the interior monologue; this person is so fond of himself he lets it all hang out, expecting everybody to admire him. Let him use big words, regardless of whether he knows their meanings.

Purpose: To use your talent for parody and be playful, enjoying the humor of pretentiousness.

Tip: Let the character be somewhere out of his waters, perhaps at a dinner party, but let him not notice that he is out of place. For example, he could brag about his accomplishments and not realize he's in the company of inventors, Pulitzer prize winners, and chess grandmasters, and let him not perceive the patronizing ironies with which his bragging is received.

You could use one the characters from "Dialogue" exercises one and five.

Check: Was the exhibitionist too easy a target? Well, you could rewrite it and make him exceedingly smart but so self-obsessed that he doesn't notice others. You could also involve the self-conscious character from the previous exercise.

9. Describe a scene in the voice of a lawyer who has acquired strange speech patterns, legalese, in her profession. (If you are more comfortable with psychotherapists, use psychological jargon in describing a scene.)

Purpose: Professions have a way of encroaching upon our lives. It's good to have an outlet to deal with that; describe how the professionals work, on their terms, with their jargon. Try to get into the mind-set and play with it.

Tip: In addition to the legalese, let there be some regionalism that occasionally surfaces, and let the person sound like a real one rather than a transcript of a legal document. This is a good chance to write something humorous, with the clash of the high legal style and some low style in dealing with an event, such as being cheated by a cabdriver in a foreign city.

Check: How does your writing sound? Although legalese in real life may sound deadly boring, I hope you're managing to write something interesting nevertheless. There's certainly enough potential for irony and parody here that the writing could be entertaining.

10. Write a couple of pages in which you reproduce a four-year-old's talk. Imagine that the child is talking about his toys, what they can do, where he got them, who brought them home, how much they cost, and so on. You can be as silly and imaginative as you like here, and you still may not be able to outdo a kid on a roll.

Purpose: To write in a child's voice. A child's point of view can refresh almost any scene. Kids express themselves in original ways, misunderstanding and yet understanding something adults may no longer bother to be curious about. A child's voice can bring energy to one's writing just as it does to an aging neighborhood.

Tip: Use a child's grammar. In a way, every child has his own grammar so you have some leeway. Some kids use the super-superlative—"bestest," "mostest." Some use double compara-tives—"differenter," "more better." Then the past tenses may be differenter—"I swimmed," "bringed," "broughted," and so on. You might also resort to indicating what consonants the kid can't pronounce. Now and then you could use "yittle" for "little" and similar sound effects. Use a child's logic as well. For example, my son has heard me talk about computer software programs, so when we went outdoors to kick a soccer ball, he said, "Daddy, this ball has a program for spinning." He perceived the ball as a technological instrument, and why not?

This exercise can be combined easily with number ten in "Point of View."

Check: Read it aloud. Does it sound simple enough? Now and then a kid will use a fancy word you wouldn't expect, but make sure the kid doesn't sound like a little professor. Are there funny shifts in logic? They are usually nice to hear.

11. For a minor (or for that matter a major) character, you might need someone with a speech disorder, perhaps someone suffering from attention deficit disorder (ADD) or paranoid schizophrenia. Write a soliloquy by someone like that, a speech in first person. The speaker could be alone in a room talking to herself, and you could pretend to be recording the speech.

Purpose: To sharpen your ability to cover a wide spectrum of human voices. There's something intriguing and provocative in someone who's undergone some shift in perception of the world and in the logic of constructing thoughts. This is all human, and in some way us. These shifts reveal our stodginess perhaps, and maybe even the oddness of our "normal" position.

Tip: Here, more than the choice of vocabulary and grammar, it's the pattern, the alteration of thoughts that creates the effect. For example, for the ADD sufferer's speech, you might jump from one topic to another midsentence and keep piling information and themes in a jumpy manner. With the paranoid schizophrenic—although there are many different forms of it, and you could certainly give us variations—evoke the logic of interpreting anything that happens as a conspiracy. Behind everything there's a deeper meaning and a threat to the speaker.

Check: No matter how odd the logic in the thoughts, can we follow at least some of it? Is it interesting? Although it might be realistic to write pure gibberish for a case of total insanity, it wouldn't be a good read. If you want to display total gibberish, be brief and move on.

12. Write a soliloquy—or a letter—in the voice of an elderly person who sounds like someone from a different era, say born before World War I. There could be wisdom here, an old storyteller's tradition, old-fashioned views, but not in a predictable way—rather in an idiosyncratic one. The longer one lives, the more time one has to develop idiosyncrasies. Invent a situation in which the old woman can rail.

Purpose: To create an elderly person's voice. The more perspectives you can get, particularly if you're writing a novel, the more you'll be able to accomplish.

Tip: If you haven't come up with a specific situation for the old woman's talk, let her tell a bit of her life story to a refrigerator salesperson or a bill collector, or let her advise her wayward grand-child on how to date or how to prepare for the end of the world.

Check: Does your writing sound like an old person speaking? If not, dig up some archaic expressions. You might hang around the elderly for a while; study the speech patterns and the attitude that must come from having lived for a long time and having used the language for decades. There could be a certain wis-dom—or attitude of wisdom—in the way the person looks at the world. She could either compress her sentences and thoughts crisply or ramble tangentially.

13. Sit quietly for a while and think of the voices that stick with you. Whose is the first voice that comes to your mind, that you can hear clearly? Now try to write, imitating that voice, the sound, in the word choices and sentence structures that would come most naturally to the character. Put the character in a situation in which she'd be most expressive with her voice, such as while gossiping or bossing someone around or shopping or fighting for her rights.

Purpose: To recall memorable voices. There's a good reason why you remember a voice. It has character—the precious ener-gizer of fiction. See how well you can render the voice and how you can apply it in your prose.

Tip: Don't be afraid of writing biographically about a real person. Worry about disguises later. First relax and see how well you can elicit this voice and what you can improvise with it. Look through the exercises in the "Scene" and "Dialogue" chap-ters and find a situation for which the voice would work. You can always repay the source of this voice by inviting her to din-ner, and then you could listen to more of it, and take notes, mentally—a wonderful recipe for losing friends and becoming an isolated writer without much temptation to go out. Does the person whose voice you're adapting for your fiction end many of her sentences with a question mark? How does she begin her sentences? Each sentence has its own miniplot (its own "spinning program"); discover how she plots her sentences.

Check: Have you mastered the speech patterns? Read it aloud, trying to imitate the person whose voice is stuck in your head. If it doesn't sound right, analyze. Think of the syntax and the vocabulary the person would use.

14. Sometimes voice pitch comes from an emotion, such as anger, depression, love, hate, fear, longing, loathing. Write in the first-person point of view acting out three emotions, whichever ones you think you could project most effectively. Write a page in each of the three emotions you choose.

Purpose: To create a voice from an emotion. If you start with an emotion, you might have both the emotion and the voice, enough to write movingly and to sound good.

And you might have a way of thinking and point of view to envision a story. In anger, most of us become loud and impulsive; in depression, quiet and philosophical. The emotion gives you a way of thinking and a way of expressing the thoughts.

The stronger the emotion, the more energy you could develop in writing. The emotion could work almost like a big bang: Out of a singular passion, a diverse universe of characters and scenes may emerge and expand with great velocity.

Tip: Imagine a situation for each emotion. For anger, you could start with a person who has been injured by someone in power: perhaps a girl who has been date-raped or an ill man who was misdiagnosed when there was time for recovery, and now when there isn't time to recover, he discovers the medical incompetence. In either case, let the anger be aggressive, striving toward revenge. Plunge directly into a scene, describing the wrong that was done.

Check: How does what you've written sound? Read it aloud. Are the voice, emotion, and character all falling into place? Have you developed a lot of energy in one of these scenes? If yes, perhaps you could keep going and write a long piece of fiction.

15. Voice depends in part on attitude. Some voices we remember perhaps more because of the attitude they express than because of the timbre and the melody of the voice. Write about an event or situation that you've established in an earlier exercise from three different attitudes—being cool, complaining, naive, charming, chronically (and artificially) excited, pretentious, humble, incurably kind, on the ropes, insulting—at least a page for each.

Purpose: To create a voice from an attitude. Attitude will bring the issue of voice directly to the character and her relationship with her surroundings. Attitude is also closely related to point of view, which depends on from where and how you perceive events.

Tip: For each attitude, immerse the character directly into a scene in which the attitude could come to the fore. It would be easiest to do this in the first-person point of view, but you could also do it in the third-person subjective, reporting the character's thoughts. Being cool, naive, pretentious, excited—all these could play out in a party.

Check: Which attitude works best for you? Use it, combine it with a story idea and a character you've developed in other exercises, or even evolve a story idea and a character simply from the attitude and the voice that fits it. You needn't have much plot; the attitude will get the character into enough trouble that a plot should follow, in her trying to extricate herself.

16. Create a cynical voice. Someone highly intelligent comments on how absurd her marriage is, or how ridiculous her job is, or how absurd her colleagues' lifestyles are.

Purpose: To use cynicism to develop a voice. A lot of strength—as well as humor and insight—can come just from a sharp, critical, ridiculing attitude.

Tip: In cynicism, you basically deconstruct something that through usage has become so accepted we no longer analyze it. Cynicism is reductive; something composite is dissolved to its basic elements. For example, you could describe football as an event in which a bunch of testosterone-driven carnivores push and shove each other in order to fondle a ball. While cynicism directed at others may appear cruel and supercilious, cynicism directed against oneself can actually sound quite charming and playful. There's nothing more delightful than getting a break from taking ourselves too seriously and defensively. There's a sense of liberation one can experience in taking oneself jocularly.

You could write about a strange family reunion or describe a failed date or whatever other situation you can ridicule. If you've developed a party story from earlier exercises, add to it here.

Check: Is there wit in your writing? Cynicism without wit is lame and uninteresting. Is your writing humorous? Humor can redeem a nasty attitude and make it dynamic and perhaps even pleasant to read. Since it's difficult to gauge one's own humor, you might give your piece to a friend, and see whether he laughs and what he says.

17. Recall a grating voice and a pleasant voice. Construct a scene in which you place yourself with these two people. Make

them talk a lot, while you, as the first-person narrator, can make comments in parentheses, giving readers bits of information about the background of each of the persons. Perhaps while doing the exercise, you could conclude why the voices are pleasant or unpleasant. What's your history with these people? Eventually we will get your voice—expressed most easily in likes and dislikes.

Purpose: To build a wide range of voices for your fiction. Likable characters are in demand for fiction as are detestable characters. It's good to be able to show how sweet someone is or how bitter, sour, dour, mellow, and so on, even in the sound.

Tip: Make the characters talk about a topic they especially like. For example, the grating one could be pretentious and talk about how popular she is or how healthy her teeth are. The pleasant one could talk about what makes her charming or fun. Perhaps she jokes, or listens, asking compassionately to hear more.

Check: Have you captured what you planned to? Even if you haven't, perhaps your voices sound convincing and have a life of their own. That could actually apply to any exercise; you may plan to do one thing but another takes over and works well in its own way.

CHAPTER ELEVEN

DESCRIPTION

Almost everything you write is in some way descriptive; if you present a character, a setting, a scene, you are describing. You describe even in dialogue, indirectly; by the way the characters talk, you might imply how they behave and what their attitudes are. So you have been describing all along, and you had an opportunity to do so especially in the chapters on setting.

The original meaning of describing (Latin, *describere*) was to copy, transcribe, record. In a way, writers try to copy what they see or imagine onto the page, in words. Since copying is impossible, they translate, from images into words. However, you don't always have to visualize what you describe; words will create a picture too, and after you pile enough words, something may begin to take shape. In revision you can judge whether you've achieved a good effect or whether to try again.

Description is made of details. The origin of the word *detail* is from French, where it had two meanings: to cut a whole into pieces, and retail rather than wholesale. I think the etymology might be useful in the sense that it provides a picture of—it describes—what a detail is: a manageable unit. It's a slice of cheese rather than a whole round—you can sample it easily, unlike the whole.

You create details primarily out of nouns. You might modify

your noun with adjectives, for nuance. Many nouns carry colors with them: grass, snow, blood, crow, dandelion. If the grass is not green, modify it; say it's yellow or brown. If the snow is not white, mention what color it is; otherwise, the reader will imagine white snow. Adjectives are secondary in importance and to be used mostly to reveal an unusual aspect of a thing. Things, nouns, are primary. Your skill—and fisherman's patience—is in choosing the right nouns, nouns that require no modification, or very little of it. Describing is often as simple as making up a list of nouns in relation to each other. For example, you might list the things that comprise a scene: "A crow sits on the fence post and watches a prairie dog squealing on his mound of soil."

Nouns are names for things, phenomena. It's desirable to know the names of flora and fauna, architecture and medicine, but use them in moderation, as much as you can reasonably expect that many of your potential readers know these names.

Being able to name things is a great virtue, but sometimes this strength might deprive you of the impetus to describe. Occasionally, it's good to pretend you don't know a name of an animal or a thing so you describe it. Try to see things with the fresh eye of someone with a poor vocabulary—a foreigner, a child. Names—and definitions—sometimes serve to dismiss a thing rather than to pay attention to it. Pay attention and learn how to express the attention in words.

Adjectives and verbs are by no means to be neglected in descriptions. You needn't cramp your writing in systematic avoidance of adjectives, although some writers (often from an ideological angle, minimalism) advise to cut most of them, except the absolutely necessary ones. Adjectives and modifiers can intensify a scene to achieve a particular color and nuance of sound. Use whatever means are available to you; catch as catch can. Don't shun from a maximalist approach, if the image you want to create is complex. Observe how Virginia Woolf describes a clock striking, in *Mrs. Dalloway.*

It was precisely twelve o'clock; twelve by Big Ben; whose stroke was wafted over the northern part of London; blent with that of other clocks, mixed in a thin ethereal way with the clouds and wisps of smoke, and died up there among the seagulls—twelve o'clock struck as Clarissa Dalloway laid her green dress on her bed, and the Warren Smiths walked down Harley Street.

Woolf uses nouns ("clouds," "wisps," "smoke," "seagulls") in such a way that you can visualize them; even her verbs (together with the nouns) are visualizable ("wafted," "blent," "mixed," "died") or auricularly imaginable. Her modifiers are either visual and direct ("green") or fancy ("thin ethereal"), and they contribute to the total picture. The different kinds of words blend into a moving whole; the senses blend too—sounds and visual images. Even her odd punctuation contributes to the description, emphasizing the blending.

The words you put together need to evoke—and sometimes provoke—images. Effective writers usually prefer direct adjectives of color ("red," "white," etc.) and other sensory materials to abstract adjectives. "Stupendous," "awful," "beautiful," and "ugly" may sound grand but don't help you paint your images. These adjectives frequently only express what effect you want to achieve in your description; they are not shortcuts, but copouts, which can't save you from the basic obligation to create paintings and music in your prose.

For example, rather than stating directly that it was terribly cold in a raging snowstorm, include the details that will convey that sensation and in addition convey a fresh picture, as does Tolstoy in his short story "Master and Man."

The wind was shaking desperately the frozen linen that hung there: shirts, one red, one white, some leg cloths, and a skirt. The white shirt especially shook frantically.

"The frozen linen" tells you it's terribly cold and evokes a picture, something an abstract mention that it was terribly cold wouldn't accomplish.

Once you have a good description like that, you might return to it; it can serve as a gauge of how things are progressing. That is, an event taking place could use an image like this as a mirror; the more intense the stage of the event, the more intensely developed the image can become. As the storm intensifies in "Master and Man," several hours and several pages later, the clothes reflect the change.

> After passing the house where the linen was hung out (a sleeve of the white shirt was by this time torn off, and the garment hung by one frozen sleeve), they came to the weirdly moaning and sighing willows. . . .

This next scene occurs several hours and many pages later.

> They rode once more through the village, down the same road, past the space where the frozen linen had hung, but hung no longer; past the same barn, now snowed-up almost as high as the roof, from which the snow flew incessantly, past the moaning, whistling, and bending willows.

In the story, one of the two protagonists freezes to death. The detail of the frozen linen no longer hanging serves as a harbinger. The previously sighing willows now whistle—this progression in intensity of adjectives of sound creates an atmosphere of threat. Details like these work like cinematic special effects, and they are essential to creating dramatic tension.

COLLECT DETAILS

Compete with the maxim "Reality is stranger than fiction." Make your fiction stranger than reality. Select strange details.

Don't go for the obvious. The way one collects butterflies, you might collect details. Whenever you observe something odd, record it, whether in your notebook or in your head. For example, I was playing with my son today when a spider startled him. I hit the spider with an anthology of experimental fiction, and the spider's body fell apart. Two severed legs kept moving and twitching; my son asked me to kill the legs. I might use the spider's severed legs twitching to augment a scene, to add a bit of a creepy edge to it. It's good to record details. You never know what will become of them. Some could be pulled out of your notes and used in fiction; some might become poems—and I think it's healthy for a fiction writer to write poems the way it is for a pianist to play etudes.

Not all your details need to come from observation. Invent some details. For example: "When he laughed, his mouth shifted to the left, and when he didn't laugh, a deep crease sank along the left side of the mouth, while his right side stayed taut." I've never seen a face like that, but it's possible and believable. I have seen people laugh on one side of their faces only; from that, I could imagine them having laughter lines on that side only.

You might use an odd fact as a detail, as in *Ghost Waves*, a novel set in Chicago, by James McManus: "She had just crossed the river. She seemed to recall being told that it flowed backward." The odd fact sets up the atmosphere. Something is amiss here. Literally, it's good to work against the grain.

In order to make fresh images, you have to shun clichés (such as "against the grain"), but not at all costs. Don't worry about clichés in your early drafts. Advance your narrative, and when you revise, weed out the clichés, find a fresher way of saying things. One way of dealing with a cliché is to recast it and spell it out. This is what I mean: Instead of "He thrashed him," Cervantes writes, "He pounded him like wheat in a mill." It's basically the same thing, but thrashed has been used so much that we don't see the original picture. You can restore that picture by analyzing it into its original images. For example, "It was a harrowing experience" can become "He felt as though harrows were about to disk him into the mud." If you don't like how the "harrowing" translates into an image, cut the image and make another one. You are resourceful—you can afford to delete an image that doesn't work. Try another one until you find what you like.

Last words—and here, they should be last, since description is a matter of practice: When you reach the limits of precise and direct description, follow the basic structure of the question, What is it like? Portray a thing in terms of other things, in likenesses and metaphors. You could occasionally even describe negatively: What is it unlike? How is it different? Use all your resources to get the job done. If you don't describe, and don't have details, your novels might end up being short stories, your short stories, vignettes. This is how you fill in the pages, not just for the sake of filling them, but for the sake of creating a world with its substances and phenomena through an ephemeral web of words. You have to have the faith of a spider, the faith that the flimsy threads of words will catch moths and even butterflies. Words do have that catchy quality. Trust them, spin them, connect branches in the wind with them.

EXERCISES

1. Describe fruits and flowers arranged on a table, a still life. Where's the light coming from? Where do the shadows fall? What does the surface of the table look like? So this won't be too static, describe the sight in the third person, from the point of view of a guest who is not sure whether it would be kosher to simply take a banana, peel it, and eat it. Perhaps the hosts are drawing attention to an antique clock on the wall.

Purpose: To be a painter. This is a basic assignment in painting classes; it could be a minor one in writing classes. Show us the fruit so we'll be hungry too. Show us the flowers so we'll want to sink our noses in them.

Tip: The visuals are the obvious aspect we share with painters. However, you have more at your disposal. You can resort to smells, textures: Touch the fruit when nobody's watching, leave your fingerprints on the haze of a plum, squeeze a peach, pop the grapes in your mouth. Moreover, you can think and associate thoughts and memories with the sensations—the taste of the tart apple brings with it a host of associations of stealing apples from your prissy neighbor.

Check: Has the still life begun to move? There's no such thing as "still" life; the linking of the two words is a sheer provocation. Unstill, distill the life, and intoxicate us with it.

2. "Paint" a nude—primary exercise for a painter, and not secondary for a writer. Imagine one of your heroes from a potential story (or use the composite character in exercise two in "Character") posing in an artist's studio. Show the muscles, the bulges, the shadows between muscles, the bones protruding. Describe the bodily attitude. You could do this from imagination, but perhaps you could persuade a friend to pose for you, or more simply, find pictures or paintings of nudes and select one for your sketch.

If all else fails, you could take a look at yourself in the mirror and do an honest self-portrait. You could give a character your body and somebody else's soul.

Purpose: To practice a basic skill. We often describe faces, hands, but rarely the whole body, naked and simple. Yet the body is there, all the time, engaged, one way or another. By describing bodies, you can convey the characters' minds in a fresh way.

Tip: This is not simple. Try various techniques. Write direct, precise descriptions of muscles, bones. Consult an anatomy book for the names. Don't overuse the names, but it's worth describing as much as you can. Resort to metaphors if you have to. If you find it's hard to stay on the surface, you don't have to; explain scars, injuries, diets. The body records a person's life, is his life.

Check: Unlike in the previous exercise (unless you're writing erotica), you can't resort to touching and tasting your subject, but you can think, remember, free-associate.

3. Describe a family at dinnertime from the viewpoint of a guest, perhaps the one from exercise one, or from the viewpoint of the mother or a child. How do people eat? What are the group dynamics? How do they handle knives and forks? Napkins? Glasses?

Purpose: To develop a dinner scene into a story. With characters seated around the table, you have perfect conditions for a conversation. The utensils and food make it possible to show indirectly how people relate to each other and to themselves, their attitudes, characters. This exercise, if done properly, is an invitation to write a short story or even a novel.

Tip: Don't worry so much about what people say, but how they speak: what sounds they make, how they move, and how their actions look. Later, you might integrate this into a longer scene, in which dialogue will be important, and the details of dining could be interspersed with the dialogue, between the lines, occasionally.

Check: Have you paid attention to body language—aggressive chewing, squeamish cutting of meat? Can we smell the food? What does the food look like?

4. Describe a character lighting a fire, outdoors or indoors. What is the event? Who is there? Concentrate on the details of the action. Engage all the senses. Fire has powerful symbolic associations, which you needn't manipulate but beware.

Purpose: To translate the visual power of fire—which is always spectacular—into words.

Tip: If you are more at ease making descriptions within a scene than out of the blue, use characters you have already developed in the exercises on character, in a setting you have already developed (perhaps the forest or a living room). Or continue the dinner party scene from exercise three; let the characters retire to the living room to drink tea or whiskey around the fireplace. Or introduce new characters—a man and a woman on a cold night, eloping. The fire might reflect how their relationship is going: passionate, wild—or they might clash over the failure of the fire, and that failure could parallel the extinguishing passions: "The spark is gone."

Here's an example of an effective fire description, from "Elk" by Rick Bass.

> It was like something chemical—the whole tree, or the shell of lichen around it, metamorphosed into bright crackling fire: the lichen burning explosively and the sudden shock of heat, the updraft, in turn lighting the lichen above, accelerating the rush of flame as if climbing a ladder. . . . Flaming wisps of lichen separated from the tree and floated upward in curls before cooling and descending.

We hear, see, and feel this fire. Maybe you can bring fire into your fiction?

Check: Do you get a sensation of the fire coming into being? Once the fire is going (if it is), do you use enough of it? If it's not lively enough, show its work, in the shadows it makes, in its sparks, in its warmth on the cheeks facing the fire in contrast with the cold backs. Keep going. Let us feel it.

5. Describe a tool—a hammer, a gun, a thermometer, a rope, a syringe—first at rest, then in action. Integrate your description into a previous setting—emergency room (thermometer and syringe) or shop (hammer) or forest landscape (saw and gun) or wherever else it might belong.

Purpose: To show what your characters do, and to some extent, what they are like, through how they handle tools. Especially a tool in action may be a fascinating sight that'll lend a lot of energy to your prose.

Tip: As you describe, if you find it hard to re-create the action of the tool in precise terms, allow yourself to get carried away; use metaphors, wild images. A tool in action usually becomes something quite wild, undergoes a metamorphosis.

Consider Richard Selzer's description of a scalpel, from "The Knife."

> At one end of the handle is a narrow notched prong upon which the blade is slid, then snapped into place. Without the blade, the handle has a blind, decapitated look. . . . But slide on the blade, click it home, and the knife springs instantly to life. It is headed now, edgy, leaping to mount the fingers for the gallop to its feast.

Following is the scalpel in action.

Now the scalpel sings along the flesh again. . . . One listens, and almost hears the whine—nasal, high, delivered through that gleaming metallic snout. . . . The flesh of the patient retaliates with hemorrhage, and the blood chases the knife wherever it is withdrawn.

Notice how his most descriptive words are the verbs: "The flesh . . . retaliates with hemorrhage," "the blood chases the knife." Don't neglect verbs. A tool works; work happens in verbs. Don't necessarily imitate Selzer, but let his example liberate you to be wildly active in your descriptions.

Check: When you use a lot of metaphors, you run the risk of overwriting. If you have gone overboard, revise and decide which metaphors, which words in your description are effective—image evoking—and which aren't. If you used no metaphors, on the other hand, you may have written flatly. If you get the impression you have been flat, let in a few monsters.

6. Use shadows to describe an action indirectly, through how it looks on the ground or against a wall. You could combine this with exercise two or four in this chapter—and with almost any exercise in the chapters on setting.

Purpose: To be able, like a painter, to work with shadows to enhance your pictures. It's good to be aware of how much light there is, where it's coming from. Work with light, and play with shadows. The less light there is, the more eerie your description can be. Streets and woods in the dark can lend an aura of threat and mystery to your scenes.

Tip: In a shadow, you can distort what is going on, make it smaller, but usually, you magnify what is going on—a slow motion can come across as a jump; feet can become large, heads small, if the light comes from below.

For example, Cormac McCarthy, in *The Crossing*, achieves a wonderful effect by paying attention to this acceleration: "There burned here and there in the dust the fires of squatters and where the squatters rose and moved about they cast their shadows lurching across the crumbling walls like drunken stewards."

Check: Have you created a strong image? Does it move? Does a shadow have a life of its own that in some way mimics the three-dimensional life but intensifies it or caricatures it?

7. Through the senses of your protagonist, let us perceive a storm. Don't neglect the feel on his skin. Go wild; use metaphors; transform the storm into something else, to create a hallucinogenic feel. What does "windswept" feel like? List many associations, jotting them down uncritically. Then rewrite and select the most effective ones, two or three. Integrate the storm into a previously finished exercise, one of the landscapes.

Purpose: To write an engaged description. If you describe a storm aloofly, without pulling us in, we will miss the most important aspect of it—how it affects your characters. So let us not only observe but participate.

Tip: Here's an example of combining direct sensation with likenesses. You needn't limit yourself just to what you see; you can improvise and jump out of the scene, and bring us back. Think about what you see; play with it.

McCarthy does this in *All the Pretty Horses*: "The wind was cool on their sweating faces. . . . Shrouded in the black thunderheads the distant lightning glowed mutely like welding seen through foundry smoke. As if repairs were under way at some flawed place in the iron dark of the world." Note how McCarthy intensifies his picture by comparing lightning to welding.

Check: Can you easily visualize the picture you have created in your description? You might want to resort to metaphors. In metaphors you express one thing through another; we always do that anyhow. Words aren't the things we talk about (unless we talk about language, and even then, we express one word by means of another).

8. Create a picture of a person through what she wears, how she carries herself, how she moves in her clothes. Maybe it's time to dress your composite character from exercise two in "Character."

Purpose: To use clothes as an aid in character portraits. If you want to show us the characters, rather than summarize and generalize them, don't avoid clothes (unless the characters are in a nudist colony). People express themselves in their clothes— these are their colors, flags, statements of independence and suzerainty to a movement, class, fashion.

Tip: Linger on clothes, in your descriptions at least, and you will create something for us to visualize. Clothes are a shield that protect a person's body; they are also a showcase, a frame, that emphasizes and reveals the body. So don't forget the body that's being enhanced, or subdued, by the clothes.

Check: Do you have a balance between the clothes and the body they suggest and imply and reveal?

9. Describe shoes and develop characters who wear them, in two variations.

First describe a pair of shoes you wear, how you feel in them, where you bought them, where they've stepped, how they got scratched; etch a bit of personal history on the leather. Now give these shoes to a fictional character you construct out of an astrological chart or a psychology textbook. Next time people ask you whether your character is autobiographical, you could say, "Maybe. Her shoes are mine."

Next: The proverb "Shoes make the man" is of course nonsense, but pretend it isn't. Go to a store, find an interesting pair of shoes, and imagine a character who would wear them happily and proudly. Write a detailed description of the shoes, the materials, colors, smell, feel, flexibility, the sounds the shoes make when worn. See whether you can construct a character out of these shoes. (This might work even better with a worn pair of shoes you find outside of a door in a hotel.)

Purpose: To portray characters indirectly. Feet are almost the most neglected part of our bodies, and at the same time the most grateful. You know what I mean if you've had a foot massage. In fiction too, you can accomplish a lot in describing people's feet, what they wear, how they move.

Tip: Don't sound predictable—red stiletto shoes, a sexy woman. Be a little whimsical and surprising.

Check: If you can't write this exercise with sufficient enthusiasm, recast it. Shoes made the man when he walked; now that he drives, the car does. Could you redo the exercise starting from the car and ending with the man?

10. Describe an object of desire in alluring terms from the standpoint of an addict. Write in the first person, to identify with the passion and the ceremony of indulging it. For example, describe a bottle of fine wine (or cognac)—the light refracting through it, the feel of the label, the cork, pulling the cork, the glass chiming, sniffing, tongue movements, gulping.

You could integrate this into exercise three or one of the character exercises.

Purpose: To be able to show desire in action, since desire is one of the prime movers in fiction. What's the allure? If what your character desires is not rendered in concrete terms and images, we may be too distant from his motivation to empathize in any way and to believe in the action that follows. The allure of the object of desire is the proof of the character's motivation.

Tip: Don't bring any moral judgment to this; don't try to demean your character through his weakness for intoxication, but give us the wonders of the object of desire in demonically seductive terms. If you are loath to imagine wine, or your therapist or minister forbids you, imagine another substance—chewing tobacco, pot, Brie, Coca-Cola with ice, a silk tie, hiking boots, a mountain bike, cats, or any other passionate fixation you could render.

Check: When you read through, do you get a sensation you'd like a drink? Is your prose attractive? Are the words seductive, melodious? If the images don't outright seduce the reader, the language might. Recast the writing; choose words to make a pretty sequence of rhythm and sound.

11. Describe an object of fear from the perspective of the character who faces it. This could be another person (a lover's wife), an animal (a stray dog, a spider, a bacillus), or a thing (a needle in the hospital in the hands of a huge nurse).

Purpose: To work with the character's motivation to get away from the threat or to annul the threat. The purpose here is similar to the one in the previous exercise, except with a negative sign in front of it.

Tip: To convince us of the risk, imagine the worst, the needle in the kidney. You might write in choppy sentences, in fragments, to create the staccato cadence of panic.

Check: When you read through and visualize what you are actually describing, do you get goose bumps, shivers, creeps?

Not that you must, but if you do, congratulations on your description (or imagination). Have you managed to unsettle yourself, create something eerie, disturbing? Great.

12. From the standpoint of a mother, describe a baby, how she moves her feet, arms, eyes, lips. Then, write another description from the standpoint of an irritable guest who dislikes babies.

Purpose: To channel the fascination of babies into your prose. Almost all of us brighten at seeing kittens, puppy seals, kids (goat children), and human babies and toddlers. Babies experience their surroundings originally; they look for new ways. We old dogs can't match them in that, but we can use the old trick of borrowing their energy and their tricks.

Tip: Practice portraying babies. They can bring a lot of cheer and humor into a scene. As in an old Dutch painting of a feast, they can be independent little creatures thriving in their liberties, in the background and under the table, while the adults obliterate themselves in their own ways.

Check: Is your description delightful? If not, make it such, unless you want to draw something sad, in which case, it could be extra sad, as tragedies in children are.

13. Describe the oldest person you know. What does she look like? How does she move? Talk? Breathe?

Purpose: To describe people of different ages. Some people can write only about their contemporaries—when they are in college, they write about college students, when they are divorcing and remarrying as middle-aged people, they write only about middle age. (As John Updike grows older, so do his characters; as Woody Allen grows older, so do his characters, except that the females stay the same age.) The ability to include the full life spectrum is at least as important as to do all the genders, if we are to represent our world democratically.

Tip: Be neither overly romantic and spiritual in your description nor overly naturalistic and squeamish. Be as accurate as possible, and suspend your immediate praise, admiration, or revulsion. While babies bring delight and freshness, the aged bring perspective and a multitemporality—their lives may go back to World War I or the Russo-Japanese War.

Check: Do we have a sensation we are in the company of your old person? Have we met her? Have we got a chance to observe her moves, her gait, breath, aura, with your help?

14. Restore several clichés to their original images the way Cervantes does the "thrashing" image. You might do "a breathtaking view," "scared to death," "busy as a bee," or any other clichés that were originally images.

Purpose: To write without fear of clichés. You can write with a greater freedom and imagistic power than if you completely avoided clichés. Go ahead, use clichés, but take them as assignments to elaborate them and create pictures.

Tip: You need not limit yourself to simply translating the cliché into its original image. Keep going. Play with the image. Write the image from a character's point of view. Incorporate it into a scene. For example: "When John came over the top of the grassy hill and beheld the Missouri River shimmering in the rising sun, he was so stunned that he held his breath. Soon he realized that his dizziness came not just from the dazzling river light but from his forgetting to draw another breath."

Check: Read your description. In some cases, the result will be a restored image, in others, it won't. It's worth a try. There's a reason why a cliché has been in currency for a long time. The seed image is strong. Is your fleshed-out image fresh? Or is it too obviously a direct translation of the cliché, and thus, still a tired, mechanical chunk of words?

15. Describe the sensations you experience with a particular illness. How do your eyes feel? How do you breathe? Do you have aches? Fever? Integrate the description into two other exercises—number two or five in "Setting I," number three in this chapter, or most directly number ten in "Setting II." When you merge two exercises, you might spark a story.

Purpose: To describe illness. Your characters can't always be healthy. If they are ill, you should be able to show us how they are ill. After all, more people die from viruses than from bullets. Disease is our main antagonist, chief enemy. And in writing, it's a topic we can't ignore. Not even the soaps do, let alone serious writing.

Tip: If a story isn't primarily about disease, disease is still a good monkey wrench. Throw it in at the crucial moment, and see what happens. In a moment of triumph, add a virus as a complication in a story.

Check: Review your description to be sure it's vivid and fresh. Delete whatever sounds clichéd, or work with it until you instill life into it (not still life, unless your character dies). Are you sure what you are telling is accurate? You might research the symptoms in a medical reference book to solidify what you are describing.

CHAPTER TWELVE

IMAGE AND METAPHOR

I n fiction, image is nearly everything; it's the connective tissue of your fiction—red blood cells that carry oxygen and energy through the story. Image and description are related, as are most elements of fiction. A description is a series of images that gives you an object, a place, a person. A description with action and dialogue creates a scene. A scene with conflict acted out is the core of plot, and plot becomes flesh through the whole series of images. It's a full circle, from image back to image. Just as in a good piece of music all the instruments work in synergy and one well-struck chord may be the climax of a symphony, one well-struck image may bring together a whole story.

Images are made of words. Nouns are the primary words— *chalk, blackboard*. You can relate the nouns by verbs—"the chalk *lies* on the blackboard." If the things denoted by nouns are not passively sitting side by side but interacting, you get the most energy out of an image—"the chalk *squeals* against the blackboard." The squealing relates the chalk and the blackboard quite vividly.

A verb can generate power in an image as in this line from *Pig Earth*, by John Berger: "The fibers of meat are still quivering from the shock of slaughter." In describing the aftermath of slaying a cow, the quivering brings out the spooky aspect of the slaughter: The cow is dead but the flesh hasn't quieted.

Making a metaphor resembles lying. It's a lot like a transformation of one thing into another, a metamorphosis, through which most creation goes. In fact, that is creation, the metamorphosis of one thing into another; and here, with the metaphor, is your chance to create something out of something.

A metaphor can intensify an image, give it a new angle, stretch it, dance around it.

"A few ambers still glowed like cats' eyes." In this line from *Memed, My Hawk*, by Yashar Kemal, "ambers . . . glowed" is already an image; "cats' eyes" gives a soul to the image. You can pause here, see cats' eyes coming out of the fire. There's something surrealistic in doubling images through metaphors and likenesses—one reality hovering over another. If you want to write strictly mimetic, realistic descriptions, you could minimize the metaphors and likenesses and write in a straightforward reporting style. Simply say what you see without jumping out of the frame of the picture imaginatively. This, though it sounds simple, requires quite a bit of self-restraint, perhaps like being on a diet at a feast, avoiding champagne and cheesecakes.

In terms of image making, there is not much difference between a likeness and a metaphor, except that the metaphor is quicker, a condensed merging of two or more images. But the mind usually connects the images, and you have the experience in likeness similar to that of a metaphor. Vladimir Nabokov uses a likeness in *Laughter in the Dark*: "As a child he had poured oil over live mice, set fire to them and watched them dart about for a few seconds like flaming meteors." Notice how much the likeness accomplishes. Instead of saying how a person had been cruel, in abstract terms, this concrete image of torturing mice, magnified by a likeness, gives us even a moment of beauty in that cruelty—not a simple external judgment, but an experience of the perverted aesthetics of cruelty.

Reading Cormac McCarthy's novels is highly instructive—each one can be used as a manual on how to make images. Here is one example from *All the Pretty Horses*: "The man sucked himself up away from the blade with the boneless grace of a dervish." "Sucked . . . up" gives you the image of the man as a mouth who sucks himself up—a great verb that accomplishes the metaphor energetically. Where McCarthy writes "boneless grace of a dervish," perhaps most of us would have relied on some form of "suppleness." But "suppleness" would be almost a mechanical choice, functional, but certainly not this picturesque and beautiful. "Boneless grace"—a concrete image, even if in the negative. We think of the whirling dervish, so the double image is highly mobile.

MOVEMENT AND SURPRISE

One principle in image making: To attract perception, use motion. Things that move are noticed more easily. They don't need to move much as is evidenced in *Rabbit Is Rich*, by John Updike: ". . . her boobs slosh and shiver in the triangular little hammocks of her bra."

Although nouns and verbs are the primary forces at work in an image, modifiers can be highly effective, as in this example in McCarthy's *All the Pretty Horses*: "They smiled shyly at him sitting there half naked and so pale of skin with the angry red suture marks laddered across his chest and stomach." "Angry red" accomplishes the bloody pain of suture marks and, much more, the radiance of the color.

An image, to be effective, needs to be surprising with unusual connections. Compare darting mice with flaming meteors (all right, now that you've seen it in Nabokov, don't).

Lon Otto, a fiction writer, is interested largely in how student writers can perceive—and convey in words—something in an original way. If your perceptions are keen, Otto believes the other aspects of writing could easily come, but not the other way around: No matter how fancy your plots, if you don't see the mundane details around you in an angry red (or in another sharp way), like a crazed painter, you will not write anything engaging.

An image doesn't have to be fancy; it can be composed of the most elemental things as in *All the Pretty Horses*: "They rode out west with the sun at their back and their shadows horse and rider falling before them tall as trees." "Shadows . . . tall as trees"—simple, elemental. We don't even need to be specific, to worry about what kind of tree. Shadow doesn't allow for too much identification detail.

Here's an example of another elemental likeness, from Cervantes' *Don Quixote*: "I shall find you even if you hide better than a lizard." Animals and plants are a great way to animate your images.

The important thing about creating images is that you need them only if they are effective. When you write your drafts and rewrite, be free to make many images—there's a joy and expansiveness in doing that. They might keep you riding the crest of your creativity, because images make new connections for you; the new associations suggest all sorts of things that can happen further.

However, later, as you revise, eliminate all the images that don't work, that are stale (like this one, but I'll leave it in, because the cliché only intensifies the staleness). It's far better to have a straightforward statement without an image than a stale image, and that especially applies to likenesses. Otherwise, an ineffective likeness, like a weed, will sap the energy out of your garden of fiction. Here, it's necessary to develop a critical faculty, nurture your judgment. Read a lot, and pause to savor each fine image and to condemn each sappy one. In your prose, ask yourself, Have I read this before somewhere? Does this sound way too familiar? If it does, delete it. It's better to have one striking image per page and no others than twenty clichéd and stolen ones. Of course, if you really like an image from a story of another writer, find a way to quote it, but don't steal it. You can always make yours.

With some of this chapter's exercises, try to work in the context of a story you already have in progress or expand other exercises. Read the exercises and first do the ones you can play with in something you're working on. Image making can give you the spark you need to ignite your imagination.

When you have the time, you will benefit from doing the other exercises too, and sooner or later, you'll be able to use them directly or to use the image-making faculty which you'll strengthen by doing them.

EXERCISES

1. Look around your room or around the subway or wherever you are. Record two images.

Purpose: To gather images for your work. Images are your seeds, your jewelry, your bullets. Out of them stories might grow. If you show off your stories, they will look better with the jewelry than unadorned. If you need to describe anything in your fiction, the image is your sharp point. Collecting images is a great investment of your time, perception, and imagination. Images help you pay attention and help you call for attention.

Tip: An image is a simple thing. It needn't be much, nor does it need to be beautiful. For example, right now, before the last period and this sentence, I lifted my gaze and saw two mosquitoes besmirching my white ceiling. I'd swatted them last winter one warm and moist night. Maybe I could use the image in a story.

Check: Do you have at least two concrete nouns in each of your recorded observations? In that case, you most likely have images.

2. Identify three skin sensations you're experiencing now. For example: What do your feet feel? Your thighs? Your back? Express each sensation in a sentence.

Purpose: To use the sense of touch to evoke an image. In almost any situation, we have many sensations. We are good at ignoring them, but sometimes we do pay attention. Now and then, noting something so basic as the skin sensations is effective in grounding the character, making readers feel with him. Emotions may be abstract when mentioned because sometimes we don't know where exactly you feel them, but we know where, to what sensory organ, sensations belong. In choosing the sense, half the job of concretizing an image is already finished.

Tip: You might simply note the things impinging on your skin—alpaca on your neck (you don't even need to mention the itch, we'll get it by association), a toenail stuck on a sock thread, a fire-ant bite bleeding again on your thigh.

Check: Have you captured the sensations you wanted? If not, try again until you're satisfied.

3. Evoke what three of your friends smell like, each one in a sentence. A friend of mine once, when he got together with a friend of his he hadn't seen in years, said, "It's so lovely to smell you again. May I?" And he leaned over and smelled her neck. "Oh yes," he said, "that is you." I don't know what that smell was like, but I certainly appreciate relying on more than the eye.

Purpose: To enhance images with smells. Cats, although they probably see better than we do, don't trust their eyes. They need to smell. Maybe you could be catty in your approach to sensation. Almost everybody can do the visuals. If you master the smells and the tactile sensations, you'll have an edge, and you'll evoke the experience more deeply, as a blind person would. Vision depends on photons, light, which is far more ephemeral, barely substantial, than what you smell, which is chemical. Through your nose, you inhale a bit of your neighbor's matter.

Tip: Combine this exercise with number three in "Description." Give the smells to the hostess and two other persons present. Perhaps asking for permission to smell the hostess brings about a chain of awkward or delightful events.

Check: Do your images evoke the smells? Ask others to read your sentences and inquire whether they have a clear picture of what you mean. If they don't, have you mentioned substances— what the smell was like, what most likely entered into making the chemistry of the smell. Don't overcrowd the images. Omit all but the evocative words. Here you're trying to be sharper, more economical, than when you write a description, in which you have more time to maneuver and eventually get at what you mean.

4. Write images of three or four kisses. What does it feel like to kiss your aunt (or another character) on the cheek? Recall the sensation of three most unusual kisses.

Purpose: To relate multisensory images. A kiss is even more substantial than a smell, for in a kiss you have the smell, the taste, and the tactile sensation. Kissing is an example of a an experience of a person that involves multiple sensations. Of course, you could describe other multisensational encounters.

Tip: In this exercise, your task is to be concise. An image takes an instant to register—a sentence per image will suffice. You might actually write several sentences to capture the essential images of each kiss and then compress the sentences to the most effective moment.

If some of the kisses have wilted in your memory, kiss someone around you on the cheeks, or your lover (or would-be lover) or spouse on the mouth. You'll have a good excuse; it's an assignment you need to complete to improve as a writer.

Check: Do you portray images we can see and taste?

5. Close your eyes. What's the first image you recollect? Relate it in a sentence. The image could include any sort of sensations.

Purpose: To recall and relate strong sensory images. No doubt, what you'll recall is something that could be visualized, reconstructed through your mental images of the sensations. And it will be striking enough.

Tip: Don't analyze why you see this, particularly not in a psychological sense. In a stream of action that you follow from a character's point of view, imitate this unexplained image recollection. And don't explain it. Move on. The reader might try to find significance in all this, but most likely, she'll get the image and move on too—but the image will stick and have its effects.

I checked what would happen if I followed the assignment. I recollected a two-foot-tall white pine—with a long dirt-covered root that went to one side—in my hands.

Perhaps you can give these images to your character from "Plot" exercise sixteen.

Check: Don't worry if the exercise didn't turn out to be totally spontaneous. The main thing is to have come up with sense recollections. Where do you think you'll be able to use them? What story? Try playing with the images in the context of several stories, if you have them, and see where the images would fit best.

6. Recollect three intense sensations of pain you've experienced. Put them in words. If you can't do so directly, try an indirect approach: What were you smelling and hearing while in pain? A sentence or two, an image or two, will do.

Purpose: To express pain vividly. Most likely, your characters must experience pain. What are passions without pain?

Tip: For example, although the pain you experience at the dentist's office with an infected molar may be mostly in the flesh, in silent sensations of a maddening itch, a sharp throbbing, the sense that might bring the pain closer to the imagination is the hearing—the crackling of the bone beneath your ear—partly because it's unexpected.

Combine this with exercise eleven in "Plot." The pain sensations could be directly related to his illness or simply serve as a comparison for what he's feeling now. Perhaps he wishes he had a toothache, or he marvels that a dangerous illness doesn't yet surface in a sharply defined pain.

Check: You may have tried to render the sensations of pain precisely. Did you succeed? If you feel you didn't, be crafty. Get at the pain in many ways; give all the senses a chance. It's like a wasp you're trying to swat, first against the wall, then against the window, and so on. See which one is most effective. You might surprise yourself. What matters here is what you finally put on the page. Of course, your initial pain was simply yours, and yours to keep, and perhaps not even to recall—good riddance. But now, what can you give your character, how can you zero in on your character's experience? The evocative power of the image is what's essential now. From your memory, you'll of course invent some kind of fiction since you can't give us your actual pain. Image making is nearly always a work of fancy, that is, fiction.

7. Recall three intense moments of pleasure you've experienced, and express them in images.

Purpose: To convey pleasure images. Of course, your characters will need pleasure. You should be able to zero in on something that evokes pleasure.

Tip: You might combine this exercise with "Description" exercise eight. Once you have the external description, jump into her thoughts, and let her think of her pleasures. This will also be an exercise in the flexible point of view, in which you move from observing a character as an object into the character's thoughts as a subject.

You might also combine this exercise with "Plot" exercise eleven: The ill man thinks of three pleasures he's had. And you might give the three pains to the woman who strolls around in her fine clothes apparently enjoying herself.

Check: Did your memory serve you better with pain or with pleasure images? Interesting to observe, isn't it? (I'm not making a rhetorical statement.)

8. What is the food you can taste in your mouth, through your memory? List these images. Mention the components of what you taste, nearly like a recipe. If you can, recall what you were doing while you ate the food. Even if you can't, pretend you can make the connection between the event and the food.

Purpose: To rely on memory to imagine something. How would you imagine what vanilla yogurt tasted like if you'd never had vanilla? Practice using your memory in image making.

Tip: You may combine this with exercise four in "Ideas for Fiction." The food tastes different now that the man is ill and he is trying to recall the original taste of the food when he used to love it and when it loved him.

Check: Have you identified the substances in the food? They are far more useful than the description of the effect the food had on you—delicious, sensational, succulent, and so on. Mention a squirted lime and something already happens in our glands.

9. In a few sentences, offer a glimpse of a fruit in such a way that we can begin to taste it, in our imagination.

Purpose: To nurture recollecting small and tasty moments. They enhance fiction.

Tip: This is how Willa Cather gives you an image of a fruit in *My Ántonia*.

> Peter put the melons in a row on the oilcloth-covered table and stood over them, brandishing a butcher knife. Before the blade got fairly into them, they split of their own ripeness, with a delicious sound. He gave us knives, but no plates, and the top of the table was soon swimming with juice and seed.

The visual image and the sound of a ripe melon splitting before the blade cuts deep is wonderfully evocative, well observed. I'm sure most of us have had the experience.

Check: Have you manifested a grape, pineapple, or mango in an interesting way? For example, sound is a bit unexpected in Cather's image. The indirect treatment of the juicy fruit, appealing to the ear rather than the mouth, contributes to the freshness of the image. If you find that yours hasn't reached a sensory effect, try different senses. By the way, just as I said that using "delicious" might not work, it did, in Cather's prose. Maybe because we have to pronounce the "sh" effect in the back of our mouths, or feel as though we were pronouncing it there, where our mouths can start to water, maybe that's why the sound of the word works. And it goes to show you what good it is to be dogmatic. I repent.

10. Construct several images you haven't seen. You can do this by putting different things together. For example, a bottle crushed by ice in the middle of a frozen lake. I "see" just the upper half of the bottle on the ice. I haven't actually observed this, but by simply juxtaposing two elements, ice and glass, it's easy to imagine that the expanding ice would choke the bottle. So try putting different things together and see what you come up with.

Purpose: To recombine your sensory experiences, which are your primary treasures in fiction, to achieve an infinite amount of possible images. You won't always have a ready-made image in your memory, nor will you have the time to hunt for images. Why not invent them?

Tip: You might use this technique especially when you transform the autobiographical materials into fiction. If you construct images and see them, you will indeed excite your imagination.

And particularly when you hit a high point in your drama, you can create a surrealist edge—place odd things together. You will be free to do this from the point of view of a protagonist in his struggle; as he exerts himself, he might have a skewed vision.

Check: Is the image strong? Strange? If yes, great. If not, why not? Put some things together that will grate, clash.

11. Here's a long exercise for the patient ones. Describe sensations in each part of your body—the ones you remember or the ones you're experiencing right now. Start with your big toes. Move on to the soles, ankles, shins. The skin on the outside and inside. Muscles. Bones. In the bones. Knees. Back of the knee.

Don't neglect small parts of the body: nails, under the nails, in your nostrils, atop your nose, eyelashes, earlobes, navel. If you don't feel anything in a part of your body, or don't remember feeling anything there, mention that. The fact that your sensory topography has neglected an area may be interesting.

Purpose: To compile a treasury of sensory images. Now and then you might dip into this reservoir to enrich your prose. If you are in the middle of a story, let your character be distracted in a tense moment by several sensations from your list. This kind of skewing of action, so that it wouldn't be totally linear, could enrich your story. Suppose in a line of dialogue, instead of directly answering a question, the character spaces out and registers her sensations. This will derail the dialogue, for a while, and make it all the more believable.

Tip: Once you're finished—and it could take days—do the exercise again. Now imagine you are feeling what you actually aren't feeling. Create the feeling through things—soap in your nostril, broken glass in your foot.

Check: Read your list. Which sensations have you captured best? Which ones worst? Could you redo the unsuccessful ones? Could you perhaps resort to metaphors—the elbow electricity, upon a struck ulnar nerve, as a migration of ants inside your skin.

12. Make metaphors. It's simple. Say that one thing is another. See how many things one thing can become. Allow yourself to be dreamy, uncritical, playful. Let yourself go. Start with a noun. For example, *book*. Complete the sentence: The book is . . . You could randomly choose another noun to fill in the blank, or you can open a book and see whether it evokes, even remotely, another word. "The book is a bird." "The book is a bird with many flimsy wings."

Purpose: To create metaphors. A good metaphor can jolt a description into life—breathe spirit into clay. Sometimes, of course, metaphors emerge spontaneously; other times, you might want to be deliberate and technical about it, especially in a revision in which you think some of your imagery could use more oomph.

Tip: Play with many nouns. Try *man:* "The man is a branchless tree with peeled bark." "The man is a reared horse." "The man is God's punishment to the forest, to the fallen paradise." It's easy to pile more and more nouns, one after another, through association of images or simply randomly.

Run ten nouns through the "metaphor mill." Make each noun become five other nouns. You'll have fifty metaphors at the end of the exercise. Some are bound to be striking.

Check: Read all your sentences. Delete the ones you don't like. If you're left with one marvelous metaphor, the exercise was worth it. You can always run more nouns through the metaphor mill. Now review several of your exercises—or stories, if you have some under way—to see where you can intensify your prose with metaphors. If you become excessive in generating metaphors, don't be sorry to part with many; keep only the best.

13. Make likenesses. What is it like? This is the basic question in image making. Create a whole list of nouns as sentence subjects. Complete the sentences.

His teeth are like _____.

His nose is like _____.

The dog is like _____.

Her eyebrows are like _____.

Her skirt felt like ————————————————.

Her skirt fell like ————————————————.

His shoes smelled like ————————————————.

Fire sounded like ————————————————.

Add other nouns you want to compare with something else in order to capture images.

Purpose: To construct likenesses. Sentence completion after "like" is the basic image-making technique; often it occurs spontaneously, but you might do it deliberately too.

Tip: Making many comparisons doesn't mean your prose will become flowery. A comparison can be sharp, vigorous, even brutal, not necessarily ephemeral and pink. Do not fear that your prose will become overrefined simply because of a great density of imagery.

Be quick to jump from one thing to another in order to capture the likeness. Do a whole bunch of these, in the context of a story.

Check: Which comparisons work? Can you imagine and visualize the comparisons? In likenesses, there should be some similarity between the two things that are compared, more so than in metaphors, which don't promise a similarity but transform one thing into another. Read your likenesses and assess them. Keep whatever looks and sounds good and use it in your prose, eventually.

14. An effective sourcebook of likenesses is the Bible. Examine characters from a story you're writing at the moment, and see where you can add comparisons to biblical characters.

Purpose: To use sources other than everyday experience. Making comparisons to the texts that have been around for two thousand years will give some kind of temporal depth and longevity to your writing, certainly more so than comparing people to the current stars of movies and soaps, who in five years, by the time you get your work published, hardly anybody will remember.

Tip: If you don't know the Bible, you can always resort to some literary classics or historical figures. Shakespearean plays are a possibility too: "Like Hamlet seeing his father's ghost, he thought that he felt her presence, even though she was dead, and he shivered." There's a danger you'll appear bookish, but so what? Aren't you writing a book? Isn't that a bookish experience? Why pretend it isn't?

Check: Does the comparison work? I mean, can we picture the likeness? It's not enough to say, "He suffered like Job." The comparison is not specific enough. Like Job in what instance? Poor Job has suffered a lot in prose, so I'd advise you to find some other biblical workhorse, but if you want to stick with Job, recall a specific moment that perhaps hasn't been used much, such as the very end of Job, where he's happy and blessed.

> So the Lord blessed the latter end of Job more than his beginning: for he had fourteen thousand sheep, and six thousand camels, and a thousand yoke of oxen, and a thousand she asses. He had also seven sons and three daughters. . . . And in all the land were no women found so fair as the daughters of Job: and their father gave them inheritance among their brethren. After this lived Job an hundred and forty years, and saw his sons, and his son's sons, even four generations.

You might say, of a character of yours, by the end of a tale of hardship, that he enjoyed himself like Job in his last days. That

would be a bit surprising, a sight of Job that we don't see much
in the regular Bible-comparison mill.

15. From one of the dictionaries of classical mythology, select
a moment you could use in your fiction. If you don't have one
of these volumes, buy one, eventually. You might want to make
this part of your library. This needn't be a major punishment—
I've just bought *The Penguin Dictionary of Classical Mythology*
for $.59 in a Goodwill store.

Now I'm reading that Aphrodite "vented her anger on the
women of Lemnos for not honoring her by making them smell
so horribly that their husbands abandoned them for Thracian
slave girls." Can you use this? Suppose you have a woman competing with others. She could at one moment wish to do something mean to them as Aphrodite did to the women of Lemnos,
and since it would be unreasonable to expect most people to
know exactly what you mean, you might, in a sentence, retell
what Aphrodite did.

Purpose: To call on Greek mythology as another source for
comparisons in your writing. Comparisons to the events and
characters of Greek mythology can be highly effective. In fact,
while making the comparisons, you might get further ideas for
plot. Maybe, after all, your heroine could make her competition
smell.

Tip: Some Greek myths have been overexploited: Prometheus
and his fire, Sisyphus and his rock, Narcissus and his puddle.
This doesn't mean you can't use these—most readers will be
more familiar with them than with some less famous myths, so
you'll communicate what you want to say faster, but the risk of
cliché will be higher. So you might want to find a different aspect
of the Prometheus or Sisyphus story, or even retell the myth, as
Albert Camus does, to show Sisyphus not as sad and suffering

but as happy in his toil. Camus accomplishes a lot in interpreting the myth: He articulates his philosophy of human happiness. When you take on a myth for a comparison, you don't need to accomplish that much, but be free to make shifts not only to illuminate what your character is doing but also to articulate your angles of vision.

Check: Does the comparison genuinely work; that is, have you found it stimulating, and does it sound illuminating in your text? If it sounds strained, and if it accomplishes nothing interesting, offers no new angle, strike it. Find other moments from mythology to apply.

16. Turn to modern mythology, science, for comparisons. Such comparisons are part of our culture anyhow. "The chemistry between them overwhelmed them." We've seen chemistry used like this too many times. So find something that's not overused. Using scientific comparisons doesn't require brilliance. The scientists have done the hard job; they have developed their stories. You can play with these stories, to make comparisons, or even to evolve your stories.

Here's an example of how Martin Amis compares a woman with an element of cosmology, in *London Fields.*

> For mother earth the escape velocity is seven miles per second, for Jupiter thirty-seven miles per second, for the sun 383 miles per second. For Sirius B, the first white dwarf they found, the escape velocity is 4,900 miles per second. But for Cygnus X-I, the black swan, there is no escape velocity. Even light, which propagates at 186,287 miles per second, cannot escape from it. That's what I am, she used to whisper to herself after sex. A black hole. Nothing can escape from me.

Besides having a jocular comparison, Amis gives us interesting information here; the information makes the novel a rich read.

Purpose: To create a parallel reality to enrich your story. There are many ways of being; I'm simultaneously an infinitesimally small speck in the universe and a giant, nearly a universe, of microbes, who are nearly a speck in me, but giants, nearly a universe to atoms and subatomic particles, and so on. Some of the logic of the universe at large, such as the forces of gravity, of course applies to the microscopic levels of nature as well. We share the logos of the universe with the universe. So comparing what we do with what happens in nature makes a lot of sense.

Tip: Reading science books to make several comparisons might not be worth the effort unless you enjoy reading the books anyway. You can rely for comparisons on the knowledge you already have; reading could help you if you need to clarify and add information.

Check: Is the scientific information interesting? Does it contribute to what you want to say? Of course, not everybody will find everything interesting, but for the moment, don't worry about interesting the reader, but about fascinating yourself with what you can do in fiction.

17. Use your personal mythology, your childhood, to further a character's development. In a moment when a character is undergoing a crisis, you might enhance his experience with images from an early memory of yours, or with your myths of what your early memories are. Surely you have sorted out your early impressions, memories, pains, sorrows, pleasures, dreams. Unless you're reserving these for your autobiography, give them to your characters.

Purpose: To call on your memories as images for your fictional characters. Your personal mythology, of course, contains a lot of thematic energy for you. In a critical moment, using some of your deeply seated images might give you a double benefit. First, you will intensify your character's subjective experience—thought, memories—and thus make him more alive, more passionately engaged in a moment. Second, the stuff that is so primal to your mind could unleash other images, and perhaps an emotional intensity, a passion, that you could breathe into your character.

Tip: It doesn't matter if the characters are different from you. You are already inventing them, putting your myth-making into them, so why not give them your early myths? You will not lose these treasures. After all, is there a law against using these twice? You might later write your autobiography and record the images again. They'll probably turn out different in different writing. Particularly when giving your early images to a fictional character, be free to invent, change, shift, play.

Check: How do the images fit in the description of the character's crisis? Do they intensify the experience? Create dimension for the crisis? Keep only the images that work in synergy with the crisis scene.

18. Develop a concrete image of an abstract notion or an undefined emotion—liberty, patriotism, nostalgia, grief.

Purpose: To use images to express abstract phenomena and ideas. When dealing with ideas, it's a pleasant surprise to find what seems to be doomed to the arena of abstractions brought into an image. See whether you can occasionally include such images in your stories.

Tip: For an example, see how Mikhail Iossel, in "Every Hunter Wants to Know," portrays his experience of freedom in the old Soviet Union as an untasted fruit: "Freedom was like the taste of avocado: I had never seen an avocado in my life; it could be bad, it could be good, it could have no taste whatsoever."

Probably all of us can recall an experience of tasting an exotic fruit for the first time and of wondering what it would taste like. The image can work even in a negative. What is absent, mentioned as absent, is still present as an image.

Check: Does the image involve the senses? Does it express the abstract notion? Does it give body and flavor to a deep emotion?

CHAPTER THIRTEEN

STYLE

There are three approaches to style in fashion: one, to emphasize the body; two, to emphasize the clothes; three, to emphasize both. No matter what approach one takes, one aims to find a style that suits one's personality.

In literature and art, style is not something superficial, something you can add to a story. A style of playing music is integral to music; a style of painting, to painting. How would you separate van Gogh's style from his paintings? Franz Marc's from his?

In style, in fact, most of the fictional matters converge. Your style is a blend of diction, grammar, sentence structure, shifts in point of view, choice of tense, direction and indirection, rhythm, philosophy (or the absence of), narrative comments (or the absence of). So it's not something like spice that you pepper your prose with. Although, of course, the spice could add to the style.

How do you choose the style? Frequently, you don't have to worry about that—after making the choices in voice and point of view and setting, the style may have already chosen you. Especially if that style feels natural to you, is you, don't worry about style, but tell your story.

Blaise Pascal praises natural style: "When we come across a natural style, we are surprised and delighted; for we expected an author, and we find a man." "Just be yourself" sounds like a cliché, but writing in such a way that you let your idiosyncrasies, your rhythms of thoughts, your whims in word choice come to the fore uncensored will probably result in something that is original. It is in fact when we look for the words that others wear that our verbal clothes become threadbare.

The natural requirement doesn't mean that you shouldn't study the language you use and play with it to test its effects and impacts. You can pay attention to style, to your benefit. Just as in dress, you can choose stylistic elements that will enhance the appearance of your body—and that will make your body move comfortably.

Some styles are beautiful. If you pay attention to your imagery, rhythm of sentences, the flow of one sentence into another, you may develop a certain gracefulness that should be a pleasure to read.

For example, Marguerite Duras writes in her novel *The Lover*, quite sensually, appropriately to the theme.

> The girl in the felt hat is in the muddy light of the river, alone on the deck of the ferry, leaning on the rails. The hat makes the whole scene pink. It's the only color. In the misty sun of the river, the sun of the hot season, the banks have faded away, the river seems to reach to the horizon. It flows quietly, without a sound, like the blood in the body. No wind but that in the water.

In writing that aims so much at beautiful imagery, there's a risk of slipping into purple prose, or even more tackily, pink prose. And Duras literally writes pinkly here, but does it so nonchalantly and naturally, that there's nothing tacky. Perhaps "muddy light" helps to enhance the beauty of the moment, gives earthy body to something that might appear ephemeral. In aiming for sheer beauty, who would think of mud? Mud might sound slimy, yucky, but here, it surprises us and lends an impression of old photographic haze to the scene. Of course, rivers have been compared to arteries and veins, but the quiet flow of a river compared to the soundlessness of blood in the body brilliantly accomplishes the old likeness in a new light, or rather, new sound. Such flow of visual imagery and hushed sound, light, color, in light and simple sentences, achieves a wonderful grace, with a very light touch. Don't worry about that in your drafts, especially if you are enjoying the sensuality of your sentences. Later, perhaps, you could edit here and there for efficiency, and if after many pages there is a monotony in how the prose flows, you might change the tempo.

Others' styles are energetic, even athletic. Here, sentences move swiftly, the points are hammered, words aren't used so much for melody as for the fast rhythm, speed. The impression given is that of authority—the writer knows where to go, without needing excuses, perambulations. In fact, the impression may be deceptive and the writer himself has moved out of the way, under the pressing urgency of events. He's like a sports commentator. However, the fast rhythm is hard to maintain—so even a style like this can benefit from some relaxation, with a bit of descriptive flourish, or indirection, a good joke here and there.

In a style, the art of omission is as important as the art of commission. Omitting some words accelerates the rhythm of a sentence. For example, "I came, I saw, I conquered." There are no nouns here. Saw what? Conquered what? Now in the original, "*Veni, vidi, vici*," the compression is even greater. There are only verbs here. Of course, in Latin as in many other highly inflected languages, the verb forms reveals the subject, so the pronoun is unnecessary, but the pronoun can be used for emphasis. *Ego veni*, etc., would call attention to "I." The saying could be in a way translated as "Came, saw, conquered," and it would work in the context where we knew who was speaking. We see only verbs, active verbs, which give immense energy to the statement. Naturally, it would be hard to write a whole story using verbs only, but now and then, for a punch, it's good to try to see whether a sentence or two would benefit from such verbal compression, to avoid verbosity.

There are moments of style you can apply when you want them. For example, it's possible to use parentheses to run a double account, one of what is happening and another of what might be happening. See this example from "The Revisionist," by Helen Schulman.

> She was a beautiful girl in an interesting way. Which means if the light were right (which it wasn't quite then), if she held her chin at a particular angle (which she didn't, her chin was in a constant seesaw on account of the gum) when she laughed or when she forgot about pulling her lips over her teeth (which were long and fine and, at the most reductive-canine) she was a lovely, cubist vision.

Besides the parentheses, Schulman uses comma splices to draw a possible angle of vision of this beautiful girl together with the actual angle that the protagonist, a moviegoer, sees of the box-office clerk. There aren't otherwise many parentheses in this story, but Schulman used them effectively when she wanted them.

So while you may have your natural style—and certainly nurture it by all means, asserting your right to your way of expressing yourself—you might avail yourself of other styles attainable through technical shifts, some of which you'll practice in the exercise section here.

Now and then you might want to write a long sentence, for the flow of it, to pile impressions and suspend a moment of thought or description in one temporal unit. For example, Bohumil Hrabal, author of *Closely Watched Trains*, does this effectively in Czech in *The Little Town Where Time Stood Still*, and the English translation mirrors the sentence length and impressions of the original.

> I hopped on the edge of the fountain to see better how nice I looked in that sailor's jacket, I looked about, no one was coming, no one was looking out of the window

to complain to Daddy, I hopped up on the fountain, and when I leaned over, I saw the lovely pleated skirt and little white sockies and shiny polished shoes, I shook out my hair, and when I looked again at myself reflected in the water, I overbalanced and fell into the fountain, and the water swallowed me up like a great fish when it swallows a tiny little one, again I tried to find the bottom with my shiny little shoe, but the bottom of the fountain was deeper than I was tall, and again I surfaced for air, but I was too frightened to call for help, because Daddy would be too cross, and I was on my way to join the angels, again I was enveloped in a bright sweet world, as if I were a bee fallen into honey.

Of course, this passage could be broken up into several sentences, but the effect of merging the possible sentences into a long sentence suits the subject matter. In a rush of drowning, all the impressions blur without a pause. A long sentence should still be readable, as is Hrabal's, and if anything, the impressions conveyed in it should be at least as good as those marked off by periods into short sentences. ". . . the water swallowed me up like a great fish when it swallows a tiny little one . . ."—this is a wonderful image that could stand on its own as a beautiful sentence; however, it's not wasted in the flood of words, but in a way heightened because it suddenly appears and disappears, drowning amidst comma splices in the fountain of words.

ABOUT THE EXERCISES

In the following exercises, the purpose will be similar unless otherwise stated; that is, the mastery of different stylistic elements that you could use as you see fit in your fiction to achieve various effects. Taking your sentences apart, in a hyperminimalist mode, and extending them further than you usually do, in a maximalist mode, might give you a chance to examine your ways of sentence making. Attention to each sentence, when you want it, will intensify and elevate your prose to a high level of performance.

The general tip for all the exercises: Play. In these stylistic exercises, see just how much you can accomplish in a certain manner. See whether you can create long sentences like Hrabal's and short ones like Caesar's ("Came, saw, conquered"). These are merely pointers, which, if you take them, might result in some wonderful techniques you may not have tried before.

The stylistic techniques are not meant to replace your natural style but to sharpen it. Departing from your natural rhythm now and then will simply refresh the rhythm as improvisations do the main themes. However, if in the process you discover that something suits you, you have not picked it up from here, but were merely reminded of a way of making rhythms and sentences that is already yours. Use all this as a way of improving your freedom and versatility on the page.

Once you complete each exercise, the check is to see what you like and what you could use somewhere. See what you don't like and what, of course, you want to avoid using. See what style you can apply—even if for only a sentence or two—to stories you have in progress.

EXERCISES

1. Write a couple of paragraphs in a highly impressionistic style. You could combine this with exercise one in "Setting I." Do it from the viewpoint of someone who has a good reason to be dreamy, someone who has just fallen in love. You needn't mention who the lover is, or that there's a lover. Pile images in long sentences, in a joyful exuberance, and don't worry if you are making comma splices, the way Hrabal does.

2. Write a page in a pointillist manner: brief images, sometimes in sentence fragments, unconnected to each other. Choose three or four themes that you alternate. You can take a look at how Carole Maso does this in *AVA*, but of course, you needn't imitate her, although do take the manner into consideration.

3. Write a page in a clipped style: no adjectives or adverbs, only verbs and nouns in the active voice, in short sentences. You could describe an urgent action in this way or a shock—maybe in the moment of dying in "Scene" exercise nine.

4. Write two or three pages in long, sensuous, sinuous sentences, with many modifiers—adverbs modifying adjectives. The point here is to be melodious, to write for the sound, the nuance, which is nearly all in the adjectives. Much has been and can be said against modifiers, but an adjective well chosen can surprise with its elegance and grace. Promenade your adjectives.

5. Write a page in a superintellectual style. Don't do it pretentiously, but for real. Use Greek, Latin, scientific, and philosophical vocabulary in all earnest. It's easy to parody this style, but see whether there's virtue in it beyond parody. Maybe there's precision and ancient wisdom in all this after all. Choose the subject matter you know best so you can improvise most freely.

Later, you could use this in many places, for example, in science fiction stories from "Plot" exercises eighteen and nineteen. You could use this to augment a dialogue: an argument between two professors trying to impress a person they are trying to seduce in a restaurant.

6. Write a page in a crude, rude, and offensive style. Use obscenities, four-letter words, poor grammar, an angry attitude.

Write this from the point of view of someone who has just been offended or hurt.

You could use some of the style you develop here to intensify "Dialogue" exercise ten.

7. Write a scene in a sensual and erotic style. Almost everything you say should involve many senses of the body as well as of the word (such as double entendres).

8. Write a page in a surreal manner. Superimpose strange things that don't belong together. For example: "One day, there was a huge crow sitting on his shoulder, and it said, 'I have your soul in my belly, you better do what I want you to do or your soul will fly away from you and you will be soulless.' At first he couldn't believe what he was hearing. The crow began to peck him on the head violently. He didn't want to lose his soul, but the pecking was unbearable, so he shook the bird off." While this may seem nonsensical (as it should since I wrote it to give an example), there is a surreal element here.

9. Write a page in a classical mode. Make frequent allusions to the Greek myths, biblical imagery. For example, in your description of the flooding in "Ideas for Fiction" exercise five, you could bring in images and stories from the myths and the Bible.

10. Write a page in the naturalist style. Describe something in its gory detail; for example, a dental visit or a wounding. Stacy Richter employs this style in her short story "The Beauty Treatment."

> There's blood all over the tops of my tits where they pushed out my J. Crew edelweiss linenshirt and a loose

feeling around my mouth when I screamed. My first
thought was fuck, how embarrassing, then I ran into the
girls' room and saw it: a red gash parted my cheek from
my left temple to the corner of my lip. A steady stream
of blood dripped off my jawline into the sink. One minute later, Cyndy Dashnaw found the razor blade on the
concrete floor of the breezeway, right where the Bitch
had dropped it.

The description of the cut is precise, almost clinical: "from
my left temple to the corner of my lip." Blood drips from "my
jawline into the sink." "J. Crew edelweiss linenshirt," a beautiful,
delicate, fashionable piece of clothing, intensifies the shock of
the blood by contrast.

11. Write a page in the superrealistic style. Scrutinize something and give us the measurements, the materials it's made of,
the price. Perhaps while describing one of your characters, you
could take this approach for a paragraph—reveal something
about her through the exact pricing and measurements of the
articles of clothing.

12. Write a scene without using any verbs. Instead of a verb,
use a dash. See whether this can make sense. You needn't start
a scene out of the blue, from nothing. Take one of the scenes
from the scene chapter, and see whether here and there you can
condense sentences by cutting verbs.

13. Write a scene with pronouns, verbs, and adverbs, but no
nouns. Can you make sense with it? Now combine it with the
scene without verbs above, or cross out nouns in several sentences in an exercise in "Scene." Perhaps you can alternate paragraphs for a while like this. See whether you can achieve a special
energy and urgency with this.

14. Write several sentences as a continuous flow of metaphors, one thing becoming another. Don't worry whether the metaphors make sense. Let things simply metamorphose one into another, as I do here for fun: I picked up a big wood-carved spoon, and as I put it to my lips, the spoon licked me raspily; it was a bull's tongue. The bull was breathing out milk steam as he gazed at me with his huge bulging eyes, but those were not ordinary eyes, they were seashells, and when I reached to touch the bull's cheek, the shells fell into my palms, and opened up, with pearls glistening blue. I looked around. There was no bull, only sharks quietly spitting out fins above me.

If you take metaphor making literally, you might not even make metaphors, but you will write surreal imagery.

15. Write a paragraph in which most words are four letters or less. You might rewrite an action scene from a story of yours. Does the scene become faster, more energetic?

16. Write a paragraph in which most of the words are ten letters or longer.

17. Write a paragraph in which each sentence is three words long. Follow it with a paragraph in which each sentence has only two words. Then make a paragraph in which each sentence has four words. You might combine this with exercise fifteen. Are you achieving interesting rhythms, like a drummer?

18. Write a paragraph in a passive voice. See how many passives you can use and still make sense. You could combine this with "Voice" exercise nine.

CHAPTER FOURTEEN

PUTTING IT ALL
TOGETHER

In my experience and that of many other writers, it seems
clear that writing a piece of fiction is a series of concrete
tasks: introducing a character, describing a setting, creating
a scene, writing a provocative dialogue, and so on. Some writers
resist the notion of exercises, but they do exercises all the time
by setting themselves such concrete assignments.

Some stories may arise from a scene, or a dialogue, or a character sketch, and the other supporting scenes can be created
along the way as you need them. Other stories may come from
a general notion of what the setup should be, and then you
gradually assemble the pieces you need, such as persons, places,
and the escalation of action.

Now that we've looked at each element in turn, let's look at
how they all unite to form a finished piece. I will show you how
a story came together for me—how I assembled various elements
created in exercise-like sketches I assigned to myself. Showing
how my story came into being may appear selfish, and perhaps
it is, but I cannot truly know or explain the creative process that
any other writer underwent to complete a story. I know only
how my own imagination made the connections necessary to
bring a story to life. And even in my own story, I cannot explain
everything. But I will try. So read the following story. Then we
can discuss how it was developed, one step at a time.

SHEEPSKIN

Since I can't tell this to anybody, I'm writing it, not just to sort it out for myself, but for someone nosy who'll rummage through my papers one day. In a way I want to be caught. But I won't call this story a confession. I should pretend that it's somebody else's story, that it is fiction. I wish I could set it in a different country—outside Croatia and outside the former Yugoslavia—and that it was about somebody else, a former self, a formerly uniformed me. I don't mean that I want a complete break with my past—nothing as dramatic as suicide, although, of course, I've entertained thoughts of it, but the thoughts have not entertained me. I have survived knives and bombs: I should be able to survive thoughts and memories.

I'll start with a scene on a train in western Slavonia. Though it was hot, I closed the window. Not that I am superstitious against drafts as many of our people are. Dandelion seeds floated in, like dry snowflakes, and all sorts of pollens and other emissaries of the wild fields filled the air with smells of chamomile, menthol, and other teas. It would have been pleasant if I hadn't had a cold that made me sneeze and squint. The countryside seemed mostly abandoned. Croats from Serbian Kosovo had moved into the villages where Serbs used to live, but they did not plant, sow, or harvest, because they had no legal rights to do so until formal land deeds were signed. Only a few could track down the Serbs who had run away.

I had never seen vegetation so free and jubilant. The war had loosened the earth, shaken the farmers off its back. Strewn mines kept them from venturing into the fields, but did not bother the flowers. The color intensity of grasses and beeches in the background gave me dizziness I could not attribute to my cold. I saw a fox leap out of orange bushes of tea. Of course, it was not tea, but many of these wildflowers would be teas, curing asthma, improving memory, and filling you with tenderness. If we had stuck to drinking tea, maybe the war would have never happened.

I leaned against the wooden side of the train, but gave up, since the magnum I had strapped on my side pressed into my arm painfully. I would have probably fallen asleep, intoxicated with the fields and the musty oil, which doused the wood beneath the tracks. As a child I had loved the oily smell of rails; it had transformed for me the iron clanking of the gaps in the tracks into a transcontinental guitar with two hammered strings and thousands of sorrowful frets that fell into diminished distances. I'd have dozed off if every time I leaned against the vibrating wall of the train the gun hadn't pinched a nerve and shaken me awake. And just when I was beginning to slumber, the door screeched.

A gaunt man entered. I was startled, recognizing my old tormentor from the Vukovar hospital. He took off his hat and revealed unruly cowlicked hair, grayer than I remembered it. His thick eyebrows that almost met above his nose were black. I wondered whether he colored them.

The man did not not look toward me, although he stiffened. I was sure he was aware of me. I had dreamed of this moment many times, imagining the first thing I'd do if given the opportunity would be to jump at the man, grab his throat, and strangle him with the sheer power of rage. My heart leaped, but I didn't. I gazed at him from the corner of my eye. He looked a little thinner and taller than I remembered. I did not know his name, but in my mind I had always called him Milos. I ceased to believe we coexisted in the same world—imagined that he was in Serbia, off the map as far as I was concerned.

I looked out the window, and the sunlit fields glowed even more, with the dark undersides, shadows, enhancing the light in the foreground. The train was pulling into Djulevci. The Catholic church gaped open, its tower missing, its front wall and gate in rubble, the pews crushed, overturned, and the side wall had several big howitzer holes; only here and there pale mortar remained, reflecting the sun so violently that my eyes hurt. At the train station there was a pile of oak logs, probably a decade old, but still not rotten. And past the train station stood the Serb Orthodox church, pockmarked. It probably wouldn't be standing if there hadn't been guards around it, night and day. The Croatian government wanted to demonstrate to the world—although journalists never bothered to come to this village—how much better Croats were than Serbs, but that was just a show. The Croat policemen sat on chairs, one wiggled a semi-automatic rifle, and the other tossed a crushed can of Coke over his shoulder.

There was a time when I would have thrown grenades into the church, owing to my traveling companion and other Serb soldiers who had surrounded and choked the city of Vukovar for months. Fearing that I would starve to death, I had minced by sheepskin jacket and made a soup out of it. The day before the soldiers invaded the city, I'd seen a cat struck in the neck with schrapnel. I picked her up and skinned her. I overgrilled her because I was squeamish to eat a cat, and once I had eaten most of her, I grew feverish. I wasn't sure whether the cat had gotten some disease from rats—I would not have been surprised if I had caught the plague this way—or whether it was sheer guilt and disgust with myself, that I had eaten a cat, that made me ill. My body, unused to food, just could not take it; I was delirious in the hospital, but there was no doubt, what I saw was not a dream: soldiers laughing, crashing wine bottles on the chairs, dragging

old men in torn pajamas out of their hospital beds. A
man with black eyebrows and a gray cowlick that shot
out trembling strands of hair above his forehead came
to my side and spat at me. He pulled the sheet off my
bed and stabbed my thigh with a broken wine bottle. I
coiled and shrieked, and he uncoiled me, pulling my
arms, and another man pulled my legs, while the third
one pissed over my wound and said, "This is the best
disinfectant around, absolutely the best. *Na zdravlye!*"

"There, pig, you'll thank me one day, you'll see," said
Milos, and stabbed my leg again.

Other soldiers came and dragged a wailing old woman
down the stairs.

"How about this guy?" one of the soldiers asked
about me.

"No, he's bleeding too much," said Milos. "I don't
want to get contaminated by his shitty blood."

A tall French journalist came in and took pictures of
me, and muttered in English.

"What are you staring at?" I asked. "There are worse
sights around."

"Yes, but they are not alive," he said. He carried me
out, while my blood soaked his clothes. He pushed me
into the jeep, and we drove out and passed several check-
points without any inspection. He took me to the
Vinkovci hospital, which was often bombed. Two nurses
pulled glass from my leg, tied rubber above and below
the wound, stitched me up, wrapped the wound—all
without painkillers. I wished I could swoon from the
pain. I ground my teeth so hard that a molar cracked.

Thanks a lot for the pleasure, I thought now and
looked at my silent companion on the train. At Virovitica, we'd have to change trains. Mine was going to
Zagreb, and I did not know whether he was going there,
or east, to Osijek.

He got out of the compartment first, and I did not want to be obvious about following him. Many peasants with loud white chickens in their pleated baskets filled the corridor between us.

When I jumped off the train into the gravel, his head covered with a hat slid behind a wall. His shadow moved jerkily on the gray cement of the platform, but I could not see the shadow's owner. Milos must have been behind the corner. Maybe he was aware of being followed.

I thought he could be waiting for me in ambush. People walked and stepped on his shadow, but they could not trample it, because as they stepped on it, it climbed on them, and I was no longer sure whether it was Milos' shadow or whether they were casting shadows over each other. Not that it mattered one way or another, but I suppose that's part of my professional photographer's distortion and disorientation that I look at light and shadow wherever I turn, and I frame what I see in rectangular snatches; I keep squaring that world, in my head, to some early and primitive cosmology of a flat earth, where nothing comes around.

I rushed past the corner. There was a kiosk stocked with cigarettes and many magazines featuring pictures of naked blondes. I stopped and pretended to be reading the train schedule posted at the station entrance so I could observe Milos' reflection on the glass over the orange departures schedule. He rolled the magazine he had bought into a flute, and entered a restaurant. I followed. There was an outdoor section under a tin roof, with large wooden tables and benches. A TV set was blaring out a sequence of Croatian President Tudjman kissing the flag at the Knin fort, after his forces captured Knin. The President lifted his clenched fist to the sky. What kind of kiss was it, from thin bloodless lips sinking through the concave mouth of an elderly stiffneck? I detest flags. Anyhow, I was not in a loving mood right then, toward anybody. In Vukovar we thought that Tudj-man had abandoned us. Maybe he was partly responsi-ble for my wantonly following a stranger down the stairs, to the lower level of the country dive. Milos sat below a window with fake crystal glass that refracted light into purple rays. I did not sit right away, but walked past him, following arrows to the bathroom across a yard with a fenced family of sheep with muddy feet, who eyed me calmly. I walked back and sat at a round table about two yards away from his.

He ordered lamb and a carafe of red wine in a perfect Zagreb accent. In Vukovar I remembered him using long Serb vowels, ironically stretching them. Maybe he was now afraid to be taken for a Serb. I couldn't blame him for that. Still, a man who could dissemble so well was dangerous, I thought.

I ordered the same thing. When I pronounced my or-der, I used the same wording as Milos, in my eastern Slavonian leisurely way, which to many people outside my region sounded similar to Serbian.

Milos looked at me for the first time and, hearing my voice, gave a start. The waiter, slumping in his greasy black jacket with a napkin hanging out of his pocket, eyed me contemptuously. His mouth was curled to one side, and one silver tooth gleamed, over his shiny fat lower lip.

He brought one carafe to Milos and one to me along with empty glasses. Milos drank, I drank. He opened his magazine to the centerfold of a blonde with black pubic hair, and then he stared at me. What was the point? Did he pretend that he thought I was a homosexual stalking him and about to proposition him, so this was his way of telling me, No I'm not interested? If he imagined he could confuse me this way so I would not be positive I had recognized him, he was dead wrong.

I had a postcard in my pocket; I pulled it out and began to write—I did not know to whom. To my ex-wife, who'd left me at the beginning of the war to visit her relatives in Belgrade? They had filled her head with nonsense about how Croats were going to kill her, and how even I might be a rabid Croat who would cut her throat. The nonsense actually served Miriana well; she got out right before the city was encircled by Serb troops and bombed. From what I heard she now lived with a widowed cardiologist whose Croatian wife had died of a heart attack. Miriana used to visit Belgrade frequently even before the war; she had probably had an affair with the cardiologist. Her running away from the fighting may have been simply a pretext for leaving me. Anyway, I didn't have her address, so I couldn't write to her—no big loss.

I wrote to my dead father instead, although this made no sense either. He had died of stomach cancer last year in Osijek, perhaps because of the war. Without the anxiety he could have lived with the latent stomach cancer for years.

"Hi, my old man. I wish you were here. Not that there'd be much to see—in fact, Virovitica has to be one of the dreariest towns in Slavonia. But the wine is good. . . ."

My meal arrived. I folded the postcard and put it in my pocket. The meat was lukewarm. Who knows when it was cooked—maybe days ago, and it stayed in the refrigerator. I grumbled as I cut.

Milos swore too, as he struggled. He asked for a sharper knife.

"This is awful! They charge so much and give you only the bone!" he said to me.

If he thought he could engage me in a conversation and thus appease me, he was wrong, although I did answer. "Yes, they figure only travelers would eat here anyway, and once they get our money and we're gone, they can laugh at us."

He gulped wine.

I navigated my blade through the stringy meat.

"Where are you from?" he asked me.

I called the waiter. "You forgot the salad."

"You haven't asked for it."

He was probably right, but I still said, "Yes, I did."

He soon brought me a plate of sliced tomatoes and onions, with oily vinegar. That helped subdue the heavy and rotten lamb taste. Funny how finicky I'd become in a hurry—not long before, I had chewed my leather shoes, certain I'd starve to death, and now I behaved like a jaded gourmet.

Milos bent down to search through his luggage. Maybe he's going to draw a gun? I thought. I slid my hand into my jacket.

Milos took out three dolls, the Lion King hyenas. What, is this possible? My torturer is buying toys for kids? He put the magazine and the hyenas into his traveling bag. Maybe that was his way of saying, I am not a guy who'd stab anybody, I'm a kind family man.

He looked toward me, and I felt self-conscious with my hand in my jacket. So it wouldn't look as though I was pulling a gun, I fumbled in the pocket and took out my pigskin wallet. The waiter eagerly came to my table. I gave him fifty kunas, certainly more than the meal was worth. "I need no change," I said.

"Excuse me, four and a half more kunas, please," asked the waiter. I gave him five coins.

"Preposterous, isn't it?" Milos said. "How can they charge that much for this? If I had known, I'd have controlled my appetite, could have bought another toy for my kids."

Was he appealing to me again? I had no sympathy for family men. My marriage failed perhaps because I had no kids. My business failed because the likes of Milos bombed my town, and here, I sat as a twitching mass of resentment. I took another gulp of wine. I first used a toothpick and then whistled through my teeth to clean out bits of meat that got stuck there.

Milos looked at me with annoyance. He clearly didn't like my whistling. So what, I thought. If it bothers you, I'll do more of it. And who was he to complain? He slurped wine as though it were hot soup. And with his sharp knife, sharper than mine, he cut through more lamb, and I couldn't escape remembering again how he'd cut into my leg.

I scratched the swollen scar through the woolen fabric of my pants. It itched to the point of my wanting to tear it.

"Do you think there are fleas here?" I asked loudly, as if to excuse my scratching, but looked at nobody.

The waiter strutted and dumped tiny coins on my table ostentatiously, probably to make a statement that it was beneath him to take my tip. The rattle of change scared two turquoise flies off my plate.

"Flies are all right," I said. Not much had changed since communism. I used to think that rudeness was a matter of fixed salaries, no incentive. But here, I was pretty sure the waiter was part-owner of this free enterprise establishment, and he was still rude, and did his best to disgust his customers. And of course customers hadn't changed either. They used to be rude, and I would continue to be rude. But before I could think of another insulting question, Milos asked one. "Hey, my friend, do you think I could buy a sheepskin jacket anywhere around here?"

This may have been a jab at me. But how could he have known I'd eaten a sheepskin jacket in Vukovar?

The waiter answered: "Maybe in a couple of hours. We are just getting some ready."

"Could I see them?" Milos was standing and picking up a thick cloth napkin that looked like a towel from his lap.

The waiter grabbed a large hair dryer from among plum brandy bottles on the shelf and waved to Milos to come along. Although I was not invited, I followed. They had identical bald spots on the pates of their heads.

Behind the sheep stall, in a shed filled with hay, on thick clothes wires hung two sheepskins, dripping blood into aluminum pots on the dusty dirt floor.

I wondered why the waiter collected the blood, why not simply let it soak the ground. Maybe he made blood sausages; maybe he drank it, like an ancient Mongolian horseman.

The waiter aimed the blow dryer at a sheepskin, filling it with air. Rounded like a sail full of wind, the skin gave me a spooky impression that an invisible sheep was beginning to inhabit it.

"This'll be a terrific jacket," the waiter said. "Give it an hour, if you can spare."

"But what about the pattern?" Milos said. "What about the buttons?"

"Fuck buttons. You can get those anyplace. But fine sheepskin like this, nowhere. Two hundred kunas, is that a deal?"

Milos stroked the sheepskin's tight yellow curls.

"The winter's going to be a harsh one," said the waiter.

"Yes, but sheep won't save us from it," I said.

Milos quit stroking, and as he turned around, he stepped on the edge of a bowl, and blood spilled over his jeans and white socks and leather shoes.

"Seeing this is enough to make one become a vegetarian," I said to the waiter. I was beginning to feel nauseous.

"I'll be passing through town in two days again," said Milos. "Could I pick it up then?"

"No problem." The waiter walked back, Milos followed. The waiter pushed in a silvery CD, and Croatian pop came on, tambourines with electric organs that shook the speakers. The music was cranked beyond the point of clarity—blasted. No conversation was possible.

Milos walked into the backyard. I thought that his Serb soul wouldn't let him listen to Croat music. He gave me a look and winked. I wondered what he meant. The waiter smirked, perhaps thinking there was a gay connection established between Milos and me. Milos went into the toilet, an outhouse next to the sheep stall.

I went behind the outhouse. There was a hole in the gray wood through which I could see his back. I put the gun in the hole and shot through his spine. His body jolted forward and then fell back, right against the wall. I shot again. Blood flowed through the spacing between the dry planks. Because of the music, I was sure the waiter couldn't hear the shots.

I rushed away from the tavern yard through the rear gate. A train was whistling into the station. I jumped on the train even before it stopped. I wondered why I was running away. I should have been able to explain my deed—revenge against a war criminal. I went straight into the train toilet and shaved off my droopy mustache that made me look melancholy and forsaken. Now in the mirror I looked much younger, despite my receding hairline and the isolated widow's peak.

I thought I'd feel triumphant after my revenge. And I did feel proud as I looked at my cleared lip. Great, I am free from my sorrow, from the humiliation. I won.

But as I sat in the first-class coach and looked at round holes burnt into the velvet seat by cigarette butts, my heart pounded and I could barely draw a breath. The smell of stale tobacco and spilled beer irritated me. I turned the ashtray over, cleaned it with a paper towel and threw it out the window. The awful mutton seemed to be coming up to my throat. I was afraid.

If I was caught, and there was a trial, public sympathy would be with me. Many people want personal revenge. Forget institutional revenge, forget the International War Crimes Tribunal in Den Haage.

When I got off in Zagreb policemen in blue uniforms with German shepherds strolled on the platform but they did not stop me. They probably did not look for me. The war was going on in Krajina; one more civilian dead in the North made no difference.

Drunken people frolicked all over town, beeping their car horns, the way they did when their soccer clubs won. As I walked I expected a hand on my shoulder, from somewhere, perhaps the sky. It did not happen. But what happened was worse. At the tram stop, I saw a man exactly like Milos. I thought it was him. Were my bullets blanks? But where had the blood come from? How could Milos have made it to the train? When he saw me, I thought I noticed a fleeting recognition, the cowlick on his head shook, but that was too little reaction for what had happened in Virovitica. It was not Milos from the restaurant. This man was a little shorter and plumper. He looked genuinely like the man from Vukovar who had stabbed me, more than my Milos from Virovitica did. What if I had killed the wrong man? We rode in the same tram car. I forgot to buy my ticket, I was so stunned. He had his punched in the orange box near the entrance and stood, with one arm holding on to a pole. What to do? I wondered, as the tram jangled us around curves, and slim young ladies with tranquil made-up faces stood between us. I could not just kill the man, although this was probably the one that I should have killed in the first place. He got off at Kvaternik Square. Now I could blame him not only for my injury but for the death of an innocent man, his double. But I could have been wrong, again. I couldn't trust my "recognitions" anymore. I hadn't felt particularly ecstatic after my first murder, not for long anyway, and I was not looking for ectasy. So I did not follow this man. I was crazed enough that I could have killed him too, but I wanted to be alone. Enough stuffy trams, oily tracks, expressionless people.

I walked home, near the zoo, just south of the stadium. In the streets I saw another Milos look-alike. Was I hallucinating? It was getting dark, true, but I looked at this third Milos keenly. They all had the same gait, same graying and trembling cowlick, same heavy black brow. I was glad I hadn't killed the man on the tram. How many men would I have to shoot to get the right one? It was absurd, and I was afraid that I was going insane.

I watched TV in my messy efficiency. Crime, if this was crime, was no news. Only Serb mass exodus from Krajina and Croat mass exodus from Banja Luka and Vojvodina made the news along with Mitterand's prostate. I drank three bottles of warm red wine and still couldn't fall asleep.

Next morning, sleepless and hungover, on my way to buy a daily, I thought I saw a Milos look-alike, leaning against the window of an espresso café, staring vacantly, as though he were the corpse of my traveling companion from Virovitica.

In the papers I saw the picture of my man, "Murdered by an Unidentified Traveler": Mario Toplak, teacher of mathematics at the Zagreb Classical Gymnasium, survived by his wife Tanya, son Kruno, and daughter Irena. Clearly, I got the wrong man. This one was a Croat, judging by his name. But then, even the man in the Vukovar hospital could have been a Croat. He could have been drafted. The fact that he did not kill me and did not drag me out onto a bus to be shot in a cornfield now gave me the idea that wounding me may have saved me. I could not walk, and since I gushed blood it would have been too disgusting for anybody to carry me onto the bus, so I was left alone. He may have been a Serb, and he saved me nevertheless. Why hadn't I thought of that possibility before? Maybe I should have sought out the man to thank him. But thirst for revenge makes you blind. Is this a real thought? I'm probably just paraphrasing "Love makes you blind." I'm filling in the dots in prefab thoughts. Can I think?

At Toplak's funeral there were almost a hundred people, so I felt I was inconspicuous in the chapel. His wife wept, and his son, about four, and daughter, about five, did not seem to understand what was going on. "Where is Daddy? I want my daddy!" shouted Kruno.

"He's going to visit the angels in heaven, so he could tell us what it's like there. He'll bring back some tiny clouds who can sing in foreign tongues, you'll see." The widow whispered loudly. Maybe she was proud of how well she was shielding her kids from the truth.

"How can Daddy fly to heaven from here?" asked Irena.

I could see why she worried about that. The chapel was small, stuffy with perfume—I detest perfume, as though breathing wasn't hard enough without it!—and too cramped for an Ascension to take place. Tanya looked pathetic, tragic, dignified with her dark auburn hair, pale skin, and vermilion lips. Her skirt was slightly above the knee; she had thin ankles, a shapely waist with round, sexily tilted hip. She was in her mid-thirties. After the funeral, I gave her a white carnation, which had fallen in front of me from a precariously laid bouquet during the prayer. (I wondered, could you make tea from carnations, at least for funerals?) "I knew your husband," I said. "I'm so sorry."

She took the flower mechanically and put it in her purse.

"Could I give you a call, to share memories of him with you?" I said.

"Not for a while. What would be the point anyway?" She gave me a look through her eyelashes, grasped her children's hands, and walked toward the chapel door. Kruno turned around, looked at the varnished casket, and asked, "How come the box has no wings? How will it fly?"

Toplak was in the phone book. I called her a month later but when she answered I put the receiver down. I was too excited, I couldn't talk. I feared that I wanted to confess to her. On several occasions I waited for hours not far from her house and followed her. Every Saturday morning she went to the neighborhood playground with her kids.

In the meanwhile, I had grown crazed and lucky in everything I did. I can't say that I was a shy man—I used to be, but photography, shoving my eyes into everybody's business and intimacy, freed me from that affliction. At the end of August 1995 I took on loans, sold a small house in Djakovo I had inherited from my father, rented a shop, and photographed a lot of weddings, funerals, births. I accosted couples in the park who seemed to be on the verge of getting married, got their phone numbers; I put up ads in all the funeral parlors, crashed funeral parties with my camera. I hired an assistant, made a lot of money. The country seemed to follow the same mood swings as I did. After Krajina was conquered and all the transportation lines in Croatia were opened again, and there were no more threats of bombing in Zagreb, everybody was on the make. Optimism, investment, spending—many people seemed to have money, while months before hardly anybody did. If I had talked to Tanya a couple of days after the funeral, I would have had nothing to show for myself, but just two months later, when I approached her at the playground while her kids were jumping up and down the slides, I could boast. It was a superb day, with leaves turning color and fluttering in the slanted rays of the afternoon sun.

I came up to her bench, camera slung around my neck, and said, "Hello, you look beautiful. Would you mind if I took several pictures of you?"

"Oh come on, that's an old line. Thanks for the compliment, but I don't think so." She did not even look at me, but laughed.

"I'm serious. I don't mean nudes, though I'm sure they would be wonderful too, but just your face, your figure, dressed. Your expression, your mood, that's art."

Here, she was taken aback by my speech, and she looked up at me, raising one of her pencil-defined eyebrows. I was standing against the sun, casting a shadow over her left shoulder but letting the sun blaze into her eyes—her hazel irises glowed with emerald undertones, like moss in a forest in the fall. Her eye colors composed well with the turning leaves, as the soul of raving colors. I wasn't lying—I did want to take her picture, and it would have been terrific.

"Do I know you?" she asked.

"Slightly, I came up to you at your husband's funeral and gave you a carnation."

"Oh yes. And even then you were about to offer something. What did you want to talk about then?"

"I was on the train with your husband that day," I said—actually, blurted out.

"Yes?" she said, and then looked over to the playground to see whether her kids were safe.

I waited and didn't say anything for several seconds. I did not want to give away any clues, but her husband was the only ostensible link I had with her—I wanted to use it, so she would not evade me and leave as a stranger. My desire for her was stronger than my impulse toward safety.

"We chatted briefly," I told her. "He told me how much he loved his family, you and the kids, particularly how crazy he was about you, how lucky to have such a beautiful wife. But that's not why I came to the funeral, to see how voluptuous you are." She grinned as though she understood that I was lying and waited for me to go on. "He went off to the restaurant, he was hungry. I was surprised when I did not see him come back to the train station, but I figured the meal must have been great if he'd miss the train out of that God-forsaken station for it. I hope, for his sake, that it was."

"Really, he talked to you about how much he loved me? I wish he'd told me he loved me. Anyway, I don't believe that he said it."

"Maybe he was shy with you."

"And not with you?" she said. "Maybe you're right. He was a moody self-obsessed mathematician. Anyhow, he was a homosexual. We hadn't slept together in two years. I don't know why I'm telling you all this, maybe just to let you know that I have reasons not to believe you."

"You seem to resent him." I was amazed. I had thought Milos was defending himself from a possible gay stalker in the restaurant, but he was actually trying to pick me up. The waiter may have been partly right to smirk and think there was a lewd connection being established.

"I know, it's irrational, but in a way I blame him for leaving us like this. Now I have to work full time, support the family, the kids are a mess, as though we didn't have enough problems."

"Did he serve in the army during the war? I've heard that in post-traumatic stress, many straight men go through a gay phase." I was bullshitting, just to appear natural, and also, to find out whether her husband was in Vukovar as a soldier, after all.

"That's interesting. Yes, he was in the army, in Zadar, and was wounded." She was studying me, and nibbling on a pencil eraser.

"What army?"

"Funny question."

"What work do you do?" I asked.

"Curious, aren't we? I teach English, mostly private lessons, and I teach at a school."

"Could I sign up for an intensive program?" I asked.

"That depends," she said.

"Don't you want to make money?"

"Sure, but there's something strange about you . . . I didn't mean it to come out like that. What I mean, I don't know you."

"Do you have to be intimate with people before you give them lessons?" I joked. It was not a good joke, but she laughed, perhaps because we were both tense.

She let me take pictures of her kids, I took several lessons, and paid well. She allowed me to take pictures of her, in her funeral dress, with the red lipstick. She could not be as pale as she'd been during the funeral, so we touched up her face with white powder to intensify the contrast with her hair. I don't know why I hadn't taken pictures at the funeral; it hadn't occurred to me then.

That was three weeks ago. I've taken her and the kids to the movies, to the zoo, and now that the first snow has fallen, I'll take them skiing. Tonight I've paid for a baby-sitter and Tanya and I took a walk in the old town, past the lanterns, in narrow cobbled streets. A cold wind chapped my lips, and they hurt, until I kissed her in a dark corridor, a moist, tingling kiss. We trembled from excitement.

When I got home, I saw that I had vermilion lips. I had forgotten to wipe them. I am still filled with tenderness, and I'm drinking red wine. I'm looking forward to another date, tomorrow night, hoping to make love to her.

I don't know why I'm having success with her—perhaps too many men are in the army, many have been killed, and there's a shortage that may be working to my advantage. Maybe she's stringing me along, maybe she's suspecting me and investigating the case. I think my guilt gives me extraordinary confidence—I have nothing to lose. I am tempted to expose myself to her, and this temptation thrills me just as much as the erotic seduction does. I am dizzy from her images—and his—swarming in my head. I should go back to the western Slavonian fields, and gather wild flowers, bury myself in their scents and colors. Then I would not need to remember and rave on the page from a strange desire to be caught. I would live like a fox in a bush of red tea.

STORY IDEA

When I got the idea for "Sheepskin," I was not looking for a piece of fiction. In fact, I was trying to get interviews in a refugee camp near Vukovar in Croatia. Because I had no press credentials, the camp director was reluctant to help me. After we talked about it for a while, he did allow me to walk around the camp and talk with people, but without the credentials I was encountering too much skepticism. I ended up talking mostly with the camp director. He told me he was a Croatian soldier when Serb forces invaded Vukovar. When he was bedridden in the city hospital, soldiers came in and dragged many people out to nearby cornfields, where they were shot to death. A soldier whom he knew in childhood came to his bed and spat at him and insulted him. "I wonder what I'd do if I saw the guy again," said the director. "I can't vouch for my actions."

As I left the camp, the question of what he'd do lingered in my head. It would have been a great subject for a piece of nonfiction to get these two soldiers together, interview them, and see what happened. But who could find the Serb soldier? Without getting together with these soldiers, of course, I could only imagine their "relationship." Since I didn't actually know the camp director, and I didn't know the soldier at all, anything I wrote about them— if I did it in enough detail—would be fiction.

I decided to write a story based on the camp director's experience. This decision became, for me, like an assignment in the "Ideas for Fiction" chapter: Write a story of revenge involving two soldiers. But the idea wasn't fully developed enough in my mind for me to simply sit down and write.

POINT OF VIEW AND VOICE

Without much preparation, I tried to write the story in the third person, and I wasn't getting anywhere. The story was too abstract—still only an idea. *I* was not in the story. I needed to bring it closer to me. I thought that by using the first person point of view, I might make this happen, bringing the characters and events into clearer focus. However, I didn't want this voice to sound like me. I needed something different.

What kind of first-person voice would work? I wondered. The man, not knowing what he would do, would probably be contemplating, making decisions, retracting them, and so on. This kind of dialectical back-and-forth thinking brought to my mind the first-person narrators of Fyodor Dostoyevsky, particularly the one in his classic *Notes From Underground*. In earlier stories and sketches, I had already played with that kind of paradoxist voice, and I was pretty sure I could do something similar.

To give you a clearer idea of the source of the story's voice, here are brief excerpts from *Notes From Underground*.

> At the time I was only twenty-four. My life was even then gloomy, ill-regulated, and as solitary as that of a

savage. I made friends with no one and positively avoided talking, and buried myself more and more in my hole. At work in the office I never looked at any one, and I was perfectly well aware that my companions looked upon me, not only as a queer fellow, but even looked upon me—I always fancied this—with a sort of loathing. I was a spiteful official. I was rude and took pleasure in being so. I did not take bribes, you see, so I was bound to find a recompense in that, at least.

Here's my attempt at a similar voice, prompted by reading *Notes*.

I'm perfectly well aware that I'm not entertaining anybody by the way I'm telling this: to entertain, one must make scenes, create the illusion that the events are really happening, like on a stage. Well, forget the stage; I have stage fright. Forget entertainment; I don't laugh at jokes.

I even deliberately adapted Dostoyevsky's phrase "I was perfectly well aware" to get myself in the right mode. And I used the same psychology: Dostoyevsky's unnamed narrator is highly self-conscious. I created my narrator to be the same way, suffering from stage fright. And I did not give him a name, to emphasize his paranoid tendency to hide, evade, and so on—which I thought could intensify his problem of attempting revenge.

This voice from a classic piece of literature, with the mental framework that comprises and evinces it, got my story moving. But still, though I could rave in the voice, I couldn't begin to see the action, to set it as if on a stage. Well, I didn't have the stage yet.

VISUALIZING THE STORY

I needed to determine where exactly the two soldiers should meet. From experience, I know that if I can visualize a setting,

I can begin to see the story in scenes. In Croatia I had spent a lot of time on trains, and I missed them. I decided I could create the sensation of travel on a train, and that this would be a way to bring the two guys together.

But I was still getting stuck. I needed to visualize the protagonist and the antagonist, particularly the antagonist. If you've seen news footage of the war in Bosnia, you've probably noticed that many people in the Balkans look as though they are having a "bad hair day." It's a common feature among people from that part of the world. I must admit that I, too, have unruly hair, and I don't do much to subdue it. So I took this image of hair and developed it. I added strains of gray and a cowlick. At last, I began to see this character. I added thick, closely-set eyebrows and imagined him talking in a slow way. Although that was not much of a character yet, the visual prop got me through. So now I could begin seeing him and letting him move around on the stage.

For the second setting, I again needed something that would convince me that I was in the story—to help me see the fictional events. To fill this need, I found a real-life source. During my last trip to the Balkans, I had eaten at a restaurant with a strange atmosphere that seemed perfect for this story. The restaurant's specialty was lamb, but the meat was lukewarm and tasted old and lardy. Behind the restaurant there were many sheep bleating in stalls, and you had to pass by them on the way to the restroom. The atmosphere nauseated me slightly as I wondered if I was eating the parents or the kids of these sheep. My salad consisted of onion and tomatoes, but mostly onion. I can easily recall the taste of this meal and the smell of the place. I was sure that bringing my characters to this odd place would intensify the story.

The setting worked, or rather, convinced me to work. I think I doubted the possibility of executing the story until I got the characters eating at adjacent tables, eyeing each other, attempting to talk.

THE NARRATOR'S CHARACTER

As I began writing, I couldn't see what the narrator looked like, but this did not seem to be a big problem. His voice and way of thinking carried me through. Later, I gave him some features (receding hairline, a widow's peak, a possessed look). From his doubting-Thomas attitude to his self-conscious, hunted-and-hunter paranoia, the character evolved for me, or devolved, into a twisted, unreliable narrator who would not be the most pleasant person. He ends up stalking the murdered man's wife. He's obsessed with her. From his angle of vision it may not even appear that he's stalking, but he is, waiting behind the corners for her walks.

I made him into a photographer, partly out of a whim. I know quite a few photographers, and it seems to me there is some professional distortion that occurs in some of them: They hunt for images, and when they are interested in taking pictures of women, there is a predatory aura about them. I can't say that I was trying to ridicule photographers of nudes, but the idea certainly came to me easily from knowing some photographers like that. Once, in Paris, my photographer friend approached a pretty woman to flatter her on her good looks and to ask her to pose for him. She laughed, and when he asked, "What's funny?" she said, "You are the fourth guy in one hour who has used these lines on me. Can't you come up with something better?"

"Oh, no, these are not lines, this is my job," he said. So I made my nameless protagonist use this approach with the widow.

SUPPORTING MATERIALS

In Poland I stayed once with a family who put up foreign tourists for a small sum. Half of their house was a sty with sheep. The host had a nice sheepskin jacket, and I asked him whether he sold these jackets. He said he had none ready, but if I was willing to wait, he'd have one in a couple of hours. Then he pointed toward the live sheep. I declined. But I did use the anecdote in my story. I gave it to the antagonist, Milos, the supposed tormentor from the hospital. Why not let him try to buy the jacket? He's a wolf looking for sheep's clothing; at the same time, he's a sacrificial lamb, since he will be killed by mistake. To create a bit of eerie anticipation, I wrote:

> The waiter aimed the blow dryer at a sheepskin, filling it with air. Rounded like a sail full of wind, the skin gave me a spooky impression that an invisible sheep was beginning to inhabit it.

I played with the image of the jacket and a ghost inhabiting it. Who is going to be sacrificed? This image seemed so central that I decided to use it for the title. I also decided that it should be developed into a motif.

ACTION

I imagined that since my story was set in the context of war, in which a lot of murder had already taken place, it would make sense to include the murder rather than avoid it. Moreover, I had written too many stories in which not enough happened, in which temptations were not triumphant. Yes, I thought, I want as much event out of this as I can get. Let it happen.

However, this struck me as a bit too linear. A guy wants revenge and gets it. Not much of a story. So revenge should be only the first climax, the deceptive one, after which a bigger one should take place. I needed a twist.

Since my protagonist doesn't trust his own perceptions, I could make him doubt that he even killed the right guy. Once I did that, it struck me that I could externalize the possibility rather than limit this doubt to the narrator's perspective. Maybe he did kill the wrong guy. This approach seemed more interesting than his simply killing the right guy, so I went with it, introducing other Milos look-alikes.

THOUGHTS, PARAPHRASES, AND OTHER MIND-WIGGLES

Naturally, since I was writing in the first-person point of view, I had an open invitation to be thoroughly subjective. I could play with the theme of subjectivity, attempting to re-create another ego with his subjectivities and vicissitudes. I could focus on the character's thoughts. The character thinks about communism and post-communism (as I describe under the subheading "Politics" later in this chapter). Then he becomes self-conscious about his thinking, since he is self-conscious about everything. He has a thought, which he can deconstruct, to show himself that it actually isn't a real thought.

To execute this strategy, I went back to an exercise I'd created in *Fiction Writer's Workshop*, my first book of writing instruction. In that exercise I ask the reader to compile a list of proverbs, then substitute the subjects with opposites and near-opposites, as Oscar Wilde often did to create his humorous observations. ("Divorces are made in heaven.") I chose the old saying "Love makes you blind," changing it to "Revenge makes you blind." It didn't strike me as a successful paraphrase, but all the better; I could use it as a source of dissatisfaction for the narrator, for he will always be dissatisfied with something. Now he could expose himself to himself by over-analyzing his way of thinking. He could, with disgust, conclude that his thinking boils down to lame paraphrasing. Although this conclusion fills him with self-loathing, it is in itself a provocative thought. Perhaps all thought is merely variation on old themes with noun or verb substitutes.

MORE SETTINGS

The soil sustains. When I am stuck, I tell myself to add more soil, more setting. For the location of the funeral, where Milos goes to establish whether or not he has killed the right guy, I wanted to use an image of a morgue chapel in Père Lachaise, a cemetery in Paris where I went once to visit the graves of Balzac, Proust, and Chopin. During my visit there was a funeral service in progress, and outside a pale woman in black and red leaned against the wall and cried. Inside there were many wreaths, and the scent of perfume and incense was so intense that as it wafted out, I got a sickening sensation in my stomach. Still I looked in, amazed at the quantity of flowers.

I was seeing and smelling this morgue as I wrote the funeral scene; I simply transported the morgue from Paris to Zagreb, the setting of the second half of my story. "The chapel was small, stuffy with perfume—I detest perfume, as though breathing wasn't hard enough without it!—and too cramped for any Ascension to take place."

IMAGES

For me, images are the most pleasant aspect of story making. They help me stick with the story; they help me see it, experience it, and their power of association suggests many things I could add.

But even more than that, I simply like details. Once I have established a story line, I enjoy coming back to various paragraphs, to extend my way of seeing what's in them; new images work for me as beacons as I try to find my way out of the dark into a clear story.

I make up some details from associations on the spot, and I import others from my previous sketches, failed poems, journal notes, anywhere I can find them. In "Sheepskin," I focused on using visual images, which seemed especially appropriate for a story about a photographer.

Months before beginning the story, while writing a poem I came up with the comparison of train rails to a guitar neck. The poem failed, but as I worked on "Sheepskin," the metaphor came back to me. I added it to the story:

> As a child I had loved the oily smell of rails; it had transformed for me the iron clanking of the gaps in the tracks into a transcontinental guitar with two hammered strings and thousands of sorrowful frets that fell into diminished distances.

The metaphor became part of the narrator's musings as he sits on the train. I thought there would be no harm in bringing the iron clank to the reader's sensory sphere of associations. Furthermore, the image of thousands of sorrowful frets falling into diminished distances fits the theme of recurrence that emerges later as one antagonist gives way to another look-alike.

As I've said many times in this book, these connections and associations are the keys to writing fiction. They are what make the process so exciting—and so difficult to discuss in books or workshops. We can examine each element in turn, each step as it arises, but when we're deeply into the creation of a story or novel, the lines blur. One element folds into another, one image leads to many others.

ECHOING IMAGES

I have often been amazed at the variety of fruits, flowers, and plants that can be used to make tea. When I was growing up, we used several types of wildflowers, but today it seems that almost anything can be used. With this idea in mind, I decided to have the narrator view the fields of vegetation as not only flammable but drinkable. Like a red fox, like fire, in a bush of red tea. During a break from writing the story, I took a hike, and I saw a fox, struck with sunlight in a dark forest, that mesmerized me like an epiphany of wild freedom. I immediately wanted the fox to stay with me somehow, to inhabit my world, and so without hesitation I put this animal into the story. At first, I used it simply as a brief image.

> The color intensity of grasses and beeches in the background gave me a dizziness I could not attribute to my cold. I saw a fox leap out of orange bushes of tea. Of course, it was not tea, but many of these wildflowers would be teas if broken by human hands and dried in the sun. . . .

I used this description in the beginning of the story. Later, while grasping for an image with which to end the story, I kept coming back to the fox, visually, in my mind. I told myself, "You've used that already." But then I thought, "Is that a problem?" No, all the better, I concluded. To use the fox as a recurring image could round off the story. I didn't mean to preach in the end, to bring meanings together so overtly, but I did want to deliver an image with the power to express yearning for freedom and escape.

> I should go back to the western Slavonian fields, and gather wild flowers, bury myself in their scents and colors. Then I would not need to remember and rave on the page from a strange desire to be caught. I would live like a fox in a bush of red tea.

There are many ways of using images. Pairing them up, from one end of the story to the other, can create an echo that spans the distance of a canyon and tells you how far you've come.

POLITICS

Though I made up the events that occur in "Sheepskin," they occur within the context of real-life events, such as the war in

Bosnia and the end of communist rule in Eastern Europe. This context gave me a platform for sneaking in general comments and observations about political realities, such as in the following excerpt.

> Not much had changed since communism. I used to think that rudeness was a matter of fixed salaries, no incentive. But here, I was pretty sure the waiter was part-owner of this free enterprise establishment, and he was still rude, and did his best to disgust his customers. And of course customers hadn't changed either. They used to be rude, and I would continue to be rude.

This comment reflects my own opinion (perhaps an overly simplistic one) about the new free-market systems in the former communist countries. At other times in the story, the narrator expresses general opinions that I do not share but that can work for him and the voice. These comments enlarge the scope of the story, adding a public, real-life quality to it.

While I was writing the story, the International War Crimes Tribunal in Den Haage was beginning its judgments on war criminals. I wondered how satisfying the mild sentences from such a distant place would be for the victims of the war. Surely these victims would want a stronger sense of retribution. This feeling helped me to explore the theme of personal revenge. It struck me that if there are five million people injured by the war, and if all of them took revenge into their hands, the real war would begin after the old one was settled. What impossible chaos this would cause! So although I had no political agenda, I did want to comment on the suspect nature of revenge after war. How would you know who was responsible? Could you always identify the soldiers? How would you know that the soldiers were free agents? Perhaps they were forced, perhaps they even practiced restraint and saved the victims to some extent. Each case is different, and conducting a full investigation for every case is impossible.

Writing the story helped me sort out some of my thoughts on the subject, almost like an experiment, so I could see for myself what revenge could look like, and what possible implications there could be in revenge that is highly individualized rather than sociologically abstract.

Fiction allows us to conduct such experiments, to jump into something that passionately concerns us and to live it through the playfulness of imagination rather than through the folly of uncontemplated action. Without fiction, I could be a warrior or a paranoid schizophrenic; instead, I'm someone who plays with words when work and family and forests don't claim me.

ABOUT THE AUTHOR

JOSIP NOVAKOVICH is the author of *Apricots From Chernobyl*, a collection of essays, and the short story collections *Yolk* and *Salvation and Other Disasters*. He has won a Whiting Award, a Richard Margolis Prize for Socially Important Writing, three Pushcart Prizes, an O. Henry award, an NEA fellowship, and a nomination for the Pen/Hemingway Award for First Fiction. His *Fiction Writer's Workshop*, published by Story Press in February 1995, was released in paperback in January 1998.

His work has appeared in *The New York Times Magazine*, *DoubleTake*, STORY, *Ploughshares*, *Paris Review*, and *The Best American Poetry '97*. He teaches writing at the University of Cincinnati, and he lives in Blue Creek, Ohio, with his wife, Jeanette, and children, Joseph and Eva.

GUIDE TO THE EXERCISES

One of the goals of this book is to show how writing fiction is about making connections. Remembered images, people, places, and events trigger imagined ones. Then you combine, shape, and reshape until you have created a new fictional world—the world of a story or novel.

Throughout the book I have recommended exercise combinations to help trigger such connections. But surely there are many combinations that I didn't recognize or consider, ones that appeal to you because of your unique background, interests, and sensibility. So, to make it easier for you to choose your own combinations, use the following index. This will help you find the exercises you need more quickly.

J.N.

CHAPTER ONE: IDEAS FOR FICTION

CHAPTER TWO: CHARACTER

CHAPTER THREE: PLOT

CHAPTER FOUR: POINT OF VIEW

CHAPTER FIVE: SETTING I: LANDSCAPE AND CITYSCAPE

CHAPTER SIX: SETTING II: INTERIOR DESIGN

CHAPTER SEVEN: BEGINNING AND DEVELOPING

EXERCISE	PAGE

CHAPTER EIGHT: SCENE

EXERCISE	PAGE

CHAPTER NINE: DIALOGUE

CHAPTER TEN: VOICE

CHAPTER ELEVEN: DESCRIPTION

CHAPTER TWELVE: IMAGE AND METAPHOR

CHAPTER THIRTEEN: STYLE

INDEX